Women for Hire

Women for Hire

A study of the female office worker

Fiona McNally

M

First published 1979 by
THE MACMILLAN PRESS LTD
London and Basingstoke
Associated companies in Delhi Dublin
Hong Kong Johannesburg Lagos Melbourne
New York Singapore and Tokyo

Printed in Great Britain by
Unwin Brothers Limited, Gresham Press
Old Woking, Surrey.

British Library Cataloguing in Publication Data

McNally, Fiona
  Women for hire.
  1. Women – Employment – Great Britain   2. Clerks
  – Great Britain
  I. Title
  301.5′5   HD6073.M4G7

  ISBN 0–333–25985–8
  ISBN 0–333–25986–6 Pbk

For Serge

Contents

Acknowledgements

Since this book has taken so many years to produce I must acknowledge a debt not only to all those who contributed information and assistance, but also to all those who encouraged me to persevere. Above all, I would like to thank my supervisor, Richard Brown of Durham University, for his limitless help and support over the past eight years. I would also like to thank all the other staff and former postgraduate students at Durham University who offered their encouragement, and who managed to persuade me that sociology could be both useful and enjoyable. I am particularly grateful to Mike Stant, Paul and Philip Corrigan, Harvie Ramsay and Caroline Freeman.

I would like to thank the following for the invaluable information and assistance which they provided: Rosalie Silverstone of City University, David Weir of Glasgow University, Martin Gannon of the University of Maryland, Lorraine Paddison of Ashridge Management College, and Monica Shaw of Newcastle Polytechnic. I am also grateful for the advice and co-operation of many employment agencies throughout the country. Particular thanks are extended to Alfred Marks Ltd, Brook Street Bureau, Lex Personnel Services and Manpower Incorporated. I would also like to acknowledge the considerable assistance provided by Major Donald Cropper of the Federation of Personnel Services.

Additional help or information was supplied by the following: NALGO, ASTMS, Ethel Chipchase of the TUC, and the Department of Employment. I would like to thank all of these and all the other organisations or people who supplied views or information. My thanks are also extended to all those who commented on the innumerable drafts of the various chapters: Mary McIntosh, Patti Carter, John Oram, Francis Absalom and Maeve Boultwood.

I would also like to thank the following for permission to reproduce copyright material: *British Journal of Industrial Relations*, the Controller of Her Majesty's Stationery Office, Oxford University Press and *Personnel Management*.

I am grateful to the Social Science Research Council for providing financial assistance for this project. I would also like to extend particular thanks to Alisa Colley and Liz Dean for executing the wretched task of typing and retyping the various drafts. Finally, I would like to thank all the temps who have contributed in diverse ways to this book, and without whom this research would most certainly not have been possible.

Introduction

Since the beginning of the 1970s there has been a steadily growing and increasingly strident body of criticism directed at the way in which sociologists have traditionally researched and represented female members of society. Much of the criticism has come from within the discipline itself, although it seems fair to say that the original stimulus for this examination of the sociological conscience lay in the neo-feminist movement which developed in the late 1960s. The main themes of this critique have been, first, that women as a group have been neglected in the principal areas of empirical research; secondly, that an implicit sexism has characterised the dominant theoretical traditions in sociology; and, thirdly, that the study of gender relationships has failed to progress beyond a narrow interest in patterns of sexual differentiation within the family context. The relatively low status of family sociology has itself impeded the development of a more sophisticated understanding of domestic relationships and organisation. The outcome of this critique has been a proliferation of literature concerned to reorient the manner in which sexual divisions are both conceptualised and investigated.

It is evident that one area in sociology which is very much in need of both a theoretical reorientation and a more abundant literature based on empirical research is the study of women in the labour market. A number of reservations may be expressed in relation to both quantitative and qualitative aspects of the existing material. Concerning quantity, one may note that the presence of women in the labour force has certainly been acknowledged by sociologists, but it is also true that the coverage has not been proportional to the degree of female participation in the work sphere. Occasionally, women have been accorded little more than footnote status in some major empirical studies of work situations where both sexes were represented. Fashions within industrial sociology have played their part in rendering women an under-researched group. A mixture of preference, availability of funds and contemporary trends has contributed to a diminished interest in organisational behaviour and a corresponding rise of interest in the field of industrial relations. Given women's relatively lower rate of union membership as compared with that of men, and given their significantly lower activity rates in the sphere of union affairs, it was perhaps inevitable that they should have become somewhat invisible in recent literature. This circumstance, however, forms only part of the explanation for the paucity of the material. It has been suggested that procedural difficulties may also account for the neglect of the female labour force:

> Women tend to work in smaller firms, and often on a part-time basis. Their rate of mobility between firms is likely to be higher than that of men. The employer may see high labour turnover as an indictment of the pay and conditions he offers, and not encourage the scrutiny of outsiders. Thus women may be difficult to 'get at' to be studied at all.[1]

The authors of this passage, however, were of the opinion that the theoretical preoccupations of industrial sociologists were of greater significance in accounting for the neglect of women workers, and I share this view. If procedural problems really represent such an insuperable difficulty for research, then it is impossible to account for the existence of many excellent studies devoted to the most personal and sensitive areas of human life.

Quite apart from the general inattention to women at work, it is also the case that within the literature which has addressed itself more directly to women's participation in the labour market certain categories of female employee have received considerably greater attention than others. It has been widely noted that the chief focus of interest has been the phenomenon of the working wife and/or mother. A great deal of research has been concerned to account for rising rates of economic activity amongst married women since the Second World War, and to assess the impact of this trend upon familial relationships. Such studies have been largely characterised by what might be termed a 'deviance' perspective, since the central aims of the research appear to have been to provide an explanation for the unexpected and to identify the degree of disruption in family life which might follow from such a trend. Whilst all energies were therefore directed towards placing the working wife under a microscope, attention was diverted away from other categories of female employees, such as those first entering the labour market.

The paucity and selectivity of the literature represent major causes for dissatisfaction with the sociology of women at work, and these problems have been compounded by a number of qualitative deficiencies. In the first place, sociologists in the past have been more than willing to take their theoretical cues from the currency of popular stereotypes. The tendency for members of the discipline to confirm rather than to inform the popular wisdom in this area has been noted by Sheila Rowbotham.[2] She claims that sociologists have proved that women are 'naturally' suited to certain types of work. They have observed that women are frequently employed in boring, monotonous and routine jobs and therefore conclude that this is because women's chief attachment is to the home. It is felt that because of this preference, the nature of the work is subjectively unimportant, just so long as it brings in enough money to pay for little extras for the house or helps to stave off the occasional feeling of isolation in the domestic environment. An example of this reasoning may be drawn from the widely recommended 'A' level textbook *The Science of Society*, in which Cotgrove discusses the reasons for the increasing participation of married women in the labour force:

> Such changes do not necessarily imply a shift of interest on the part of women away from their traditional role as wives and mothers to a growing interest in and preoccupation with work. Although this may be a trend for women who have a professional training and career, the great majority of working wives use work instrumentally as a source of income to be spent on the home – on refurnishings and decorations, durable consumer goods, holidays and clothing for the family, and only secondarily because they are lonely or bored . . . The increase in working

wives is, in fact, perfectly consistent with the growth in home-
centredness. Such women put their families first and are not
interested in promotion.[3]

In putting forward this opinion, Cotgrove articulates a widely held
view of women's attitudes, often confirmed in conversation or by
observation. Yet the apparent unwillingness to explore more
systematically the many sources of female home-centredness, where
it exists, must be challenged. According to this popular stereotype
Britain's post-war economy offers women the opportunity to realise
their modest ambitions, and women passively, naturally and happily
accept subordinate status in the labour market. Another viewpoint
might, however, stress the lack of choice and opportunities which
necessitates resignation to one's fate and which renders an
attachment to the home an understandable response to the fact of
limited alternatives.

It is this inattention to the economic opportunity structure for
women which represents a second major weakness of the literature.
Whilst we now know a great deal about the growth of suburban
housewives in the labour force, and whether or not this has created
problems for their families, until recently we have had a
correspondingly poor understanding of trends in the market position
of women as a group. Insufficient attention has been paid to the
function of women as a reserve army of labour and to the way in which
changes in the economic climate of the country have affected their
individual or collective bargaining power. There has been little
attention to the barriers to satisfaction and/or advancement which
prevail in the workplace, such as limited training opportunities or
discrimination by employers and unions. The analysis of women's
participation in the labour force has instead concentrated on the
constraints arising in the domestic sphere – attitudes of husbands
and relatives, obligations towards children and other dependants.

The net effect of the sociologist's predilection for popular
stereotypes and inattention to the broader economic context of
female participation in the labour market has been the reinforce-
ment of a partial and unsatisfactory understanding of women at
work. Moreover, the failure to examine systematically the factors
influencing women's attitudes towards their jobs has enabled the
belief to prevail that women attach little importance to promotion or
to interesting work. Indeed, one may say that the nature of women's

orientations to work represents the most conspicuous area of neglect as a subject for empirical investigation.

It is true that the recent growth of interest in women's position in society has done much to rectify the problem of general neglect. The claim that women in the labour force have been ignored becomes increasingly untenable given the amount of new publications which are concerned to describe and account for sexual differentiation within the labour market. It remains the case, however, that there are very few published studies which examine women's attitudes to work in a particular occupational context in a systematic manner. The aim of this research, therefore, is not only to offer a descriptive account of a mode of female employment hitherto neglected in the literature, but also to undertake an investigation of the diversity of factors which influence women's attitudes to work.

The particular focus of this study is represented by women in routine white-collar employment. Women constitute an overwhelming majority of those employed in this sector of the labour market and clerical work is the single most common form of occupation among women. For these reasons alone, the subject of female participation in the white-collar labour market merits a great deal more attention than it has so far received. The present research is to some extent concerned to remedy this deficiency by undertaking a synthesis of what can only be described as an impoverished and extremely scattered literature. However, even if one assembles the scraps of information in order to develop an idea of the nature of women's participation in this sphere of the labour market, an important lacuna still exists, namely, an understanding of the attitudes which women actually hold towards this kind of work. The research is therefore centrally concerned to identify and to account for women's orientations towards routine white-collar work. Fundamental to this particular focus of the study is the assumption that factors both within the workplace and beyond it are of relevance for an understanding of work attitudes. To this extent it represents a departure from the work which has already been done in this area of female employment.

In order to highlight the configuration of circumstances surrounding not only occupational choice, but also changes in attitudes to work, I decided to conduct my research amongst female temporary clerical workers – those whose services are hired by firms from private employment agencies. Although the inevitable criticism which could be made of this strategy is that such workers may be greatly unrepresentative of women as a whole, or even of other clerical workers, it must be pointed out that the intention is not to provide information from which to generalise about all women, but to offer some insight into the diversity of factors which influence women's perceptions of their jobs. Moreover, the phenomenon of temporary work illustrates *par excellence* the manner in which women can manipulate and actively manoeuvre within a structure of limited economic alternatives. As we have seen, all too often women have been characterised as passive, reacting agents, with limited occupational aspirations created by their socialisation experiences and domestic circumstances. For many women, it may well be the case that work is regarded as an unfortunate economic necessity, or that it is seen as very much a secondary activity to the main business of running a home and looking after children. This should not blind us, however, to the possibility that discontentment with the home environment may drive some women to seek alternative satisfactions in the labour market, or that other women may experience boredom with their work for want of responsibility, interest or variety. Their attempts to find solutions to their problems, even if sometimes founded upon an incorrect appraisal of the available alternatives, belie the notion that there exists a typically feminine orientation to work. To a very great extent, the study of women in temporary clerical employment illustrates this capacity for an active pursuit of personal satisfaction from work as well as the necessity for compromise in the face of restricted opportunities.

This study, then, incorporates a shift of focus away from the domestic circumstances of working women towards the nature of their work situation and their attitudes towards their jobs. It does not assume that female orientations to work are fixed solely by their upbringing and education and later by their domestic obligations, but explores the extent to which they are sustained, modified or frustrated by the experience of work itself.

In view of the points elaborated earlier, it will be apparent that it is essential to give consideration to a much wider range of sociological issues than the research findings themselves directly illustrate. If one is to avoid the tendency towards oversimplification and stereotyping noted above, then one has to draw upon a whole range of information pertinent to the subject of female clerical workers. Chapter 1 is an analysis of sociological literature which deals implicitly or explicitly with the question of women's work attitudes. Chapter 2 examines the existing literature concerning white-collar work. The majority of studies have focused on males occupied within this sector, but have nevertheless generated a great deal of information which is of direct relevance in the present context, particularly in relation to sources of satisfaction and dissatisfaction with white-collar work. Chapter 3 concentrates exclusively on female office workers. It is essential to take full account of women's experience in the permanent sphere of office work if one is to comprehend the resort to temporary employment. It has been necessary, because of the dearth of relevant sociological literature, to draw mainly upon non-academic sources of information. It is not difficult, however, to document fully the disadvantages attaching to female status in this sector of the labour market, and material from a wide range of sources has been used to show how women experience and react to restricted opportunities.

Chapter 4 examines the phenomenon of temporary labour and the role of the private employment agency. Although the principal focus of this research is represented by those employed in a temporary capacity, it is important to consider the activities of the agencies themselves and the extent to which they help or hinder women's attempts to ameliorate their work situation. Chapter 5 incorporates the findings of my research among female temporary clerical workers. The discussion is based upon the results of a postal questionnaire issued in 1971–72 to women working in three areas of the country, and the results of a short period of participant observation which I undertook in 1971. The intention is to examine not only the general characteristics of women in temporary office work, but also the extent to which this mode of employment represents an occupational safety valve for women whose work opportunities are otherwise greatly circumscribed. The findings are also used to illustrate the proposition that women's experience of work represents an integral component of their attitudes towards it. In this way, I intend to demonstrate the redundancy of the idea that a woman's attitude towards work is usefully accounted for purely in terms of her gender or position in the life cycle.

Finally, the broad conclusions of this study are presented and are discussed in relation to both past and present orientations in sociological literature.

1

Women's Attitudes towards Work

While it has long been understood that women's labor-force participation is responsive to such major life-cycle events as education, marriage, divorce, bereavement, childbearing, and geographic mobility, the study of the motivational side has been neglected. Thus, when we turn to the theoretical work on work aspiration in women, and the empirical literature it has spawned, we find it both stagnant and unimaginative. Work aspiration (or occupational choice, or career commitment – rarely are these concepts distinguished) is usually treated as a discrete event like the menarche, which occurs at some time in adolescence and never again.[1]

Despite the recent growth of literature concerning post-war trends in female employment and the characteristics which differentiate male and female occupations, we remain remarkably ignorant about such issues as occupational choice and sources of work satisfaction among female employees. According to Judith Long Laws, much of the literature which is available in relation to these themes is theoretically obsolete and informed by a deficient methodology.[2] It also tends to display an uncritical acceptance of certain myths and assumptions concerning the character of women's orientations towards paid employment. In this chapter, therefore, I am concerned to identify the sources and nature of these deficiencies and to indicate ways in which the study of women's attitudes towards work might usefully be re-oriented.

One of the most pervasive themes in the literature is that women, as compared to men, display a consistently attenuated level of occupational aspiration. This position derives considerable strength from the findings of sociological and government-sponsored enquiries into the occupational choices and aspirations of male and female school-leavers and graduates. One of these, the Schools Council Sixth Form Enquiry, carried out in 1967, found that there were marked differences between the sexes in their chosen occupations.[3] A study by Hutchings and Clowsley of sixth-form boys and girls found that even where scholastic achievements were of a similar standard, girls tended to hold lower levels of expectations than boys.[4] An investigation of attitudes amongst sixth-form girls in London and the South-east found that their subject choices at school had followed traditional lines and that there was a reluctance to enter into certain types of science-based careers. The authors concluded that 'girls showed a great unwillingness to combat prejudice and a preference for work in which they would be welcome'.[5] Studies of the occupational plans of male and female graduates have revealed similar patterns. A report produced by Sheffield University in 1970 showed that female graduates planned to take up a much narrower range of occupations than male graduates, and that some form of teaching was the chosen career of 60 per cent of the women as compared with only 31 per cent of the men.[6]

These and other studies have provided a great deal of empirical support for the argument that women are characterised by a qualitatively different orientation towards work from that exhibited by their male counterparts. However, whilst there is a reasonably full documentation of the existence of these differing expectations and aspirations at the point of entry to the labour market, we know a great deal less about the ways in which these attitudes are formed. Although it has long been acknowledged that more could be done by teachers, career officers and employers to encourage greater ambition and a willingness to enter careers not traditionally associated with women, it is only recently that there has been a more studied attention to the social processes which mould girls' work aspirations.[7] As both Laws and Acker have pointed out, in the absence of a fuller understanding of the social construction of girls' seemingly limited occupational horizons, it has been all too easy to ascribe their attitudes to a motivational deficit in the female personality.[8] Explanations of this nature are unsatisfactory not only because they ignore the varied and complex patterns of social interaction which give rise to particular attitudes, but also because they can assume the character of self-fulfilling prophecies.

There is a further reason why caution should be exercised in the attempt to draw conclusions about female work orientations from studies of young girls at the point of entry to the labour market. It may be suggested that because these studies demonstrate so positively the relatively lower job expectations of girls at this stage in their lives, the possibility that these attitudes may be susceptible to change at a later date may be overlooked.[9] The findings which were referred to earlier inform us only about the *expectations* which girls have *prior* to their entry into the labour market. It cannot be assumed that what holds good for schoolgirls and female undergraduates also holds good for women in paid employment or for women on the point of re-entry into the workforce.

One theme which appears with considerable frequency in the literature is that women's attitudes towards work are directly related to their position in the life cycle. Thus variations in attitudes are assumed to depend primarily on differences in age, marital status and the presence or absence of dependant relatives. While there can be little doubt that position in the life cycle is likely to have some bearing upon work attitudes and aspirations, there are a number of reasons why this approach to the analysis of women's job orientations is not entirely satisfactory. Firstly, there is the danger that it may lead to a neglect of the impact of work experience itself upon attitudes to work. Secondly, it is a perspective which can sometimes lean rather too heavily upon stereotypical assumptions about female dispositions and priorities. This is particularly true of the way in which the occupational attitudes of single female employees are presented. In a number of studies, the young single girl is often presented as an instrumentally oriented worker, with a difference – marriage is her central life-interest:

Women have largely gone into office jobs that require little skill and carry small responsibility . . . A large proportion are young, unmarried women and for many of them clerical work is 'just a job like any other' taken up in the interval between leaving school and getting married. It is known that girls are especially attracted to clerical work because of its social status, and also, it may be surmised, because of the opportunity it affords for meeting desirable marriage partners in the blackcoated class. In short, the strictly vocational nature of office work is here very much attenuated.[10]

A similar perspective may be found in the work of Mumford and Banks:

Why is so much of clerical work being taken over by women? The answer seems fairly obvious. Women – or rather girls, for the great majority are under twenty-five – will, at present, accept routine jobs that are unlikely to lead anywhere. For most of them matrimony is their principal objective or interest and work is regarded as temporary and incidental, rather than central in their lives. Because of this they are willing to put up with tasks that seem intrinsically dull and for the same reason they are not unduly anxious for promotion . . . This passive acceptance by women of low grade, routine work may, of course, not continue in the future.[11]

The notion that the occupational distribution of young women is readily explained in terms of their own preoccupation with matrimony is extremely unconvincing. It is an argument which has been framed with an apparent disregard for the existence of inertia and discrimination amongst employers in relation to the provision of training and promotion opportunities for girls. It is also seemingly blind to the obstacles which confront those young women who entertain the possibility of moving into occupations not normally associated with their sex. In short, it is a perspective which totally ignores the realities of the labour market, or – what is more important, perhaps – it ignores the subjective reality of the labour market for the workers concerned. As Hunt has pointed out, the conviction that 'better the devil one knows than the angel one doesn't' can be a powerful incentive to remain in a job, even though it may seem highly dull and routine.[12]

Recent findings tend to undermine one's confidence in the utility of this traditional conceptualisation of single women's attitudes still further. First, Hunt has noted that girls in the 16–19 age group are prominent among those who are not very satisfied with their jobs and she considers that this is because 'this group includes many who were in their first jobs which might not have come up to their expectations'.[13] Similarly, in their study of female operatives in the electronics industry, Wild and Hill found that job dissatisfaction was more common among single girls.[14] Thus, contrary to what might be supposed from the quoted passages, there *are* single girls who experience a shortfall between their expectations and the openings available to them. This situation can generate feelings of dissatisfaction which are not offset by the prospect of a marriage partner popping up over the nearest filing cabinet. Secondly, Hunt found that 78.6 per cent of single working women under forty expected to go on working after marriage, and that in reply to the question, 'If you were to stop work after you were married do you think you would start again later?', 63.7 per cent of these same women said that they would. These figures represent something of a rebuff to those who believe that the horizons of young unmarried girls do not extend beyond their wedding day, for as Hunt herself says, it is the birth of the first child, rather than the date of marriage, which has become the point at which women give up paid employment, and then only temporarily.[15]

It is quite legitimate to suppose that the attitudes to work of single girls will reflect to some extent their out-of-work preoccupations. However, there is evidence to show that the future prospect of marriage for such women does not preclude job dissatisfaction or the desire to find a more stimulating work environment. It should not be assumed that young girls simply adapt to seemingly mundane forms of occupation because their interests lie elsewhere. What should be investigated is the degree to which single women find themselves in occupational cul-de-sacs and whether or not this leads to resignation and an emphasis on substitute sources of satisfaction.

Whereas the single female is thought to use work instrumentally either to find a husband directly or to purchase the means necessary to bring the hunt to a swift conclusion, the married woman is represented as using work as a way of financing home improvement. As the home has increasingly become the central life-interest of many post-war couples, so there has been every incentive for the female partners to add to its attractions and comfort by providing an additional income. In the past, much research has demonstrated the apparent utility of this model. Viola Klein, writing in 1965 claimed: 'Money is undoubtedly the largest incentive for married women to go out to work. Three out of every four women interviewed gave this as the main reason for having a job.'[16] The husbands in her survey agreed that their wives' motives for working were mainly instrumental: 'From the answers given by husbands of working wives, it is evident that their wives' earnings are more often regarded by them as a subsidiary, as a help to buy "extras", rather than as essential contributions.'[17]

Although one cannot dispute the universality of the finding that the desire for money is of considerable significance among the motives for working amongst married women, one must lodge certain objections to the image of acquisitive womanhood which the research has undoubtedly encouraged. First, many sources of data have shown that working wives are not solely motivated by the quest for money. According to the work of Zweig, and of Hunt, such factors as 'the emotional, pressure of loneliness' and the monotony of housework are also of considerable weight in propelling women into the labour force.[18] Hunt states: 'More than one attraction was named by the great majority of those who named any at all, and nearly two-thirds of those mentioning financial advantages mentioned at least one other advantage.'[19] Hunt also canvassed the opinions of non-working wives, and while 64 per cent cited the desire for money as a reason why they would be going back to work, 40 per cent of her respondents named boredom at home and 25 per cent gave the desire for companionship as reasons for this decision.[20] Klein herself, while emphasising the overriding significance of the pecuniary motive, was at pains to point out that other factors, such as social isolation and the monotony of unrelieved housework, often contributed to the decision to seek paid employment.

This factor – dissatisfaction with certain aspects of the home environment – has received very little attention from sociologists until the last few years. Consequently, any attempts to assess its relative significance in the configuration of reasons for the increase in working wives have been largely speculative, and have probably underestimated its importance. In her pioneering study of women's domestic situation, Ann Oakley found that 70 per cent of her respondents were dissatisfied with housework, and concluded that 'Housewives experience more monotony, fragmentation and speed in their work than do workers in the factory.'[21] We may suppose that this is not wholly a modern phenomenon, but certain post-war developments may have increased the social isolation of the housewife and made her tasks seem more thankless than previously. The increasing isolation of the housewife has gone hand in hand with the increasing physical isolation of the nuclear family. Young and Willmott's study of working-class family life demonstrated very clearly how the physical and social characteristics of the modern housing estate can render a young wife very lonely indeed during the daytime with little else to do but cleaning, shopping and babyminding.[22] Even where a housewife has occasional social contact with neighbours, the very superficiality of these relationships may only serve to heighten her sense of deprivation of meaningful social interaction.[23] It is not surprising then that more and more women take up paid employment with a view to injecting some interest into their lives.

According to Ann Oakley, the available evidence suggests that: 'questions about married women's reasons for taking jobs tap the normative tip of the iceberg – that women say they work for the money because this is the socially acceptable reason.'[24] Like Hunt, Oakley is of the opinion that women may tend to advance reasons which they think they ought to give, rather than those which they really believe. Married women are not expected to express profound dissatisfaction with their status as housewives – to do so might be to cast doubt upon their personal adequacy – and consequently they give answers which in no way detract from their capacities as homemakers and mothers. In view of the limited amount of recent data relating to working wives and their attitudes, it is impossible to come to any firm conclusions as to whether their responses are more likely to be rationalisations of their genuine feelings, or whether we should dismiss this idea as unwarranted speculation. The point cannot be resolved, it seems, until we have a great deal more research which attempts to probe the responses of working wives in much greater depth. In the meantime, the frequency with which sources of dissatisfaction with the home environment are mentioned by them is a finding which should not be overshadowed by the apparent significance of the pecuniary motive.

A second objection to the economic model of the working wife is that it helps to perpetuate the notion that women are only supplementary earners. Since the overriding impression is that of women exercising a choice over whether or not they go out to work and that their decision to work is born out of the desire for little extras for the home rather than of necessity, the view that employment for women is always subsidiary is thereby reinforced. According to Jean Gardiner, it is this view of women which 'perpetuates both lack of training and low pay for women workers and the traditional sex division of labour and responsibility within the family'.[25] Not only is this sociological vision of an ideological nature, but it also neglects the fact of lack of choice among those who have to work because they are the sole supporters of their households. Furthermore, even if one chooses to disregard the evidence that the bulk of the earnings of working wives typically goes towards necessities such as rent and housekeeping rather than on 'extras', it is impossible to disregard the implications of the spiralling inflation of recent years. Many couples became accustomed to a certain standard of living during the 1950s and 1960s and more recently married couples no doubt based their expectations upon the example of their predecessors. Until the late 1960s, it is probable that within the middle-income groups there was no driving necessity for the wife to work, but that if she did, then a somewhat higher standard of living could be maintained. Soaring inflation, rising rates of taxation and interest have brought about a situation where it has become harder and harder for a husband to sustain his family's standard of living on his income alone, and have made it correspondingly more and more necessary for his wife to work as well. To the extent that this is actually happening, then the view of working wives as temporary, supplementary earners becomes increasingly untenable. One recent development may perhaps be taken as indicative of the changing significance of the wife's income, namely the falling birth rate. Although the birth rate has been falling ever since 1964, it has now pitched to an unprecedentedly low level. Demographers rarely agree among themselves as to the causes of fluctuations in the birth rate and there has been a great deal of controversy concerning this latest downswing. However, economic factors are usually of some significance, and a declining birth rate may thus be regarded as in part the aggregate of individual couples' responses to changing economic fortunes in the society as a whole. One such response is to limit the total number of children that one has, and another is to postpone the birth of the first child. Some demographers are of the opinion that there is a high incidence of the latter response among recently married couples, which is having its effect on the birth rate. It is possible to argue, therefore, that since the loss of a wife's income and extra expense incurred by the birth of a child represents a source of potential hardship at the best of times, contemporary economic circumstances are such as to make it necessary to postpone having a family until such time as this would constitute no serious threat to a couple's standard of living. According to an article by Frances Cairncross in the *Guardian*, evidence from the United States suggests that more and more couples are practising this 'new home economics':

> It looks suspiciously as if couples in the United States, at least, are well aware of the opportunity cost of having children, and trade off the wife's job satisfaction and earning power against the satisfaction of having a family.[26]

It may be that this practice is more likely to occur where the wife's occupation is highly rewarded and accorded high status, for, as Adkins and Piepmeier point out:

> Only when women attain equal or greater social recognition for economic activity than for childbearing, will the balance change and production of children become the less important activity.[27]

The relationship between fertility, education and employment among women is a highly complex one, and there is very little way of knowing whether fertility patterns are the outcome of education and occupational experiences or whether they determine them. It does seem, though, that the analysis of recent trends in the birth rate leads strongly towards the conclusion that wives' earnings have now acquired strategic importance in the maintenance of the standard of living of contemporary couples. To the extent that trends in the birth rate reflect the heightened importance of the wife's earnings within the household economy, we must regard the notion that wives' incomes are of purely marginal significance as increasingly redundant.

Furthermore, it is possible that changes in the practical significance of wives' earnings may have been accompanied by changes in women's work attitudes. As work increasingly becomes a normal and essential component of a married woman's daily existence, the nature of work conditions, levels of remuneration and job satisfaction may assume increasing importance at the subjective level. Married women may become less willing to compromise in the face of limited opportunities and inferior rewards.

Thus, whilst it may readily be conceded that attitudes towards work will be influenced by the stage reached in the life cycle, it is also necessary to explore the impact of the work situation itself and any recent economic changes which may have a bearing upon the way women perceive their jobs. It is also desirable that sociologists devote more attention to the sources of job satisfaction and job dissatisfaction among women, both single and married, than they have done to date. Unless more work is done in this area, the notion that marriage and motherhood represent the height of women's ambition will prevail.

If one examines the literature which addresses itself to the nature of women's attitudes to work it is evident that there is a tendency to construct *a priori* models of female motivation which are thought appropriate to the population of women under investigation. In some cases a woman's position in the life cycle is held to be the crucial determinant of attitudes. In others, social or educational background are accorded primary significance. Recent debates concerning the concept of orientation to work lead one to be cautious in accepting one-sided explanatory models of this kind. These debates have involved arguments as to whether workers may be said to display a consistent set of priorities in the rewards they seek from work and whether these priorities, if they exist, derive primarily from the work situation or from out-of-work factors. The main protagonists agree that worker behaviour in general is a function of influences deriving from both sources, but Goldthorpe's contention that a fairly stable set of priorities or orientation to work arises to some extent *independently* of the work situation is disputed by Daniel.[28] The latter maintains that workers exhibit different sets of priorities at different times, such that job choice, job satisfaction and job leaving are not necessarily influenced by the same factors. Thus for Daniel the key question is not 'what do people want from work?' but 'at what point are they interested in particular rewards?'[29] Consequently, it becomes necessary to focus on the way in which the experience of work itself generates different sets of priorities at different points in time.

The two main contenders in this argument have yet to reach agreement on these issues. However, those who have attempted to resolve the debate on their behalf have come to the conclusion that whilst the concept of orientation to work is not as redundant as Daniel would have us believe, it is inappropriate to give too much emphasis to workers' priorities when they enter a job as the determinants of subsequent attitudes. Brown, for example, agrees with Daniel that one must pay considerable attention to the context of choice and action since this may well lead to the modification of a person's priorities:

> consideration must be given to the priorities among workers' objectives and aspirations, and to the way the order of priorities may be influenced by practical possibilities of realizing them, or what could be termed the conditions of action as perceived by the actors themselves. Workers who would like to have interesting jobs with high pay may give low priority to the former objective because they realize that they are unlikely to find both; but this order of priorities may change over the long, or even the short term.[30]

This observation highlights the point that a preparedness to read between the lines is particularly important in the measurement of job satisfaction. As Baldamus has suggested, when workers express satisfaction with their work it may be that these satisfactions are only 'substitute goals or rationalisations which are a function of deprivation, not an independent variable in the motivation to work'.[31]

Many studies of women at work have failed to heed this principle. Respondents' attitudes have been taken at face value and little interest has been shown in the way in which the opportunity structures which confront women in various occupations interact with patterns of expectations and priorities. In addition, factors which are independent of the work situation are held to be the primary determinants of attitudes. In a critical assessment of this literature Richard Brown concludes that:

> In contrast to existing studies of 'orientations to work', therefore, what is needed is an extension of enquiry beyond the conventional dichotomy of work and a limited range of non-work factors to include, in particular, patterns of socialization and the nature of the labour market. Consideration of the ways in which

'orientations to work' for the majority of women might be generated, and sustained or changed, also draws attention to the constraints on their possibilities of action – constraints which for many are so restrictive that the explanatory value of the notion must be called into question. Job 'choice' or behaviour at work would be much the same whatever the 'orientation to work'.[32]

Throughout history, men and women alike have been constrained into the adoption of certain attitudes and patterns of behaviour by their upbringing and by the nexus of structural and ideological forces encountered in adult life. It is clear that the apparently attenuated occupational ambitions of many women in today's world must be examined within this wider context of restricted opportunities. However, it is essential to recognise that acquiescence is neither an inevitable nor a universal response to the fact of limited options. The processes which make for widespread adherence to the prescribed norms are deep-rooted and substantial, yet this does not preclude resistance nor the desire for individual or collective change. The lesson to be learnt from history is that women are capable of resistance to structures of oppression in diverse ways. Their discontent may express itself in open protest and militancy, or it may take the form of a manipulation of the opportunities available. It is important, therefore, to examine not only those factors which promote acquiescence, but also those which foster an active posture. The next two chapters will be concerned with both sets of factors in the world of white-collar work.

2

The World of White-Collar Work

The paucity of information concerning women in white-collar occupations is a function of a more general lack of sociological interest in this sector of the labour market. Revolutions, when they occur, are usually accompanied by a torrent of controversy. Yet the remarkable growth of the white-collar labour force during the twentieth century, which amounts to a truly dramatic change in the occupational structure, has received scant attention. Those writers who have examined this development are all agreed that it is one of revolutionary dimensions. Crozier describes it as 'a veritable administrative revolution comparable to the industrial revolution of the nineteenth century.'[1] Bain writes: 'The growth of the white-collar labour force is one of the most outstanding characteristics of the economic and social development of the twentieth century.'[2]

In spite of such superlatives, our knowledge and understanding of the evolution and contemporary character of the white-collar labour force remains fragmentary and inadequate. Perhaps this has something to do with the very nature of white-collar occupations. They have been characterised as dull, boring and dehumanised, in short as having all the classic properties of alienation. Yet even if white-collar work were appropriately labelled as monotonous or alienating, and certain doubts must attend such a judgement, it would be quite wrong to conclude that the incumbents of these occupations were equally uninteresting and therefore unworthy of attention. Just as this sector of the labour force includes a tremendous diversity of skills, we may also assume that here is to be found a vast range of attitudes to work and relationships at work. On numerical grounds alone, the white-collar labour force merits close analysis. According to Bain, the number of white-collar workers increased by 147 per cent between 1911 and 1961. During the same period, the number of manual workers rose by only 2 per cent.[3] Growth in the numbers of white-collar workers and in their proportional representation within the labour force as a whole has been particularly dramatic since 1951. Elliott notes that there were 5.74 million white-collar employees, amounting to 29 per cent of all employees in industries and services in Great Britain in 1951. In 1971, they totalled 8.88 million and accounted for 42 per cent of workers in industries and services.[4] According to Lumley, the annual average increase in their numbers in the early 1970s was 1.3 per cent.[5]

Some confusion, however, surrounds the use of the term 'white-collar work'. Broadly, it may be used to distinguish all non-manual occupations from manual ones, connoting differences in working conditions, career prospects, method of payment, and even orientations to work and towards trade unions. More narrowly, the term may be used as a shorthand for all lower and intermediate categories of non-manual work, thus making a further distinction between such groups and professional and managerial employees. According to this meaning, the terms 'white-collar work' and 'clerical work' are interchangeable, and I shall adopt this usage for the purposes of this book.[6]

This chapter chronicles the origins and subsequent development of white-collar work and focuses on some of the sociological literature relating to those currently employed in a clerical capacity. This affords an insight into the general nature of white-collar employment which is essential for an appreciation of the status and location of women in this sector of the labour market.

The origins and early development of white-collar work

Although the marked growth of white-collar occupations is associated with the period of rapid industrialisation and expansion in world commerce in the second half of the nineteenth century, the origins of white-collar work date back much further. As Benet has pointed out, the word 'clerk' has the same root as the word 'cleric', and throughout the Middle Ages clerks were a part of the church organisation, their job being to maintain records and perform routine book-keeping. Gradually, clerks developed more secular associations with the world of commerce, achieving a measure of security and status as the employees of the new entrepreneurial class.

With the expansion in the scale of manufacturing and commercial enterprise in the second half of the nineteenth century, there came a tremendous demand for those equipped with clerical skills. In Britain, the expansion of the empire and overseas markets accentuated this demand still further since workers were urgently required to process correspondence. At the same time, the natural habitat of the clerk came into being – the office.[7]

These old-style clerks of the nineteenth century, almost exclusively male, held a highly personal relationship with their employers. This may have had something to do with the fact that clerks were often sons of the owners of the enterprises, undertaking training with a view to eventually taking over the business themselves. Those who were not in such a favourable position nevertheless remained loyal to their employers, hoping that the rewards of long service and faithfulness might be perhaps a stake in the business, or at least promotion and gradual increments of pay. Lockwood writes of the relationship between the clerk and his employer: 'In many cases it took the form of a "gentleman's agreement". Needless to say, this relationship was often exploited by the employer and great expectations frequently came to nothing.'[8] Wright Mills' description of the American counterpart is strikingly similar, a picture of servitude and dependence.[9] It seems that many were willing to submit to these conditions because in so doing they might gain respectability and the external trappings of a gentleman. Both employers and manual workers despised clerks for their lofty aspirations in this regard. There was little glamour or excitement in the clerk's daily round of activities. It is possible that the clerk of the past obtained some job satisfaction. No doubt he took a certain pride in his book-keeping, just as an industrial apprentice might derive a certain pleasure once he had mastered the intricacies of his craft, but this was small compensation for a lifetime of underpaid servility. The appeal of clerical work for many persons lay in its potential for secure employment, a feature of white-collar work which has persisted, at least for female employees, throughout most of the twentieth century.

Braverman has suggested that whilst there was considerable diversity in the character of clerical occupations during early industrial capitalism, their incumbents had little in common with the clerks of the late nineteenth and twentieth centuries. This distinction derives partly from the fact that early generations of clerks were virtually untouched by the twin processes of rationalisation and mechanisation.[10]

Despite their numbers and the demand for their labour the clerks of the nineteenth century rarely attempted to display their bargaining strength. Trade union activity was anathema to those who wished to distance themselves from the industrial proletariat. In any case, problems of organisation arose from the fact that they were scattered throughout a great number of offices and business enterprises. The development of white-collar unionism during this century is therefore all the more interesting seen against this background.

The feminisation of white-collar work

Before one attempts to account for the growing association between women and clerical work it is appropriate to offer further explanation for the expansion of clerical occupations which began in the late nineteenth century. According to Braverman, this development may be regarded in part as a reflection of the growing importance of the accounting of value, itself a consequence of the growing complexity of capitalism and the growth in scale of capitalist enterprise.[11]

However, Braverman suggests that the proliferation of paperwork under monopoly capitalism has not resulted simply from a desire to maintain accurate records of company transactions with a view to monitoring the transference of value. He considers that it has also derived from an assumption that dishonesty prevails in intercorporate dealings and characterises the outlook of company employees. In order to insure themselves against the possibility of double-dealing on the part of clients and workers, companies have instituted systems of checking and cross-checking with corresponding implications for the amount of clerical work to be discharged.

Whilst Braverman provides an interesting and thought-provoking interpretation of the growth of clerical work in the late nineteenth and twentieth centuries, the widely documented existence of white-collar 'fiddles', even at the present time, leads one to doubt whether the aims of capitalist accounting are always realised in practice. Yet no matter how one seeks to interpret the expansion of paper processing, there can be little doubt that the remarkable growth of clerical occupations has been paralleled by an equally remarkable transformation in the sexual composition of the clerical labour force.

It is curious that office work has come to be thought of as a typically feminine occupation when one considers the fact that in the nineteenth century it was essentially a masculine preserve. In 1851 there were precisely nineteen female commercial clerks, and women represented only 0.1 per cent of all clerks.[12] In 1971, however, women accounted for 71.9 per cent of all clerks, and according to Lumley, in 1966 they constituted about 46 per cent of the entire white-collar labour force. Male secretaries were highly opposed to the intrusion of women into the office world in the nineteenth century. Alexander Dumas was a secretary before he became a playwright and novelist, and he warned women that 'if they put one foot inside an office, they would lose every vestige of femininity'.[13] Lockwood is less inclined to take the view that such work was ever considered masculine. He maintains that clerical work was already stigmatised as unmanly before women began to enter this form of employment in large numbers, hence the origin of the phrase, 'Born a man, died a clerk.'[14]

The proliferation of white-collar jobs in the late nineteenth century was an important factor in the move towards the recruitment of women into clerical work. It was also a matter of technology, for not only were there more jobs, but there were more tasks as well, as a result of the introduction of typewriters and telephones into offices.[15] Typing and telephoning were considered eminently suitable tasks for women and as long as women were confined to these activities, male clerical workers were not concerned for their own security and status. It was not long, however, before women began to make inroads into what had hitherto been regarded as male territory. The ability to write in shorthand was a skill jealously guarded by the male sex, but during the 1880s women began to attend courses and were soon offering their services as 'shorthand-typists'. This development dealt a severe blow to the self-esteem of the male clerical worker since there were few aspects of his work left which were not now performed by women as well. Office work was now coming to be regarded as women's work and it was already widely felt that women's work consisted of occupations which did not make too many demands on the intellect or physical capabilities.[16] In addition, women were quite prepared to work for less money and so the male clerk's economic security was also threatened.

With regard to the 'supply' side of this development, it should be noted that these women were drawn from a fairly narrow range of the population. Most came from middle-class backgrounds and worked out of sheer necessity, having no husband to support them and in many cases no financial assistance from their families. The alternatives – teaching, governessing and nursing – held few attractions, especially since these often necessitated 'living-in'. Consequently, many women were glad of these new opportunities to obtain a measure of independence from their families and employers. The recruitment of female labour into office work therefore did not represent a massive advance towards emancipation so much as an extension of the opportunities by which the unsupported middle-class woman might avoid destitution. Certainly, employers were little interested in furthering the cause of women's liberation. In hiring female labour they were motivated by expediency and cost efficiency. Conditions were very harsh for the new army of office girls, their freedom being curtailed in a number of ways, such as not being allowed to leave the office building during working hours. The notion that women only worked for pin money was a useful ideology in that it helped to justify low remuneration.

The First World War created still more white-collar jobs, and it was at about this time that novelists began to display an interest in the phenomenon of the female clerk. In his book *Angel Pavement*, J. B. Priestley maps out the clerical career of a young spinster, focusing on her frustrated ambitions and secret fears.[17] In Christopher Morley's *Kitty Foyle* the heroine is rather more successful in achieving her plans for a fully-fledged business career.[18] These novels reflect the fact that the recruitment base for office workers had now grown somewhat wider. Even those families where a young unmarried daughter was not a financial liability now encouraged their female offspring to undertake a clerical career.[19]

Many girls from working-class backgrounds likewise sought jobs in offices in preference to the drudgery of domestic service. Benet suggests that the fact that office girls were typically single, young, much more independent and often more 'daring' in their appearance has much to do with the contemporary image of the typist or secretary as a man-hunting good-time girl.[20]

In 1931, according to Rhee, men still outnumbered women at the lower levels of white-collar work. Thereafter, women formed the majority of such employees so that office work had become well and truly feminised by 1951.[21] This development had not been without effect on the male clerical population. On the one hand, it had brought clear disadvantages in terms of depressed status and pay. This to some extent accounts for the development of a more militant stand among male clerks than had been the case in the nineteenth century. The growing competition for jobs led to the formation of white-collar unions divided not only along occupational lines, but also according to gender.[22] On the other hand, many men gained from the feminisation of the office world. Corresponding to the growth of routine non-manual jobs was a proliferation of lower and middle management positions. Since these necessitated prolonged training and extensive qualifications, women were effectively disqualified from such jobs and confined to the lower levels of the office hierarchy.

The last category of women to enlist in the office battalions were married women. This development was mainly a consequence of the growing need for white-collar workers at the time of the Second World War. For some women, the problem of dependent children was then solved by the provision of state nurseries. The growth of the service sector of the economy after the war entailed a sustained demand for female labour. The idea that a married woman's permanent location should be the home never really managed to re-establish itself as the increasing number of women who entered this and other forms of work after bearing children clearly demonstrated.

The rationalisation of the office

During the twentieth century, and especially since the last war, office work has been substantially transformed. This has involved both the increasing specialisation of functions and the standardisation of administrative procedure. The process has been a gradual one, but real enough to lead several writers to draw a parallel with the processes of industrial rationalisation. Wright Mills writes of the 'alienating conditions of modern work' with respect to the commercial enterprise. If this were to be regarded as an appropriate description of contemporary office work, however, it might be necessary to think in terms of the gigantic, impersonal bureaucratic structures that Wright Mills regards as the typical modern office. Where workers are little more than extensions of elaborate accounting machinery, automatons of the commercial venture, then it is possible that here we might find feelings of social and self-alienation:

> The modern office with its tens of thousands of square feet and its factory-like flow of work is not an informal, friendly place. The drag and beat of work, the 'production unit' tempo, require that time consumed by anything but business at hand be explained and apologised for.[23]

The spread of rationalisation in America has been uneven, but it would appear that it developed earlier and more rapidly than it did in Britain. Lockwood, writing in 1958, was inclined to contest this image of the modern office. He maintained that the proportion of clerical employees who were likely to find themselves in this situation was very small, and that in any case the traditional social relationships of the office militated against the development of impersonality and bureaucratisation.[24] He also pointed out that small administrative units were still the norm in the area of white-collar work. Crozier, writing in 1963, similarly felt that French organisations had yet to experience the full impact of rationalisation.[15]

Although in the past the pace of administrative rationalisation has been slow and uneven, there does seem to be a heightened interest in methods of office organisation at the present time. This appears to have been prompted by the spiralling costs of labour, equipment and space. One can gain some idea of the probable response to these economic pressures from the special reports on office organisation which appear with growing frequency in the quality press. In 1976, and again in 1977, *The Times* ran a series of articles which were entirely taken up with the themes of productivity and efficiency in the office, and which reviewed a wide range of strategies by which management might achieve these goals. These included work measurement and job evaluation schemes; the calculated and systematic use of office space; and the introduction of bonus and incentive schemes.[26] In a similar report published in the *Guardian*, one finds ominous echoes of the Millsian scenario:

> There is no doubt that most office workers are slow to adapt to open planning. They usually complain about the noise and the distraction, but there is evidence that productivity generally improves and people are happier in well-designed open-plan offices. In many ways, people in open-plan offices are more like free-range chickens while those in traditional cellular offices are like battery chickens. It just depends how you like to lay your eggs.

Later in the report, still further emphasis is laid on the boost to productivity if the chickens are housed in open-plan offices:

> It is this last advantage [improved throughput] of open planning that one suspects is really the biggest disadvantage as far as some office staff are concerned. When people complain that they do not like working in open-plan offices, what they may really mean is that they do not like to be seen not working, coming in late, going early, being told off, flirting, dozing, or doing any of the hundred and one things it is possible to get away with in conventional cellular offices.[27]

It may well be that with the passage of time one will be obliged to discard Lockwood's version of the office and to accept the view, adopted by Braverman, that there is little distinction between the modern office and the factory. A more determined pursuit of cost effectiveness by management is certainly likely to encourage a major modification of the office environment and its traditional relationships in the future. It should not be forgotten, however, that there are still thousands of offices which have more in common with the counting-house than with the factory. Both Lockwood and Braverman have pointed out that the opportunity to rationalise clerical processes is very much a function of office size. Until such time as the small administrative unit has been swept away, there will always be some offices which defy comparison with the factory, by virtue of their more traditional organisation and their more intimate character.

The mechanisation of tasks

Since the nineteenth century more and more machines have been introduced into the white-collar environment in order to cut the cost of clerical work and in order to meet the growing need for clerical services. However, at the present time capital investment per member of office staff is relatively low compared with that found among industrial workers. In Britain, average investment per office worker is £500 compared with £5000 per industrial worker. The reason for this disparity is not simply a matter of differences in the character of work performed:

> in the past office staff has been cheap and fairly efficient, and the scope for spending on capital equipment for the office was limited. Today costs of office staff are rising while the general level of competence is falling.[28]

Since the last war, office costs have risen dramatically. In 1950 they represented only one-fifth of the total costs of a typical business, whereas today they represent half. It is this development which is likely to lead to a much more extensive use of office machinery in the future.

Some writers take the view that the growth of office mechanisation has eliminated the traditional distinctions between non-manual and manual work. Mechanisation, especially where it is coupled with administrative rationalisation, is said to have eliminated mental processes or else to have routinised them in such a way that clerical workers now stand on an equal footing with blue-collar labour. Clearly this assertion merits close analysis, since, as Lockwood has pointed out, machinery alone cannot transform the clerk into a factory hand.

According to Lockwood, there are few office machines which

dictate the tempo of the work and to which the operator is merely an appendage. Normally it is the other way round, machines being an extension of or aid to the operator.[29] This is also true of many of the machines which have been introduced since Lockwood wrote *The Blackcoated Worker* in 1958. The calculator, for example, can hardly be said to have transformed either the work situation or the status of the clerk. Lockwood believes that there are cases where office work has become like factory work, that is, where the application of mechanisation and rationalisation have together converted the clerk into a machine-minder, but he considers that such instances are rare. In his view, therefore, the degree of office mechanisation has not proceeded far enough to warrant a comparison between the clerk and the factory operative.

Braverman's description of the contemporary office, which postdates Lockwood's book by some sixteen years, presents a very different picture. Braverman considers that the modern office is now virtually indistinguishable from the factory. He suggests that the clerk has become a 'helpless attendant' of a highly-mechanised, high-speed process, and lists a large number of technological innovations in the character of clerical functions in support of his arguments.[30] However, one is inclined to doubt whether this version of the modern office has universal application. Certainly there have been major technical advances in office equipment during the last decade. These include word-processing systems, micro-computers, automated filing systems and visual display units. Many of these innovations bear comparison with the most advanced factory mechanisation, and in some cases they do entail the subordination of the operator to the machine. Yet it is doubtful whether it is legitimate to regard these as the typical equipment of the average office. Whilst they are certainly being used by the larger companies, and whilst the number of more rudimentary machines is rapidly proliferating even in the smaller offices, it is more accurate to describe office automation as the shape of things to come. The availability of a large pool of cheap female labour has acted, and continues to act, as a brake upon the extent of capital investment in the office. Business-machine manufacturers are increasingly at pains to acquaint managers with the advantages of mechanisation, but there is every indication that managers are very slow to respond. Even in the future there are likely to be offices where extensive mechanisation would not prove cost effective.

As yet, it is difficult to assess the impact of increased mechanisation and automation upon the demand for white-collar labour. A survey conducted by the Ministry of Labour found that the net effect of office automation up to 1 January 1965 had been to reduce the number of office jobs by only three-quarters of one per cent. It predicted that in any case by the year 1975 more new jobs would have been created than those which had been eliminated. It also suggested that the growing application of computers merely offset a growing shortage of office staff.[31] Since this report was produced, however, the cost of clerical labour has risen very markedly, and some of the more recent forms of office mechanisation are quite clearly intended as aids towards the planned reduction of staff costs. This is particularly true of the word processor. In an article in *The Times* on 15 September 1976 entitled 'The £4,000 typist substitute that will soon pay for itself', the chief of office administration at a Lloyd's underwriting agency was reported as saying that without her word processor she would need the assistance of at least one full-time typist or perhaps two. Machines of this nature do not necessarily create redundancy, but they most certainly curb the demand for labour because of their revolutionary impact upon levels of productivity.

The silicon chip is a new development which may well have a profound impact on the demand for office labour. This is a tiny wafer of silicon on which it is possible to put as much information as was once stored by a huge computer. This chip facilitates the production of very small, very cheap data-processing systems and thus places automation within the range of even small firms. Although the full impact of this development belongs firmly to the future, the government has already expressed concern regarding the employment consequences of micro-processors.

It seems that it is the lower grades of white-collar work which have been most noticeably affected by the twin processes of mechanisation and rationalisation, and it should be noted that it is these very categories which are overwhelmingly dominated by women.[32]

White-collar unionism

In spite of the general dearth of sociological literature relating to white-collar workers, there are quite a few studies of the growth of

TABLE 2.1   *The growth of total white-collar and manual unionism in the UK, 1948–64*

	1948 (000s)	1964 (000s)	% change 1948–64
Total white-collar unionism	1964	2623	+33.6
Total manual unionism	7398	7442	+ 0.6

SOURCE G. S. Bain, *The Growth of White-collar Unionism* (Oxford University Press, 1970) p. 25. © G. S. Bain 1970.

white-collar unionism. The expansion in membership is essentially a post-war phenomenon, and, as Bain has noted, the figures are impressive – see Table 2.1.

However, if one considers changes in the density of membership, that is the relationship between actual and potential membership, then, as Bain has pointed out, the figures are far less dramatic. For during the period 1948–64, the density of total white-collar unionism only increased from 28.8 per cent to 29 per cent. In fact, the apparently remarkable growth represented by absolute numbers merely reflects the growth in the number of white-collar occupations.

More recent figures, however, show that there has been a definite expansion in membership density since the mid-1960s. Bain and Price state that there was a 9 per cent increase in density between 1964 and 1970 and that density rose to as much as 39.4 per cent in 1974.[33] The increase in union density after the mid-1960s proceeded at a faster pace than the growth of white-collar employment.

Lumley has pointed out that if one were to include staff and professional associations within the category of white-collar unions, the current overall density would be approximately 50 per cent, a figure which compares favourably with that of 52.7 per cent for manual workers.[34] Statistics relating to white-collar unionism are notoriously difficult to interpret, however. Quite apart from the kind of problems which they pose for a sociologist sensitive to meaning, other difficulties arise over the question of classification. For example, Bain has noted that one-fifth of total white-collar union membership belongs to unions which cater for both manual and non-manual workers and separate figures are not always available. The figures also conceal wide variations in membership density between different occupational categories. Nevertheless, the figures do present us with a rough guide, and in themselves offer a striking contrast with the low degree of unionisation in the nineteenth century. The history of the growth of white-collar unionism includes many developments which have already been discussed, such as feminisation, but an important feature is the declining economic position of the clerk relative to that of the industrial labourer.

In terms of average earnings, male clerical workers now lag behind not only skilled but even semi-skilled manual employees.[35] In terms of fringe benefits, the clerk has traditionally been in a superior position to that of the labourer, although even here a narrowing of differences has been reported.[36] More and more manual workers are covered by pension schemes (although these are usually based on basic rather than on average earnings), receive sick pay and have longer holidays. With reference to the latter, Scott and Deere comment: 'Office staff entitlement seems now to be little different from that of many manual workers.'[37]

In recent years, one of the main pressures making for an improvement in the work conditions of manual workers has been the introduction of statutory and 'voluntary' incomes policy. The granting of longer holidays is just one of the ways in which employers have sought to circumvent the pay restrictions imposed by successive governments. Although, as Lumley has stated, the narrowing gap between manual and non-manual workers in terms of pay and fringe benefits cannot by itself account for the growth of white-collar unionism, it nevertheless remains an important background factor: 'Many white-collar employees see the relative advance of the blue-collar labour force as due to strong organisation, and so they seek to emulate this in order to defend their position.'[38]

Some writers, however, prefer to attach more weight to the actions of government and employers than to other factors in their analyses of trends in white-collar unionism. Bain, for example, while not wholly discounting the significance of changes in the relative status, income and security of white-collar workers, is of the opinion that these factors are of only negligible importance:

If this has left white-collar workers unhappy, it does not seem to have encouraged them to unionize. At least, it is not possible to demonstrate any connection between the economic position of various white-collar groups and the degree to which they are unionized.[39]

In his view, employment concentration tends to promote the growth of white-collar unionism, but more important determinants are the extent to which employers are prepared to recognise the unions, and the willingness of the government to introduce policies which enable the unions to exert pressure for recognition. He therefore concludes that the activities of employers and governments in these respects will determine the future growth of white-collar unionism.

It is clear that the factors which account for the growth of white-collar unionism are highly complex and extremely difficult to interpret. One should not overlook the fact that the various factors will affect white-collar workers very differently, depending on their market position and orientation to work. Crompton has pointed out that the class situation of the white-collar workforce displays a heterogeneous and ambiguous character, and that consequently it is necessary for theoretical approaches in this field of enquiry to reflect this diversity if they are to have any value.[40] Silverman, who has conducted research into the relationship between clerical ideologies and organisational factors, also considers that it is most important to emphasise the heterogeneous nature of the white-collar workforce: 'If we are to advance from speculation, the pressing need would now seem to be the attempt to dismantle the notion that there exists a unitary occupational group of "white-collar workers" or "clerks".'[41]

Work satisfaction

The awareness that occupations on the shop floor have grown further and further away from traditional notions of craftsmanship has led to a great deal of interest in what sources of job satisfaction, if any, remain for the contemporary manual worker. There has been a corresponding literature, if not quite as extensive, relating to the changing nature of work satisfaction for the white-collar worker. Central to many of these studies is the distinction between intrinsic and extrinsic sources of job satisfaction. No matter what other changes may occur in the work situation of the white-collar worker, it is claimed, he will normally derive, or expect to derive, his primary satisfaction from intrinsic factors such as interest in work, opportunities for exercising responsibility, skilled and varied tasks, and to that extent, the clerk differs markedly from the manual worker, who is supposedly bound to his work by the cash nexus. In their investigation of the embourgeoisement thesis, Goldthorpe and his colleagues compared attitudes to work among manual and non-manual workers in the Luton area. They found that the performance of work tasks and work roles was a direct source of satisfaction significantly more often among non-manual workers. Expectations from work in terms of social relationships, promotion prospects, and relations with superiors were also markedly different between the two groups.[42]

Crozier considers that whilst white-collar work is fast assuming some of the disadvantages which are associated with manual work, such as lack of autonomy, it nevertheless facilitates identification with the ruling classes and has many compensations.[43] Crozier feels that it is important to distinguish between 'interest in the work' and 'satisfaction with position'. The former, he maintains, derives from an employee's location in a hierarchy of functional prestige, whereas the latter derives from a person's ability to manoeuvre within the system. The overall picture of white-collar attitudes that emerges, says Crozier, is one of:

> persons relatively lukewarm toward their work and their positions, but whose opinions are nevertheless varied and do not correspond at all to the image of the downtrodden small bureaucrat, robot of modern civilization, disseminated by the literature of the years between the two wars.[44]

The most important contribution of this study is its focus on relative satisfactions and degrees of interest among white-collar workers themselves. Although these differences are not fully explored, he does point out that male employees are slightly more satisfied than females, as are those who have more seniority over those with less. In another study, he found that great rivalry prevailed amongst groups, and that each group asserted its interest in its work as a means of demonstrating superiority:

Members of higher-level categories received as a traumatic shock the news that their colleagues in lower-level categories were really interested in their work; this was the point whose significance they made the greatest effort to minimize even when quantified results were submitted.[45]

There are grounds for thinking that the white-collar worker is not entirely untainted by instrumental thoughts. Mercer and Weir, in their study of four groups of white-collar workers, maintain that whilst their respondents attached importance to intrinsic features of their work, it would be highly surprising if they did not. For after all, a person's self-image is closely bound up with his or her occupation, and it would be tantamount to an admission of personal failure if one admitted to no satisfaction in one's job.[46] Moreover, their research findings show quite clearly that there is a strong emphasis on work as a source of economic reward, although the extent to which this is so varies according to the occupational group. Whilst a question relating to current sources of satisfaction showed that these are overwhelmingly the intrinsic aspects of work, a question concerning the most attractive features of a prospective job revealed that economic considerations were of equal if not greater importance for many of their respondents. Their findings draw attention to the fact that it is erroneous to assume that employees display a consistent set of priorities in their attitudes to work.

The multi-dimensional character of attitudes towards work among white-collar employees was explored in an early study by Nancy Morse. She distinguished between intrinsic job satisfaction, financial and job status satisfaction and level of company involvement. With regard to intrinsic job satisfaction, Morse found that for most people jobs which were more varied and which required more skill and decision-making were more satisfying. An important finding, however, was that work which was deficient in these qualities was not necessarily a cause for complaint. This was because in some cases perceptions of job content might be positively influenced by the experience of satisfaction with other aspects of the work situation, or because the level of expectation held in relation to job content was fairly modest. Thus Morse concluded that satisfaction was not determined simply by job content, but also by the surrounding context of other satisfactions and by individual levels of aspiration.[47]

Mercer and Weir have also stressed the relative character of perceptions of work among white-collar employees. Although it is often argued that 'boredom and monotony are the major occupational hazards of the clerk', they are somewhat wary of such typifications.[48] They, like Morse, and also Crozier, found that seemingly boring, repetitive work was not necessarily a cause for dissatisfaction.[49] They maintain that 'valid satisfaction (relative to the expectations of those involved) may, in fact, be derived from work which *appears to the outside observer* to be boring, monotonous and repetitive'.

There may well be more than a grain of truth in these words. It should never be forgotten that studies of white-collar workers are typically undertaken by those who occupy more prestigious positions in the occupational hierarchy. When academics cast their eyes downwards upon the serried ranks of clerical workers, perhaps there is a subconscious feeling that 'there, but for the grace of God, go I'. Just as the more exalted clerks in Crozier's study found it impossible to accept the fact that the lower orders found genuine satisfaction in their work, it is equally possible that sociologists cannot tolerate the idea that intrinsic job satisfaction is not peculiar to highly-qualified occupations. From the remote and lofty observation platform of the sociologist, routine non-manual work may seem a colourless enclave of boredom and monotony. He should be more prepared to put his prejudices to the test by undertaking a close examination of the white-collar world. All too often, these subjective judgements are a reason for ignoring it.

Indeed, the world of entertainment appears to have devoted more attention to the clerk than have industrial sociologists. I have already mentioned the proliferation of novels in the 1920s which explored the life of the female office worker. In the cinema industry, too, the office has provided the setting for many a film. Some, such as *The Rebel* and *The Apartment*, have emphasised the alienating conditions of the office environment. In the former, Tony Hancock attempts to overcome perpetual boredom by doodling caricatures of the other male clerks in the huge open-plan office where he works. In the latter, Jack Lemmon is so intent upon escape from a similar environment that he is obliged to offer his apartment to senior executives for their extra-business, extra-marital activities, in the hope that they will reward him with promotion. *How to Succeed in Business Without Really Trying* presents a rather different image. Here, employment as a clerk, far from being dull and monotonous, is an occasion for song and dance, and the journey to the top of the organisation is smoothly and swiftly accomplished.

Whilst sociology has never glamourised the white-collar world to this extent, it nevertheless offers a similarly wide-ranging set of images. At one end of the spectrum is Wright Mills' gloomy pessimism, a vision of frustrated hopes and alienation, and at the other, Crozier's qualified optimism, a belief in greater opportunities for the clerk to determine his own work situation. It hardly needs to be said that more information is required before we can reasonably assess these very different interpretations. One thing is certain: the female office worker remains something of a mystery, since few of these studies have focused on her directly. In the next chapter, I shall endeavour to make up for this discrepancy.

3

Women in the Office

Nine o'clock in the morning on a cold winter's day in the city . . . and everywhere you look women are striding briskly to work, bare-legged in zero degree weather . . . Most of these women are striding toward their typewriters and yesterday's unfinished dictation, toward a banking job where they count money rather than make it, toward work with no future except more of the same. Married or unmarried, ambitious or not, they are making their daily rendezvous with a world in which women are largely *tolerated*, on the grounds that men can no more be expected to use a typewriter or answer the telephone than to wash socks or clean house.[1]

In spite of the fact that nearly half of all white-collar workers are women, few sociologists have considered it worthwhile to turn the spotlight on their experiences and attitudes.[2] They are often excluded from empirical studies of clerical workers, or else accorded footnote status of a mainly statistical nature. Some studies attach little or no importance to the sexual composition of their subjects, their authors seemingly of the opinion that the gender of a white-collar worker is of no consequence for attitudes to work, location in the office hierarchy, opportunities for promotion, or indeed any other aspect of the work situation.

A notable exception is Mumford and Banks' *The Computer and the Clerk*, which, although primarily a study of the social impact of computerisation in two firms, incorporates an extended discussion of sex differences in attitudes towards and responses to the introduction of automation. Although the authors point towards considerable diversity in the attitudes of female clerical workers to changes of this nature, women, on the whole, are characterised as less work-oriented than men, and as placing more importance on the social ambience of the workplace. To a large extent Mumford and Banks regard this attenuated interest in the work *per se* as a product of young girls' preoccupation with marriage and social activities beyond the workplace. The extent to which these 'short-term personal work goals' are socially constructed within the work context itself, however, does not represent an important focus of their study. Consequently it is not at all clear whether employer discrimination or other forms of social interaction in the work context reinforce or even create this apparently diminished interest in the character of the work.

Another well-known study of white-collar workers, Lockwood's *The Blackcoated Worker*, tends to give minimal attention to female employees and generally subscribes to some rather stereotyped images.[3] Crozier's study of white-collar workers in six Parisian companies presents us with a picture of women workers concentrated in the more routine positions, but does not offer any satisfactory explanation as to why this should be so. Although he recognises that women were prominent among people holding an inferior status within the firm, which in his view might account for the presence of apathy and indifference among them, one gains little insight into the mechanisms which confine women to the lower levels of the office status hierarchy.[4] Apart from these studies, there are very few 'established' pieces of research which have concerned themselves wholly or in part with the subject of life in the female ghetto. There is no shortage of references, however, among the many volumes of feminist literature, which add up to a picture of frustration, servitude and exploitation.[5] Benet's *Secretary* is the only published book known to the present writer which is exclusively devoted to the subject of the female office worker.[6] There is no attempt to disguise the feminist orientations of the author, but it represents a truly comprehensive and thoughtful investigation which succeeds in exploding many of the myths concerning female clerks and secretaries. Since it does not incorporate any systematic analysis of their attitudes and work situations, however, it is unlikely to gain academic respectability, especially because of the author's journalistic background. The same is probably true of Korda's discussion of sexual gamesmanship in the office, *Male Chauvinism: How it Works*, which affords a rare insight into the fantasies and prejudices of male executives in the American business community.[7] Wright Mills, who is of course academically respectable, wrote a fascinating book about white-collar workers, but while his section on girls in the office is highly illuminating with regard to how they were perceived by novelists in the 1920s, we learn very little about the contemporary situation.[8]

There is every reason to suppose that the future will yield a torrent of literature on the subject of women in the office, mainly because the feminist movement has brought about a heightened interest in the subject of women generally amongst sociologists. It seems inevitable that they will shortly focus on that field of work which accounts for over one-quarter (29 per cent) of all female employees, and one hopes that their findings will dispel many of the assumptions which for too long have lingered in the minds of managers and academics alike. For the present, however, one is obliged to rely heavily upon a great deal of non-academic source material in order to construct a picture of female white-collar employment. At an advanced stage of this research, I was fortunate enough to gain access to two studies of a sociological nature, both of which are as yet unpublished. One of these is Silverstone's *The Office Secretary*, and the other is Shaw, Elsy and Bowen's *Office Girls: Education and Job Choice*. Both represent a marked departure from earlier studies of office life in that they focus primarily on women and are not based on the assumption that women's attitudes to work are fixed by their out-of-work preoccupations and circumstances. The findings of these studies have proved invaluable for the purpose of providing strong support for observations based upon non-academic sources of information.

A further source of information was provided by the numerous American and British journals which publish articles concerning personnel policy and work attitudes. Since many of the studies have been conducted from a managerialist perspective, however, they possess certain limitations from the point of view of the sociologist.

The following discussion covers a great many aspects of female employment in white-collar work. The ultimate aim of this section, however, is to demonstrate the ways in which the decision to engage in temporary as opposed to permanent employment may be regarded as a response to a range of problems encountered by women in this sphere of the labour market.

Female white-collar workers – a general survey

The occupational distribution of female office workers

At the present time, more than two million women in England and Wales are employed as clerical workers, and there is every sign that their numbers will continue to grow.[9] According to the DES, in the late 1960s 40 per cent of girl school-leavers aged under eighteen went into this kind of work.[10] Recently there has been a marked increase in the proportion of girls entering clerical work, so that in 1973 this was the occupational choice of no less than 60 per cent of girl leavers[11]

Table 3.1 illustrates the principal trends which took place in the proportion and distribution of female office workers during the period 1911 to 1971. It is necessary to mention the fact that Price and Bain interpret white-collar work in its very broadest sense to include, for example, sales personnel, whereas we are strictly concerned with clerical workers, but their data is of considerable interest in that women's minority representation among the ranks of managers and administrators is clearly a constant feature of the white-collar world. In contrast, their representation among the humbler ranks has actually grown more than three-fold during the same period. According to the 1971

TABLE 3.1. *The proportion of female workers in white-collar occupations in Great Britain, 1911–71*

Category of white-collar work	Percentage of females					
	1911	1931	1951	1961	1966	1971
All white-collar workers	29.8	35.8	42.3	44.5	46.5	46.2
Managers and administrators	19.8	13.0	15.2	15.4	16.7	18.5
Higher professionals	6.0	7.5	8.3	9.7	9.4	10.0
Lower professionals and technicians	62.9	58.8	53.5	50.8	52.1	51.9
Foremen and inspectors	4.2	8.7	13.4	10.3	11.4	12.8
Clerks	21.4	46.0	60.2	65.2	69.3	71.9
Salesmen and shop assistants	35.2	37.2	51.6	54.9	58.7	59.4

SOURCE R. Price and G. S. Bain, 'Union Growth Revisited: 1948–1974 in Perspective', *British Journal of Industrial Relations*, vol. XIV, no. 3, table 7, p. 348.

census, women represented: 63 per cent of all clerks and cashiers; 83 per cent of all telephone operators; 86 per cent of all office machine operators; and 99 per cent of all typists, shorthand writers and secretaries.[12]

The jobs of comptometer operating, filing, copy-typing and telephone answering are not renowned as stepping stones to the director's chair, while the job of secretary is sometimes alleged to lead in that direction, but quite incorrectly so. The jobs that women do in the white-collar world on the whole preclude upward movement, and in the case of those positions which theoretically offer some opportunities for advancement through the ranks, men rather than women tend to benefit. Blackburn's study of bank clerks is illuminating with regard to this latter point: 'Careers in banking are for men; the routine work such as machine operating is for women. This distinction is basic; women are employed for "women's work" and it is only the outstanding women who can progress to "men's work".'[13] Blackburn states that the banks regard men and women as 'two different classes of employee', and that this attitude is particularly noticeable in recruitment literature where the banks encourage young men to aspire to careers in management, and young girls to aspire to jobs as secretaries, supervisors or super-clerks: 'the keen and intelligent girl may ultimately undertake the duties of: Cashier, Ledger Supervisor, Income Tax Clerk or Correspondence Clerk'.[14]

Blackburn concludes that any change in this sex-differentiated structure of banking occupations will only come about if there is a shortage of male recruits. While recent legislation is designed to foster improved opportunities for women in jobs such as banking, the fact that more and more women seem to be handing us our money over the counter these days has probably more to do with the diminishing supply of male school-leavers who opt for banking, rather than a pioneering attitude on the part of the Big Four.

Sullerot has noted that the concentration of women in the least-skilled, least prestigious, lowest paid white-collar jobs is the rule in most Western societies, especially in the public sector of employment. Even in 'go-ahead' Sweden, 73 per cent of women in public employment are found in the lowest categories, whereas 73 per cent of the men are found in the higher categories.[15]

The work of Fogarty *et al.* offers considerable insight into the promotion prospects of secretaries. Part of their research is concerned with the occupational background of ninety-six male and ninety-six female managers in a large company. Apart from the fact that women are 'a distinct minority' among top management, less than 20 per cent of the women managers came up via the secretarial route, whereas well over a third 'came in with some expertise already established as a result of specialist training or experience in other work'.[16] Men on the whole took longer to reach management status than women, but some of them had been 'plodding up the ladder from the humble beginnings of errand boy or junior clerk', whereas no women had worked their way up from such modest levels on the occupational ladder. Thus, the fact that there is a diminishing number of opportunities for long-range upward mobility in the white-collar world appears to be especially true in the case of women. The findings of this study suggest that entry into management without specialised training will be a very rare experience in the future for either sex.

Stassinopoulos is inclined to regard women's relative absence from the higher echelons of the white-collar hierarchy as something of a blessing in disguise. Unlike men, they are not vulnerable to any stresses and strains in their work, because they possess 'freedom':

> They are not trapped by a career ladder to which they must hang on like grim death, struggling from rung to rung, hoping against hope to succeed 'old Boggins' as deputy assistant acting temporary manager, and dreading the day when a rung snaps and plunges the climber into the proletarian abyss.[17]

It may well be true that most women are not constrained, as many male breadwinners are, into risking their physical and mental health for the sake of moving up a few grades in the office hierarchy, but this is small consolation to those women who do aspire towards more responsible positions but who can find no way round the obstacles which stand in their path.

Pay and conditions

Evidence from a number of sources shows quite clearly that female clerical workers are paid less than their male counterparts, even when one excludes the effect of overtime earnings. The New

Earnings Survey of 1977, for example, showed that the average hourly earnings of adult male full-time clerical workers was 167.1 np, whereas that of women was 129.3 np.[18] Further confirmation of the existence of a marked differential is provided by Shaw, Elsy and Bowen. Whereas 54 per cent of their male respondents earned £1500 — £2000+, only 7.8 per cent of their female respondents fell into this bracket. They also found that this differential could not be accounted for simply in terms of the relatively greater age of their male sample.[19] Within the broad occupational category of clerical work women's earnings do vary, depending on the particular skill and level of responsibility, but as a group their earnings are significantly lower than those of men. An IDS survey of women's pay and employment shows that part of the reason for this discrepancy is the existence in many companies of 'men's work' and 'women's work', which are differently graded.[20]

With regard to sickness pay and occupational pension schemes, women clerical workers are once again found to be in an inferior position. According to the 1970 New Earnings Survey, 93 per cent of males in non-manual office and communications occupations were covered by sick pay schemes, and 70 per cent by occupational pensions schemes. The corresponding figures for women were 85 per cent and 36 per cent respectively.[21] With regard to annual holiday entitlement, women clerks again hold a less favourable position. Although the majority of both men and women employed in full-time clerical work can expect to receive between three to four weeks annual holiday, the New Earnings Survey of 1974 found that whilst 53 per cent of men in these occupations received four weeks or more annual holiday, only 32 per cent of women did so.[22] Benet considers that women not only receive inferior pay and fringe benefits, but that their working environment is usually less favourable than that of men:

> It has recently been shown that women tend to receive the same proportion of office space as they do of pay – 20 per cent to 50 per cent less than that of men doing roughly the same work in the same office . . . The higher the concentration of women in a particular area of the office, the lower the standard of decor.[23]

Union membership

Throughout the twentieth century women white-collar workers have exhibited a lower overall density of union membership than men. It is often supposed that this discrepancy may be explained partly in terms of female personality traits. For example, one writer has suggested that 'women are generally more conservative than men'.[24] Bain, however, considers that the difference between the sexes in respect of union density cannot be explained in terms of innate or learned dispositions. In his opinion, the lower proportion of female employees who belong to unions must be accounted for in terms of the occupational and industrial distribution of the female workforce. He points out that there is a direct relationship between union density and size of establishment, and that since female employment (in manufacturing industry) is 'skewed in the direction of small establishments', we would expect them to exhibit a lower rate of union membership. He also proposes that 'the greater the degree of employment concentration the greater the density of white-collar unionism'.[25] Women, however, are less numerous in those industries which have a high degree of employment concentration, and more numerous in those which have a low degree of employment concentration. He concludes that women do not possess inherent qualities which make them more difficult to organise and agrees with the view of Lockwood that: 'the proportion of women in clerical unions is usually roughly equal to their representation in the field of employment which the unions seek to organise.'[26]

The idea that women in white-collar work are less union-minded than their male counterparts is also undermined by the fact that there is a higher proportion of unionisation among women than among men in the public sector. Moreover, a historical perspective casts considerable doubt on the notion that the propensity of women white-collar workers to organise is finite. Table 3.2 shows the trends in both union membership and union density for the period 1948–74. It is evident from these figures that whilst women still lag behind men in terms of both criteria of unionisation there has nevertheless been a very considerable growth in female white-collar unionism since the war.

There is no way of knowing whether the growth of female

TABLE 3.2   *Sex differences in white-collar unionism in the UK, 1948—74*

Membership of white-collar unions (000s)											
Male				Percentage increase		Female				Percentage incre	
1948	1964	1970	1974	1948–74	1970–4	1948	1964	1970	1974	1948–74	1970–
1267	1681	2143	2593	+104.7	+21.0	697	1003	1447	1629	+133.7	+12

Union density (%)											
Male				Percentage increase		Female				Percentage incre	
1948	1964	1970	1974	1948–74	1970–4	1948	1964	1970	1974	1948–74	1970–
33.8	33.4	40.0	44.5	+10.7	+4.5	25.4	24.9	30.7	32.6	+7.2	+1.9

SOURCE Derived from R. Price and G. S. Bain, 'Union Growth Revisited: 1948–1974 in F spective', *British Journal of Industrial Relations,* vol. XIV, no. 3, table 8, p. 349.

membership and union density has been due simply to greater activity on the part of the unions in their drive to recruit new members, or whether changes in the situation of female clerical workers has brought about a heightened interest in union membership. At any rate, this development does represent a challenge to stereotyped thinking, as do instances of union militancy among certain categories of white-collar workers.[27]

A recent example of militancy, involving secretaries belonging to NATSOPA, provides a useful insight into the way in which attempts to secure better wages and conditions can be frustrated by the indifference of union hierarchies. In 1977, according to a report in *Spare Rib*, secretaries working at *The Times* decided to press for higher wages. Seven months after this decision was taken, the women concerned were still waiting for the union to arrange a meeting with the management. The secretaries were reported as saying that they had been instructed to stop writing to the branch because they were annoying the union. In the meantime, the secretaries had embarked on a vigorous campaign to publicise their cause, which included such tactics as sticking up posters and writing slogans on letters.[28]

There are no grounds for supposing, therefore, that female white-collar workers are simply more conservative than men. However, it is important to bear in mind that female clerical workers are highly stratified. There are tremendous differences between the filing clerk and the executive secretary, not only in terms of their social and educational background and degree of training, but also in terms of their work situation, status and in particular their relationship with employers. Lumley considers that the close contact between the secretary and her employer generates a strong feeling of company loyalty on the part of the former which militates against her identification with the office proletariat.[29] Thus, a knowledge of the sources and character of differentiation within the ranks of female office staff is relevant to an understanding of variable patterns of unionisation among this group.

The office secretary

Official statistics often make no distinction between typists, shorthand-typists and secretaries, as though one could legitimately regard life in the all-girl typing pool as identical to life in the inner sanctum of the senior executive's suite of offices. Nothing could be further from the truth. The twin processes of technology and business rationalisation have brought about a division of clerical functions into two separate components, executed by two different groups of employees. The first category comprises the true secretary – the boss's personal assistant who, whilst performing a degree of routine work such as typing, taking dictation and filing, spends a great deal of time organising her employer's daily activities. The other category of worker is engaged almost exclusively on routine paper work, and is increasingly located at some distance from the corridors of power. The only aspect of their work situation which is common to both groups is that men typically hire them and fire them, administer and control them, and in some cases, regard them as sexual entertainment. It is essential, therefore, to consider them separately, and this section will be devoted to those who are situated at the apex of the status hierarchy of female office workers.

On becoming a secretary

There is no need for a woman to prove herself equal: she is acknowledged equal, and different. The making of a home, its happiness, beauty and comfort is for younger married couples today a partnership of equals. For girls who look forward to this, at a time when people are getting married at younger ages, what careers are there which provide the dignity of intelligent work without prolonged years of study and several years of practice to ensure competence? Perhaps the most obvious is a secretarial career?[30]

Ever since Remington introduced his first female typewriters in 1873, secretarial work has been considered an ideal occupation for women. It has attracted women of all social backgrounds and ages, and will no doubt continue to do so for many decades to come, despite the frenzied activity of office-machine salesmen who would like to persuade employers that word-processing machines are more productive. There is not a great deal of systematic evidence in published form relating to modes of recruitment to secretarial positions, but it is possible to identify several different routes into this occupation.

First, it is possible to become a secretary by undertaking a specialised training course at a private college. The reputation of these colleges, their typical recruits and the degree of emphasis placed on purely vocational skills vary enormously. They range from the select finishing-school type of establishment which offers a training in grooming, gourmet cooking and etiquette, in addition to instruction in secretarial skills, to the more matter-of-fact locally-attended private commercial college. The former variant represents the natural extension of boarding school for many daughters of the upper middle class, its curriculum reminiscent of the training in accomplishments for mid-nineteenth-century characters in search of a husband. One suspects that the latter variety is more likely to recruit ex-grammar school girls (or their contemporary equivalents from the comprehensive schools) or those from private day schools.

A second mode of entry is via a college of further education, where the emphasis is strictly on skills appropriate to the office, although there may be provision for specialised courses involving the use of foreign languages and the chance to learn secretarial skills among many others in a general business studies course. It appears that many of the women who undertake these more specialised courses subsequently enter secretarial work only by default. In the spring of 1978 I spoke to a group of girls who were pursuing a bilingual secretarial course at a college of higher education in the South-east. Without exception, the secretarial component of their course was regarded as entirely secondary to the task of developing linguistic proficiency. Not one of them expressed any interest in following a secretarial career and all envisaged an occupational future which would grant them the opportunity to use their language skills. However, their optimism was not shared by their language tutor:

> Their bread and butter subject is their shorthand-typing. They're not going to go in and get jobs as linguists. In very few instances will they be able to say to a firm, 'Look, I can speak French and German. I can write it. I've got my Grade II in this and my intermediate in the other – employ me as a linguist.' Very few *graduates* in languages are employed as linguists.

In the case of girls such as these, secretarial work is seen as a last resort. Yet while this view may be based on a correct appraisal of the limited opportunities to be found in secretarial jobs, it appears to be matched by an equally incorrect assessment of the likely outcome of their training. It seems highly probable that the ranks of secretaries include many girls like these, for whom the last resort has actually become a way of life.

A third route is the graduate secretarial course, the development of which betokens the limited pool of opportunities for female graduates. It is possible to take such a course at one or other of the establishments named above, but some institutions of higher education offer special courses for women graduates. There is even a first-degree course in secretarial studies at Strathclyde University for girls who have anticipated the likely outcome of three years devoted to the complexities of Middle English. The course includes the usual training in shorthand, typing and business machines practice (involving 'machine laboratory work'), plus a selection of courses in business studies. It is hard to see what distinguishes this BA in secretarial work from any other high-powered course in office skills, although the Director of the Centre, Mary Dunn, clearly believes that her products will become indispensable in the offices of the future:

> The Centre has a firm belief that modern management, constantly on the go, facing pressures their predecessors never dreamed of, needs the assistance of secretaries whose education

and training is of university level. This is not to underestimate or in any way denigrate the many competent experienced secretaries who have not been to university nor indeed had any formal higher education. But such women will become rarer . . . The top positions in future are likely to be held by the University and Polytechnic trained girls, and the most important jobs will go to the graduate secretary.[31]

It seems unlikely that the prophecies of the Director will be fulfilled, when one considers the findings of Silverstone concerning the attributes which employers value most in their secretaries. She claims that most employers operate with a set of minimum requirements with regard to the education and secretarial qualifications of potential secretaries. Furthermore, they tend to place much more emphasis on ability in such traditional skills as typing and shorthand than on business acumen or knowledge of finance, banking and economics.[32] This being so, one would suppose that given a choice between a girl equipped with a BA (Secretarial Skills) and a more conventionally qualified secretary, both displaying equal dexterity on the typewriter and the notepad, an employer would be more likely to choose the girl whose training had not aroused 'great expectations' with regard to income.

A fourth route into this occupation is by attempting to gain or to work one's way towards a secretarial position on the basis of skills acquired at school. One would have thought it unlikely that this method would lead to the high-status, well-paid jobs without some form of further training being undertaken en route. Silverstone maintains, however, that in central London the general shortage of office staff tends to enhance the opportunities for advancement among those having only the bare minimum of qualifications.[33] Over half of her secretarial respondents had worked their way up from positions as typists, clerks, shorthand-typists or general office workers.

These represent the principal routes of access to secretarial positions, although there are many other ways in which it is possible to train. Both private and state institutions run part-time courses and evening courses, and many crash courses are available in the larger cities. Some firms are willing to train girls themselves or to sponsor them for courses at local colleges. The government operates a training opportunities scheme which enables those who wish to train somewhat later in life to do so at the government's expense.

The battalions of secretaries are thus highly differentiated in terms of training and also in terms of social and educational background. It is likely, however, that many of them will have been encouraged prior to their entry into the labour market, to foster ambitious hopes for the future:

> Promotion opportunities for secretaries are legion. The fascinating world of business is alive with endless possibilities for still greater advancement. Secretarial experience is often the 'way in' to interesting and highly paid posts in big firms and organizations. Many prominent women in the advertising world started their working lives as secretaries, and the knowledge they gained during those early years led to the wider horizons of advertising . . . Women executives in senior Government positions have graduated from the ranks of secretaries. A large percentage of successful business women also started life this way.[34]

The advice manuals for prospective secretaries are filled with tempting visions of the future, usually based on the careers of most exceptional women. Girls are frequently informed in these books that it is but a short step from the job of personal assistant to that of junior executive, and that devotion to one's boss and company will inevitably reap the due rewards. All this is quite at odds with the facts. According to Silverstone, most employers do not consider that there is a natural progression from secretarial to executive duties, and any such movement necessitates a specialised form of training.[35] Advertisements similarly tend to propagate the 'Marcia Williams Myth'. For example, one advert placed by the Department of the Environment reads: 'I never dreamt when I became a Senior Personal Secretary here just how closely I'd be involved with affairs of national importance.'[36] Upon closer examination of the copy, this involvement with top-level affairs turns out to be somewhat more humble than first impressions would indicate:

> You take notes for your boss at high level meetings, arrange appointments for him (and remind him to keep them!) and

organise his Diary generally. Depending on whom you're working for, you could be dealing with telephone calls and correspondence from Cabinet Ministers, MPs, important businessmen and specialists of every kind.

A great many advertisements tend to activate the career ambitions fondly nourished by the secretarial colleges, although the majority apparently recognise that the exercise of power will be experienced at most vicariously by the average secretary.

The theme that the ultimate ambition of a secretary should be to attach herself to an important boss is a recurrent one in the advice manuals. The importance of her work is determined by his prestige and position, rather than in terms of any ultimate standard of competence:

> You want to be a secretary – a top secretary, the able assistant to an important executive. You know that as a secretary you'll enjoy a busy, exciting career. And when Mr Important Executive brags that credit for his success goes to you, his secretary, you can beam proudly, knowing that your contribution is, indeed, a valuable one.[37]

In view of the fact that the manuals place so much emphasis on obtaining important glamorous jobs in close proximity to important glamorous men, it is not surprising to find that prospective secretaries have very clear preferences regarding the type of employers they would like to work for. In a survey by Williams and Root, a top ten of employers emerged from the responses of a sample of women secretarial trainees, the results of which are shown in Table 3.3.

At the bottom of the list were building societies, building firms, gas and electricity offices, London Transport and trade unions, with not a single mention between them. The authors conclude that:

> The reasons for the overwhelming popularity of the top ten employers are probably fairly complex, but their frequent exposure in the mass media, linked with glamorous situations and young people, may be an important contributive factor.[38]

TABLE 3.3. *The type of employer which trainee secretaries would most like to work for*

Rank	Employers	Number of mentions on 'popularity'
1	Airlines	70
2	Travel agencies	51
3	BBC	50
4	Film companies	47
5	Fashion houses	36
6	Advertising agencies	26
6	Newspapers and magazines	26
8	Hospitals	25
9	Hotels	21
10	Doctors and dentists	16
10	Oil companies	16

SOURCE R. Williams and M. Root, 'Has Your Company Got Secretary Appeal?' *Personnel Management,* November 1971, table 1, pp. 33–5.

During the process of becoming a secretary, therefore, a girl may be exposed to mouth-watering images of the future. If she is not actually encouraged to displace the boss, she will inevitably be told that there is room at the top for those with ambition and ability.

The image of the perfect secretary

I should say that the six qualities I require in a personal and private secretary, in addition of course, to basic secretarial skills, are: Fragrance: an unsavoury secretary would render my work quite impossible. Punctuality: a late secretary is an abomination. Tidiness: I consider slovenliness to be a cardinal sin. Alacrity: a slow-witted woman is worse than one who chatters. Intelligence: this is of supreme importance. Speed: I always require everything done the day before yesterday.[39]

The perfect secretary is expected to combine in herself a mixture of abilities and qualities in much the same way as the perfect wife. Not only must she be capable of certain minimal speeds on the typewriter and when taking dictation, just as wives must display a certain bare level of competence with a frying pan, but she must also 'understand' her boss, just as a wife must be sensitive to her husband's whims and moods:

> Study him closely; tread warily during the first few weeks; get to know his likes and dislikes, his every mood. Find out the best time to interrupt him, if interrupt him you must. Gradually adjust your methods of working to fit in more easily with his. A lack of understanding will mar your success as a secretary.[40]

In view of the similarity which exists between the duties of wives and secretaries in relation to their male superiors, Benet has referred to the girls of the office as 'substitute wives'. In both cases, women spend a great deal of time performing the drudgery, whilst men make the decisions. Both types of work involve endless routines of tidying up which begin again as soon as they are completed. Both types of work are increasingly mechanised with the result that secretaries and wives are becoming potentially more and more productive rather than less burdened with routine tasks. Furthermore, each woman's status derives from that of her man. Benet points out that there *is* a crucial difference between the wife and the secretary, and that is their security of tenure:

> Even the weakest marriage is longer-lasting than a work partnership, and much harder to get out of. Wives can use money, sex, the children, bad temper, and an almost infinite number of other weapons to get their way, but insecurity keeps the secretary sweet.[41]

In view of the strong market position of contemporary secretaries, one cannot be quite so certain that insecurity alone would prevent them from voicing their grievances. It seems more likely that their loyalty and submissiveness, where it exists, may be attributed in part to the emphasis on these qualities encountered during training. There is a prevalent opinion, found especially in the manuals, that the boss is always right, even when he is wrong. Intending secretaries are frequently informed that the strength of the boss's right-hand woman lies in her ability to defer to his judgements, and that any errors on his part must be communicated to him in the most roundabout way possible. Any weaknesses on his part must be 'understood' and managed. The secretary who expresses dissatisfaction with her employer's time-keeping or manners is in danger of jeopardising her 'highly personal relationship' with him, if not her future as a Golden Girl Executive.

The perfect secretary, like the perfect wife, knows her place. Not only are girls cautioned to know their station, but bosses are told how to ensure that this shall be so. In her advice to employers, Lewis-Smith writes:

> Every secretary should have a job desċription, carefully written and linked where relevant to her boss's (or bosses') job descriptions. Make sure she knows exactly what is expected of her and how you like your office run. Lay it on the line! A lot of secretaries just don't know.[42]

In this handbook, managers are further cautioned to make sure that they can distinguish between 'Jobs only you can do; jobs your secretary could do with guidance/training; [and] jobs no manager should do, e.g. filing.'[43]

The extent to which secretaries are willing to do 'jobs which no manager should do' is quite remarkable. One survey discovered that 80 per cent of secretaries were willing to run errands, and 74 per cent were willing to do the shopping for their bosses and their families.[44] Perhaps it is these sort of activities which are thought to distinguish the exceptional girls from the merely capable ones, or, as one textbook informs its readers, 'little things mean a lot'.[45]

The perfect secretary exudes an antiseptic femininity. There is great attention to the cultivation of this quality in the manuals and, one suspects, during training. The ideal secretary must not only achieve a perfect balance between appearing attractive and competent, but must also ensure that all her bodily functions are in good, working order:

> Is your hair sparkling clean and free from dandruff? . . . Do you see to it that your breath is clean and sweet smelling? (especially after a meal with onions)? Do you bathe daily? Do you use a good deodorant every day? . . . Are your clothes spotless and free from perspiration odour? . . . Do you shave underarms and legs regularly?'[46]

Woe betide the girl who isn't using Amplex. If her best friend won't tell her, then her boss surely will.

The would-be secretary is cautioned against any attempt to appear sexy or glamorous, particularly when attending an interview. In the opinion of the manuals, such a presentation of self would automatically disqualify the candidate. Since the boss's secretary is his personal status symbol, her appearance reflects on him, and therefore he no more wants a blonde, mini-skirted bombshell for his First Lady of the Office than he would want such a woman for his wife.

Not much is known about the preferences of bosses themselves in this matter. It is quite likely that they feel that sex must not rear its head during dictation sessions, although it may be quite acceptable when flaunted by the pretty little filing clerk down the corridor. Accordingly, there may be a tendency to hire girls who are not overtly sexy – to keep the flamboyantly attractive ones at a safe distance in the typing pool where they can do no harm to the business-like image: 'An attractively turned-out secretary is not only a decorative asset; her tasteful appearance marks her as being pretty smart – and the boss as quite a clever fellow for having chosen her.'[47] The perfect secretary is thus like the perfect office – unadorned and uncluttered, yet contributing towards the establishment of a comfortable environment for the careworn boss.

The perfect secretary must never be idle – a busy secretary denotes a busy executive . . . or does she? Korda believes that this obsession with being continually on the go is nothing more than 'a hysterical charade played out . . . for other people's benefit.'[48] Most girls who are active all the time are simply experts in the art of 'making work', they are merely keeping up appearances for the sake of their own and their boss's image in the eyes of others. The manuals give a great deal of advice on how to be super-efficient, although it is equally possible to regard this information as useful tips on making work for the otherwise inactive secretary:

> When Evelyn's boss had to go to an office in an out-of-the-way part of the city, Evelyn thoughtfully worked out the shortest route and typed up the directions so that he would have no difficulty changing trains and finding his way. These are the thoughtful little acts that relieve an executive of bothersome details and impress upon him that you are capable of more than routine work.[49]

This extract also draws attention to the fact that the perfect secretary must be something of a mother figure. When she is not tidying up her desk for the nth time, or striving to produce a perfect letter, she must be trying to look after her boss. She should ensure that he does not get lost on trips to remote parts of the city, she should buy his favourite sandwiches for his coffee break, and she should make excuses for him to other people.

The perfect secretary is thus not only required to maintain high standards of proficiency as a human word processor, but is expected to evolve a relationship with her employer where she must act out the roles of wife and mother, and where deference is the key to success but not to promotion. There is something curiously old-fashioned about this superwoman of the textbooks and training courses. In many ways she is the twentieth-century version of the male clerk of a former age – a picture of uncomplaining servitude made tolerable by never-to-be-fulfilled aspirations for the future. A number of what are thought to be essentially female characteristics have been grafted on to the image of the ideal secretary, but the past and present versions display a remarkable similarity.

Barriers to promotion in secretarial careers

As we have seen, many trainee secretaries are encouraged to regard the years spent at the typewriter as a preliminary stage in the process of becoming a junior executive, yet few girls ever cross the big divide without taking a special course of training. In this section, the factors which render secretarial work more of a cul-de-sac than a stepping stone to the bright lights will be considered.

One of the main factors which confine women to the lower rungs of the office ladder is the belief among employers that females tend to be 'unstable' employees. Employers are reluctant to promote or to train employees whom they feel are unlikely to stay with the firm very long. This attitude bedevils the occupational progression of women in the field of non-manual work and yet it is based only on half-truths. It is true that the majority of British evidence supports the notion that women in employment generally exhibit higher turnover rates than those of men, but this is not necessarily the case with all occupational groups, nor is it true of all age groupings. Pettman, in a review of research literature bearing upon this issue, concludes that the 'hypothesis relating turnover to the sex of the employee is, as yet, neither substantiated nor refuted'.[50]

One is inclined to doubt whether many employers who subscribe to the hypothesis have actually undertaken a thoroughgoing review of the relevant research data. It seems likely that their attitudes are based rather upon fallacious or simplistic perceptions of women and their attitudes to work. Wild and Hill have listed what they consider to be the most commonly advanced reasons for female labour turnover:

a. The existence of a restless 'roving population'.
b. The large number of young people employed.
c. The inherent irrationality and unpredictability of women.
d. The availability of other jobs.
e. Pregnancy or illness.
f. The existence of better paid jobs elsewhere.
g. Domestic difficulties.
h. Leaving the district.[51]

Although they concede that there may be truth in some of these reasons, the first four are dismissed as common fallacies. The remaining four are not fallacies, in their opinion, but 'f' and 'g' are factors over which firms could exert some control if they so wished, thus reducing the volume of turnover and avoiding 'wastage of labour'. Pregnancy, illness and geographical mobility are beyond the firm's control and 'render a certain amount of labour turnover virtually inevitable'. According to their own research findings relating to a sample of female operatives in the electronics industry, 51.7 per cent of leavers were quitting their jobs for reasons which were theoretically within the firm's control. Furthermore, job dissatisfaction was pronounced amongst those who were leaving for these reasons. In other words, the pull of a better paid job elsewhere was often matched by the push of the boring, unsatisfying, depressing nature of the job they were leaving. Similarly, a study by Harris and Clausen of labour mobility amongst men and women found that of the six reasons which accounted for the highest proportions of job changes by women, dissatisfaction with the work itself was third highest on the list.[52]

The attitudes held by employers in relation to job turnover amongst women appear to have something of the character of a self-fulfilling prophecy. Since employers anticipate that women are likely to leave their jobs, they do not give them responsible positions, nor train them for more interesting and more skilled work. Many women become frustrated and bored in these undemanding occupations and eventually leave for what they hope will be greener pastures, and in the process confirm the views of the employers that women are unstable members of the labour force.

According to Silverstone's research among London secretaries the only strategy which bosses have evolved in order to try to stem the tide of labour turnover is to offer higher and higher salaries. Employers in London, it appears, believe quite erroneously that 'a high salary . . . is the most effective way of attracting and keeping staff'.[53] It has not occurred to them that turnover might be reduced by opening up promotion channels for secretaries, or simply by giving them more responsibility. Apparently the turnover rates are very high in London, which Silverstone feels is partly due to the preponderance of young women, some of whom leave their jobs to get married and have children, and some of whom are simply dissatisfied. Again, employers do not appear to have reacted to this in what would seem to be an obvious manner by trying to recruit older women. Older females are much more likely to remain in their jobs as Table 3.4 suggests.

A second problem which may be encountered by the ambitious secretary is male prejudice. The notion that women exhibit high rates of turnover is at least based on some degree of fact, but the notion that 'women are not cut out for business', the view that 'they have not got what it takes', can make no appeal but to the

TABLE 3.4 *Turnover – percentages of full-time employees employed by their current employer for less than 12 months – April 1976*

Age	Women non-manual workers (18 and over)
18–20	24.7
21–24	20.9
25–29	15.7
30–39	13.6
40–49	8.4
50–59	4.5
60–64	2.1

SOURCE Department of Employment, *New Earnings Survey, 1976*, part E, table 145 (London: HMSO, 1977). Reprinted by permission of the Controller of Her Majesty's Stationery Office.

stereotypes which inhabit the mind. The lesson of both world wars was that women have to be seen doing a job before they are believed to be capable of doing it, and at the present time, very few women have been seen executing management functions. Employers often declare that they are more than willing to promote their secretaries and to give them more responsible positions but one looks in vain for evidence that they follow their intentions through. One study, carried out in 1972, found that 79 per cent of bosses considered that their secretaries were worthy of promotion, yet only 45 per cent said that they would be willing to promote them to a junior management position.[54] Korda is of the opinion that there is more than a hint of male chauvinism in the office. He considers that the characteristics which would be rewarded in an aspiring young man would be severely censured in an aspiring young woman. A man is assertive, a woman is bitchy; a man shows signs of knowing when to take the initiative, a woman always wants her own way; a man requests the opinions of his more experienced colleagues, a woman is a troublesome nuisance who has no confidence in her own judgements. According to Korda, if a woman is not permitted to progress up the career ladder by displaying those attributes which are required of men, she is obliged to use feminine wiles to get her there. For this, she will be accused of being temperamental and emotional, and told to stop acting like a woman.[55]

An interesting theory regarding male chauvinism in the office and its implications for female advancement is suggested by Benet. In her opinion, there has been something of a managerial revolution during the past few decades, not in the sense that Burnham meant, but in a direction identified by Bell.[56] Although managers today represent the largest property-owning group among the population, they cannot compare in this respect with the owner–managers of early industrial capitalism. Unlike the latter group, neither the position nor the status of modern management is assured. Accordingly, the chief executive of the 1970s attempts to resolve his status anxiety through the pursuit of success, and by surrounding himself with the symbols of achievement. One of these 'status trappings', writes Benet, is the secretary. The display of sexual superiority which her presence affords the boss confirms him in a position of power and authority. An employer is unlikely, therefore, to undermine his status, albeit anchored on delicate foundations, by promoting his subaltern to a position similar to his own, or by transforming in any way the master/slave colouring of their relationship. This theory would certainly seem to go some way towards explaining the reluctance of many managers to offer their secretaries more exalted positions in their companies. At the same time, it is possible that many men simply cannot tolerate the idea of a woman as an equal in the sphere of executive functions.

The presence or absence of discrimination is exceedingly hard to prove and one is usually unable to do more than infer its existence in a particular situation from the evidence available. A belief in the presence of discriminatory attitudes within a work context may, however, be an important component of women's assessment of their chances for promotion. According to Shaw, Elsy and Bowen, the majority of their female respondents considered that women in clerical work could not gain promotion as easily as men:

> Of the various reasons given, discrimination by men against women is cited most frequently and the next most frequent response is that preference is given to men. These two responses were given by 48% of all women responding.[57]

A third reason why secretaries rarely become management executives is that some of them do not seek promotion of this kind. It may be that their career aspirations are tailored during training, and subsequently during social interaction with bosses and other secretaries. If the trainee secretary learns and accepts that the greatest achievement is to secure a job in close proximity to a famous, important, glamorous man, it is quite possible that she would never wish to attain anything beyond that goal. For such women, promotion takes on a quite different meaning – it is synonymous with the acquisition of a job as handmaiden to Mr Big. These girls enjoy the kudos which attaches to this role and do not entertain thoughts of moving into the arena of decision-making. It is this kind of secretary who considers that there is no comparison whatsoever between her functions and those of her boss. For her, the secretary and her boss are as distinct as chalk and cheese in terms of their responsibilities and abilities, and to think otherwise would constitute delusions of grandeur. The girl who was voted Top Secretary in 1972 represents an example of the kind of secretary who regards herself as functionally different if not inferior to her employer: 'I couldn't, for example, do my boss's job. He is a man with a string of technical qualifications, and my role is to relieve him of as much non-technical work as possible.'[58] This girl was the private secretary to the engineer and manager of a Water Board, and whilst one would not dispute that her employer's job probably involved the application of a great deal of specialised knowledge, there is a clear implication here that the secretary has taken over at least some of the managerial functions, which would seem to be at odds with her self-image. It is this kind of self-image, however, which tends to perpetuate the status quo.

According to Silverstone, most secretaries recognise that promotion is unlikely to mean anything other than working for a higher status boss. However, few of her respondents placed any value on this qualified form of promotion, whereas most of them attached a great deal of importance to that kind of promotion which entailed greater responsibility and more interesting work.[59] Indeed, when one assesses the definitions of secretaries themselves, in accounting for the rarity of their progression into high status, highly rewarded responsible posts, it would seem that it is their resignation to the inevitable rather than a low level of ambition which is the most important determining factor. Furthermore, as Silverstone points out, the existence of two types of promotion, one for male 'junior' executives and the other for female secretaries tends to structure the perceptions of employers as well: 'If it is accepted that secretarial advancement is achieved by working for more eminent people, then there is no need to incorporate secretaries into the normal promotion hierarchy of an organisation.'[60]

Finally, it is appropriate to dispense with the hypothesis that secretaries do not seek and therefore gain promotion because they are more interested in seeking husbands. Lockwood, it will be remembered, goes so far as to say that young girls regard the office itself as a marriage market – a view which carries the implication that the quest for a partner displaces any interest in career progression. According to Benet, however, no more than 5 per cent of office girls in the US and England meet their husbands in the 'enormous file', and in her opinion this poor record would surely discourage many husband-hunters from trying this method.[61] This is not to say that office romance is a phenomenon which only exists in the minds of novelists and David Lockwood.

Evidence on this subject is extremely thin, since most studies of white-collar work as of other occupations have maintained a strictly clinical interest in modes of interaction in the workplace. If one is prepared to accept the rather unconventional methodology used by Quinn in his study of 'The formation, impact and management of romantic relationships in organisations', which consisted of interviews with people with time to kill in airport lounges, then it would seem that office affairs are widespread. Of the 130 men and women he accosted, all had either had an office affair or had witnessed one 'close to'.[62] However, he found that the most common type of affair was 'the fling', which was in essence a search for excitement or sexual experience, and one which people entered into with the expectation that it would last only a short time. He also found that the most common affair was one which involved a male boss and a female subordinate, but not an immediate subordinate. This view is shared by Benet and Korda, who consider that most bosses prefer to maintain their office sex and romance either on the plane of fantasy or else at a safe distance, rather than to have it thrust upon them during dictation sessions. Thus, whilst one would not deny that there are sexual undertones to office life, it is necessary to distinguish an interest in flirtation and affairs, which after all involve both men and women, from husband-hunting. The existence of the latter has not been satisfactorily documented and it is time that this ridiculous perception of the female secretary as office predator is dismantled once and for all. While it persists, it constitutes part of the ideological ammunition of those who wish to keep the secretary in her place.

Sources of work satisfaction and work dissatisfaction among secretaries

According to Benet, office girls have experienced dissatisfaction with their jobs for over half a century.[63] In her book she cites the findings of an American study conducted in 1925 which investigated the social and educational background of office girls, and their aspirations for the future. Amongst those girls who were leaving their jobs, the most important reasons for the decision to resign were that they wanted to go back to school, they wanted a change, or they saw no future in their current occupation.[64] Then, as now, marriage did not come very high up on the list of reasons. It would seem then that despite the limited range of alternatives to office work and the fact that it compared very favourably in terms of remuneration and status with other work for girls, women at that time did not invariably stay with their office jobs and count their blessings. In Benet's opinion, the fact that office life disappointed girls almost from the very beginning partly explains the falling marriage age during the twentieth century. According to her, many girls have regarded marriage as an escape route from the drudgery of the office. Although this is an interesting idea, which reverses the traditional stereotype that women's boring jobs reflect their preoccupation with finding husbands, it is impossible to verify this assertion in view of the absence of any relevant historical data. From a purely speculative point of view, one would have thought it unlikely that girls in the 1920s and 1930s regarded marriage in this way – as some kind of last resort – when one recalls the social and economic climate of the period. Feminism was at a low ebb, and where it existed it was reformist rather than revolutionary, seeking to elevate the domestic conditions of the wife and mother rather than to challenge the traditional role of women. Marriage was regarded as an altogether natural destiny. Jobs on the whole were scarce, and it was deemed more appropriate for men to fill them. It is possible that the unappetising nature of office work was one factor which propelled some girls towards matrimony, but it is important to recognise that this would have been only one of several reasons, and the same must be said of all subsequent generations of office girls.

As we cautioned in the previous chapter, it is essential that one does not typify or label certain types of work as boring, monotonous or unrewarding without reference to the attitudes of the workers themselves. The next task, therefore, is to investigate the work attitudes among secretaries more directly – to document the extent of job satisfaction and dissatisfaction, and to consider possible explanations for the patterns which emerge. The picture which seems to emerge from the evidence available is one of girls who for the most part enjoy their jobs, but who are clearly dissatisfied with certain aspects of their employment situation. It seems fairly clear from the available surveys that a principal source of job dissatisfaction among secretaries is the lack of opportunities for promotion or for the exercise of a greater degree of responsibility. The conclusions of an Alfred Marks Survey conducted in 1974 were as follows:

> One rather distressing conclusion we have to draw from this survey is that the executive secretary has not progressed in terms of responsibility since we last took a look at her five years ago. Although we were looking at the job descriptions of 104 of Britain's top secretaries, there was a high incidence of limited job satisfaction and misuse of highly trained and effective woman-power.[65]

This opinion is shared by Silverstone, who found that there was a feeling of disillusionment among her secretarial respondents which could be partly explained in terms of 'the great lack of promotion opportunities'.[66] They placed a high value on jobs which offered variety and interest, freedom from supervision, responsibility, a sense of achievement and opportunities to use their initiative. Yet secretarial jobs, by their very nature, do not display these characteristics. In response to the frustrations which this situation yields, many secretaries frequently change jobs in the hope that they will discover a firm which will offer them a more interesting, responsible post. It seems that the sense of frustrated ambition experienced by many secretaries is exacerbated by the expectations of achievement generated by their social and educational backgrounds. Top secretaries in particular are usually drawn from the middle class and have emerged from grammar or public schools with a handful of 'O' and possibly 'A' level passes and it is not unknown for them to have a degree.[67] According to Benet, of those college graduates in the USA who do not join the teaching profession, about 10 per cent become secretaries and clerical workers.[68] As far as Britain is concerned, there can be little doubt that there is a certain lack of congruence between educational achievement and the realities of occupational choice for women in this country, with the consequence that a number of well-qualified girls are obliged to take up secretarial work in lieu of any alternatives. Certainly, the significance of a 'Graduate Girls' secretarial employment agency cannot be dismissed lightly. If the Director of the Centre for Secretarial Studies at Strathclyde University is correct – that the secretary of the future is more rather than less likely to have a degree – then assuming that the opportunities for promotion and the exercise of greater responsibility among secretaries remains static, dissatisfaction is likely to increase.

A second source of dissatisfaction among secretaries is the experience of under-utilisation. A number of secretaries find that they are never fully occupied, and this generates acute boredom. Silverstone found that the majority of her respondents always or nearly always had work to do, but a series of letters on this subject in the correspondence column of the *Guardian* in 1974 suggested that boredom was by no means unusual.[69] In the opinion of one manager who wrote to the *Guardian*, the under-utilisation of the secretary is the result of a number of features of office life.[70] First, it results from the unwillingness of many managers to share the services of a single secretary. This would be tantamount to losing one's special parking place in the car park, or one's access to the executive dining room. Employers regard their personal female assistants as one of the perks of the job and are therefore unwilling to relinquish exclusive rights to such a very important status symbol. Secondly, some bosses regard their secretaries as a 'worktime version of the little woman at home' and expect them to do no more than look pretty and make tea from time to time. 'Such "MCPs" would scoff at the view that a secretary should be a colleague and an equal.' Thirdly, secretaries tend to establish demarcation lines and restrictive practices which represent 'massive obstacles to a more flexible use of their services'. Fourthly, secretaries are often under-utilised, but this may be offset by the number of occasions on which they are very much over-utilised. This is often a reflection of the boss's own workload, but it also indicates the haphazard nature of work organisation in many offices. Finally, most secretaries lack the training necessary for more involved work in their departments. Once they have completed the typing, shorthand and filing, they often lack the training which would enable them to execute more responsible tasks. Furthermore, even where they possess the training they are seldom encouraged to make full use of it.

According to one article in a management journal, 'secretarial under-employment is a phenomenon often recognised by efficiency experts'. It goes on to cite a former editor of a secretarial magazine who considers that the under-employment of a secretary increases as her boss rises in the executive galaxy:

> Typically where a boss needs a secretary most is when he's on
> the lower end of the echelons, and where the volume of work he
> will produce that requires transcribing and typing will be heavy.
> As the boss moves up the ladder, his needs may change, he may
> not produce as much documentation, he will probably travel
> more – and she may just sit around and do his Christmas card
> list. But even if she has little to do, he's still entitled to a
> secretary.[71]

A further source of job dissatisfaction among secretaries has
been identified by Silverstone. It appears that many secretaries
feel that the status of the occupation has declined in recent years.[72]
The same finding emerged from an Alfred Marks Survey in 1974:
'These senior women clearly feel that their own position is being
eroded by the general deterioration in standards. Such
deterioration is clearly affecting the usefulness of the secretarial
career as a stepping stone into management levels for women.'[73]

As far as the London situation is concerned, it appears that this
belief among senior women is not without foundation. According
to Silverstone, the age structure of the female secretarial
workforce in that area is extremely unbalanced towards the
younger age groups, as compared with the age structure of the
female working population as a whole. The result of this imbalance
is that employers tend to offer quite senior positions to girls who
are both young and relatively inexperienced. Owing to the chronic
shortage of office staff in central London, employers have no
choice in the matter. Many of Silverstone's respondents regarded
this development as highly damaging to the status of executive
secretaries.[74]

In this situation, where girls who have barely emerged from
their training colleges are free to style themselves as experienced
secretaries, it is not surprising perhaps that the older woman feels
threatened. She has spent years clawing her way to the top,
bending over backwards to please male executives, becoming
expert at producing the instant smile for boorish clients, producing
gallons of tea and coffee, and what does she find? . . . the bosses
now prefer beauty and youth to experience. Some little teenager

manages to find a shortcut into *her* office, yet all she has to offer is speedwriting and a certificate from one of those crash courses in typing!

These apprehensions on the part of the older woman secretary exactly parallel the fears which male clerks of the 1880s entertained when their occupational territories were invaded by women. Then, as now, these anxieties found expression in the formation of quasi-union organisations. In 1970, the Executive Secretaries Association was founded, and it has developed a very selective recruitment policy. Those applying for membership have to be over twenty-five, have shorthand, and they have to be working for top management only. Although the Association has several aims, it is very much concerned with establishing the superior status of the secretary, as its founder points out: 'Anyone who can type these days calls herself a secretary. We call them typists.'[75]

Thus, while it is clear that the status of a secretary (or rather, her lack of it) within a particular company is an important key to her work satisfaction, it is also important to take into account the status of the occupational group as a whole when considering an individual's attitudes to work.

A fourth source of dissatisfaction, according to Silverstone, is the submissive, self-effacing role which many secretaries are obliged to assume. She maintains that some secretaries resent playing traditional feminine roles in the office – 'the little woman' with notepad instead of frying pan. Many of them are conscious that they are human status symbols – there to buttress their boss's ego rather than to play a significant part in the execution of his duties.[76] The secretary's day is riddled with domestic acts ranging from pouring out the boss's coffee to tidying up his desk, and even the most exalted personal assistant is required to adopt the handmaid posture on occasions. Some of the chores which secretaries are asked to perform by their bosses would not even be demanded of wives. A contest organised by WOW (Women Office Workers) in 1977 to determine the most ridiculous chore asked of office workers by their bosses elicited some very bizarre entries. One secretary maintained that she had to take her boss's toupee to be dry-cleaned and re-styled. Another said that she had to clean her boss's false teeth. The winner of the contest was a secretary who had to pluck out her boss's grey hairs and who at one stage had been required to shave off his moustache, taking photographs of 'before' and 'after'[77]

However, in the opinion of Bernard Marks, Chairman of the Alfred Marks Bureau, the supporting role which secretaries are expected to play represents a major source of job satisfaction:

> Whatever our friends in the Women's Lib movement say, it is, in my view, an absolutely natural, classically appropriate, role for women. They want to feel needed, they want to feel wanted, they want to feel that they're contributing towards the success of the man. It's rather like being an office wife – and that, really, is the way of describing a secretary's role.[78]

According to one of the surveys conducted by his organisation, 80 per cent of secretaries are quite satisfied with their supportive role and have no desire to take over from their bosses. At the same time, they would like to play a more important and valuable part in the boss-secretary partnership.[79] Even Marcia Williams, who is often supposed to be personally ambitious, has said that she prefers the supportive role of the secretary, and is ambitious for the people she works for rather than for herself.[80]

It is important therefore that one does not overstate the degree of work dissatisfaction which secretaries subjectively experience. Most of them, like most wives no doubt, are basically satisfied with their role, although they may feel that the work tasks themselves are rather boring and repetitive, and would prefer to be more closely involved with the execution of their boss's own activities. Moreover, even though there are some anxieties about the future status of the occupation, the levels of remuneration and the prestige of the work compare very favourably with other female-dominated occupations. In this respect, the position of the modern secretary greatly resembles that of the male clerk of the 1880s. The latter, it will be remembered, often held a very lowly status in his own firm, yet there was the consolation of knowing that he was much better off than his blue-collar counterparts. The secretary of the 1970s may compare her situation with different occupations, and judge herself to be better paid, and to have the benefit of superior working conditions, or she may look down the corridor at the typing pool battalions and think how lucky she is not to be confined to a machine all day, far from the more exciting environs of the executives' suite. All this does not mean that the secretary is never exploited, discriminated against, under-rewarded or prevented from realising her ambitions, but one is obliged to recognise the fact that her job may yield her a great deal of satisfaction and meet all her expectations.[81]

Is the secretary really necessary?

The role of the secretary has remained very much unchanged for the last fifty or so years, but the spectre of technology hangs like the sword of Damocles over the traditional boss–secretary relationship. The introduction of the dictating machine has already shown that shorthand is theoretically obsolete, and now the IBM's word-processing machine, introduced in 1965, threatens to transform completely the office environment. This is intended to speed up the production of correspondence, albeit at considerable cost, by mechanising it and concentrating it in specialised 'word-processing departments'. In theory, the boss no longer needs a personal secretary, since all the tasks which do not involve shorthand and typing can now be performed by one girl who is employed to keep the diaries of several executives.

According to Thackray, however, salesmen have not had an easy time persuading employers that their secretaries are interchangeable with machines:

> Industry sources suggest that each salesman has a quota of one and a half word-processing centres a year to sell. The biggest obstacle they face is 'to avoid the confrontation with the executive who has to give up his private secretary. For him that can be traumatic', says Daniel O'Connor, marketing director for Remington Rand. One Montgomery Ward executive who was faced with the loss of his secretary to word processing complained, only half humorously, 'It's like getting a divorce. We've been together for six years.'[82]

It is not only bosses who fear the threat to their status implied by the introduction of such machines. Thackray maintains that secretaries are often vocal in their opposition to the idea of word processing, since it entails the destruction of their special relationship with one man, if not their relegation to a typing pool.

Word processing is not the only phenomenon which threatens to displace the secretary, or at least to transform her work situation greatly. Computers are technically capable of performing many of her tasks such as processing correspondence and reports:

> The time could come . . . when a central office computer could mastermind all office communications, which would include the handling of correspondence for outside and the monitoring of inter-office contacts through television and videophone . . . The only dictation the secretary would then take would be for very personal or confidential correspondence, and if correspondence is analysed there is very little which falls into this category.[83]

Although one might have supposed that these developments were very much a thing of the future, Braverman has maintained that the disappearance of the secretary is imminent. In his view, the 'drain on the corporate pocketbook' represented by the practice of granting secretarial assistance to even the lowliest of executives has grown to such proportions that 'major surgery' lies just around the corner.[84] A similar view is adopted in a BBC publication entitled *Office*, in which it is also suggested that shorthand will either be dead or else regarded as an oddity by the 1980s.[85] Whilst both sources present a convincing account of the reasons why the secretary may one day follow the same path as the dodo there is little evidence to suggest that the process of extinction is well under way. A weakness of Braverman's account is that it depends very heavily on the views expressed in management periodicals and he fails to make a clear distinction between the strategies which are advocated and those which are currently practised.

No matter what the future holds, one may be certain that for the present, training schools continue to emphasise the importance of high speeds at shorthand and typing, while bosses continue to resist the displacement of their personal status symbols by impersonal machines. And as Thackray points out, although there may be a tremendous 'cumulative inefficiency' in the traditional boss–secretary relationship, it does afford certain gratifications to both parties, which no machine of the future is likely to be able to match.[86]

The paper jungle – a review of other forms of female clerical employment

While there has at least been some concern to investigate the working life of the secretary, the interest shown in the vast armies of filing clerks, copy and audio-typists, comptometer and keypunch operators, and other assorted paper processors of the office has been entirely minimal. The growth in their numbers has corresponded to the enormous growth of paperwork during the twentieth century, and yet their situation remains very much a mystery.

Few generalisations can be made about the girls who are employed in the lower grades of non-manual work, but it is possible to identify certain aspects of their work situation which tend to differentiate them as a group from secretaries. In the first place, their work is much more likely to be mechanised, or in the process of becoming so. Although a great deal of the secretary's day is spent over the keyboard, the great range of other, non-mechanical tasks which she is expected to perform are held to distinguish her from the 'mere' shorthand-typist. Moreover, there does seem to be some evidence that many bosses are highly resistant to the intrusion of technology into the relationship which they share with their secretaries. Yet employers are often more than willing to harness machine-power to the routine grades. In recent years, the division of labour has infiltrated much of the office, while leaving the secretary's job as yet intact. With the exception of certain categories of clerk, and supervisors, many of these office girls are defined in terms of the machine they operate, in much the same way as many blue-collar workers. Although the degree of machine-pacing may be less pronounced in the office, the extent to which routine office workers use machinery is quite substantial. Machines now exist for almost every task, ranging from the 'Addressograph', which speeds up the process of addressing envelopes to clients on mailing lists, to sophisticated duplicators, which produce thousands of perfect copies at the touch of a button.

Secondly, the jobs of many members of the office proletariat, as Benet calls the lower-grade workers, are likely to be much more routinised than that of the secretary. Part of the latter's job is to be able to cope with the unexpected – be this a sudden change of plan on the part of the boss, or having to make an unusual errand. There is a great deal of routine in her job, but there is no one standing close at hand, making sure that the tasks are done in a strict order. Those who are solely occupied with the typing of invoices or the filing of insurance claims, however, encounter little variation in their day-to-day tasks, and they are often subject to the control of a hawk-eyed supervisor who attempts to ensure that they adhere to the prescribed order of duties. The unusual, in their case, is more likely to present itself in the form of a new girl in the office, the installation of a new duplicating machine, or a change in the procedure for making coffee, all of which arouse some initial controversy and are then quickly forgotten as life goes on as before. In this type of job, the newcomer is obliged to conform to the existing way of doing things, whereas the secretary is expected to evolve the method which suits her best.

A third feature which distinguishes the routine grades from the secretary is their degree of proximity to the management, both spatially and socially. The great majority of females employed in the lower grades of work are physically segregated from the environs of the executives. This is probably less true of smaller offices and less likely to be the case with higher grades of clerks. Where, however, there is a concentration of females engaged on principally mechanical tasks, they are often situated in a special work area at some distance from the executive suite. Routine clerical workers, on the whole, do not hold highly personal relationships with the management, and indeed they are not expected to. Their immediate boss is much more likely to be a female supervisor, and their contact with executives may be minimal.

The office battalions, therefore, are in several respects somewhat distinct from the secretaries, and the differentiation also extends to remuneration, as any glimpse at the situations vacant columns will confirm. There are also only limited opportunities for promotion, even that kind of promotion which secretaries experience, namely being appointed to work for a rising star in the executive firmament.[87] A filing clerk is a filing clerk, no matter whether the paperwork comes from one of the salesmen or from the managing director. These girls also differ from the secretaries in terms of social and educational background and training. With regard to the latter, there are many office jobs for which no special qualifications are required, and there are many others where the appropriate skills may be learnt on the job in a very short space of time.

Yet while these girls may experience lower pay and status than their diary-keeping sisters, they enjoy certain advantages over the girls on the factory floor, with whom they frequently share a similar social background. The average hourly earnings of the routine non-manual female worker do not greatly exceed those of the female manual operative, but their working conditions are very dissimilar. Both may experience a great deal of tedium, but the noise and the dirt of the factory are seldom matched by the conditions of office work. Office workers are vulnerable to certain health hazards, deriving not only from the use of machinery but also from their exposure to chemicals, but the risks involved are somewhat different from those encountered in the factory environment.[88] For example, they are unlikely to find themselves trapped in a piece of machinery nor are they likely to experience prolonged exposure to cancer-producing substances. They are also less likely to have to clock in at work or to lose pay in the event of late arrival or because of a visit to a doctor. The routine office worker is more likely to have certain fringe benefits such as pension schemes or sick pay benefit. Furthermore, they are not obliged to wear unflattering overalls and headgear. Whilst a routine office worker's lot may not always be a happy one, therefore, in the extent to which it affords opportunities for varied, interesting work, it does at least compare favourably in certain respects with the lot of the female factory operative. Were this not so, one would be unable to account for the fact that a majority of women opt for office employment at the point of entry to the labour market. Although Braverman has insisted that modern clerical work is virtually indistinguishable from factory employment, one is obliged to recognise that there are subtle differences between these two modes of employment which, from the point of view of the school-leaver at least, render them qualitatively distinct.[89]

Although one may draw a distinction between female manual workers and female clerks and office machine operators, and between the latter two groups and secretaries, it is important to recognise that clerks and operatives are themselves stratified. In his book on white-collar work, Crozier points out that there is a definite hierarchy of office staff. At the very bottom, he maintains, are the filing clerks, who represent 'the most dependent of all employees'. Contrary to what one might expect, all the filing clerks in the Parisian insurance companies which he studied were men, but this did not alter the fact that their job was accorded little status by other employees. These male filing clerks had a number of things in common – their social origins, their relative youth, physical isolation from other workers and a low salary. Crozier is inclined to regard their detachment from the rest of the office staff as something of an advantage: 'It is a closed world. But, within that world, file clerks enjoy a certain amount of autonomy. Each file clerk is assigned an area for filing; within that area the battle against disorder is his alone.' A further advantage, in Crozier's opinion, is the fact that the file clerk stands up to do his work: 'Therein lies, in a certain sense, his glory, but also his servitude. For his work is tiring.'[90]

Having been employed on many occasions as a filing clerk myself, I would be inclined to hesitate before characterising such work as in any way glorious, although I did derive some satisfaction in one instance when I managed to put to rights a filing system which had been a spectacle of ·utter chaos when I first arrived. More often than not, however, filing can be backbreaking, exhausting work, particularly in the enormous record departments of hospitals, insurance companies and other organisations where there is a daily deluge of paperwork to be carefully put away. In time, no doubt, filing clerks will be replaced by the automated memory banks which do not stop for coffee and a chat, or place information in the wrong location when they are feeling bored with the job. Another technical development which threatens to make the filing clerk redundant is the microfilm system. According to one estimate, this type of system can save 98 per cent of the space needed to accommodate conventional filing systems, and it is therefore likely to be particularly attractive to firms at a time when rents are soaring.[91]

The next group of workers which may be identified are keypunch operators, whose work involves the preparation of data for computer analysis. In Crozier's study keypunch operators were usually women, and Benet notes the same of English and American firms.[92] In terms of skill and training, such work represents an advance on filing, although it does not require a lengthy term of apprenticeship, and firms are often willing to train girls themselves. Crozier maintains that whereas file clerks represent the white-collar equivalent of the unskilled manual labourer, the keypunch operator is more like a semi-skilled machine operator. Accordingly, they enjoy higher rates of pay and somewhat greater status. They are annexed to the machines of the future whereas the filing clerk is being replaced by them. Since there is a high demand for their skills, which are wholly transferable, Crozier considers that the keypunch girls are less obliged to conform to the norms of the company they work for than their unskilled sisters in the enormous file. Benet, on the other hand, claims that this type of worker is 'extremely vulnerable to changes in the economic climate' and that new machines constantly threaten her job security.

This type of worker is usually segregated from other office employees, and Benet suggests that this fact has had certain consequences for recruitment policy:

> Sequestered in the computer room, she could look how she pleased . . . Indeed, for the first time in office history, she could be black. Some companies even managed to tie in computerisation with 'equal opportunity' employment policies, getting credit for training and hiring underprivileged girls, and staffing their computer rooms cheaply, while not having to cope with unfamiliar notions like black receptionists. The number of non-whites in clerical employment in the U.S.A. went up 77% between 1960 and 1967, compared to a 23% increase in white clerical workers.[93]

No corresponding figures are available for the UK but the statistics furnished by Benet certainly highlight the function of routinised, mechanised office work as a source of employment for the disinherited of the American Dream. Very little appears to be known about the work attitudes of keypunch operators, although Crozier found that they, along with the typists, were the workers who seemed least interested in their jobs, yet were the ones who were least likely to complain about their position. He attributes this in part to their lowly status in the office hierarchy, although one could interpret this in other ways. For example, Benet suggests that this is a mode of work *par excellence* which enables the young working-class girl to move 'out of the file-clerk or factory-worker class'. The work itself may not be subjectively experienced as interesting, but it does afford 'opportunities to girls who would otherwise have had a hard time making it to the office at all'. Hence the co-existence of a lack of interest in the work itself, with a lack of inclination to complain about the position obtained.

Typists, like keypunch operators, are increasingly segregated from the rest of the office staff. Typing pools first appeared in the 1920s, and as Benet points out, this was partly the result of the development of audio-machinery, which obviated the need for bosses to be located near to their typists.[94] They were also the result of the application of 'scientific management' to the organisation of office procedure.

Studies of typists are very few and far between, and several of those which do exist are unsatisfactory for a number of reasons. First, there is a tendency to regard typists and secretaries as a homogeneous group and thus to generate data which offers no insight into the character of jobs which are wholly based on typing, nor an understanding of the attitudes of those who perform them.[95] Secondly, the preconceptions of the researchers are sometimes allowed to prejudice the results. As an example of the latter problem, one may cite a recent study of typists working in banking. Although the authors profess an interest in the work motivations of such employees, the nature of the work itself is prejudged to be lacking in intrinsic satisfaction, and consequently discussion turns upon a narrower range of variables thought to promote satisfaction or dissatisfaction.[96] However, there are a number of other studies which do not display these weaknesses and which suggest that there is a considerable reservoir of discontent among female typists. A study of women in typing pools by Stansfield found that there was no expectation of any satisfaction from work, and his respondents stressed the following as sources of dissatisfaction: the lack of perceived importance of their work, the lack of personal communications and the fact they rarely received any thanks for what they were doing.[97] A study of audio-typists by the Alfred Marks organisation revealed a pattern of widespread boredom and frustration. Forty-nine per cent of the respondents stated that they were bored with their work, mainly due to the lack of personal contact, and there was a general feeling that their work lacked status. Nearly half the sample could not think of any ways in which their work could be made more interesting, and as many as 70 per cent stated that they would prefer to be a secretary or a shorthand-typist. A majority of those who sought this change in status mentioned a desire for more personal contact or more variety, interest and responsibility.[98]

Speaking from personal experience, I find that this type of work has very little to recommend it. In the typing pool, one is well and truly machine-bound, and the noise and the physical separation of girl from girl tend to inhibit all conversation when work is being processed. This is even more pronounced when the typist is wearing headphones. Typing is often very tiring, since it necessitates sitting up fairly straight all day, although electric typewriters render the incessant drumming on the keyboard rather less fatiguing – if one's firm is willing to provide them. Typing can be particularly irksome when it is all figures, such as with invoice-typing, since more time seems to be spent pulling levers and pressing margin buttons than with producing figures, and there is not even the satisfaction of having something vaguely interesting to read. The degree to which work output is monitored varies from the situation where a supervisor merely checks that the girls remain anchored to their machines all day, to the situation where a supervisor actually counts the number of invoices, index cards or whatever, that each girl produces. Even the typing pools which have certain minimum demands in terms of productivity, however, are unable to set a fixed pace to the work, in the same way that many factory floor machines can dictate the pace of their operatives. It is this factor which permits the occasional daydream, or an aside to one's neighbour, which may help to pass the time between breaks.

Since the work is almost always predictable, the things that go on when the keyboards are silent assume great importance. It is easy to become quite irrational, to see life out of all proportion, when the source of entertainment is not the work in hand, but one's co-workers or the occasional male visitor from another department. The social life of the office can generate a great deal of satisfaction, but at other times it can lead to extraordinary bitchiness over the most minor of events. There can be intense rivalries but there can also be a deep sense of solidarity which sometimes forms the basis of a restrictive practice. If girls in the pool sometimes express no desire for a different position, this does not necessarily betoken short-term personal work goals, but may indicate their involvement in the camaraderie of the typing pool and a recognition that without further training, an alternative position would be unlikely to represent any improvement on their current one.

One type of work which in my opinion represents a considerable improvement on non-stop typing is that entailed in the position of the clerk–typist. This usually involves typing and filing, but also many other tasks which, while they are concerned with the processing of paperwork, afford some variety and change of tempo. As a temporary, I was employed on several occasions in this capacity, and always found the work itself quite interesting due to its varied nature, and the fact that it was not unusual to process work through from beginning to end, whereas typing pools afford little insight into the origins or destiny of the paperwork. As a clerk–typist, I was never housed in an all-female ghetto, far away from the management, as I was when working as a copy-typist or filing-clerk. Indeed, I was always included in the activities on special occasions which involved the senior staff, such as Christmas parties and the final toast of farewell to a departing executive. My experiences in this capacity suggested that routine white-collar work does not necessarily preclude interest and variety. The more one's job approximates to that of the traditional clerk, the more one is likely to experience its traditional satisfactions.

Clerks are in many ways the labour aristocracy of the paper jungle. Although they are defined in the *Oxford English Dictionary* as those who are employed to keep accounts, the range of skills which they are expected to perform is quite substantial, and in this respect they differ markedly from the copy-typist or the filing clerk. They tend to occupy a rather ambiguous position in the office hierarchy, as Crozier himself noted:

> More than anything, being a clerk signifies being clearly defined as neither this nor that, but rather as belonging to a mass of multifaceted personnel who have developed a more or less large number of bureaucratic skills which are called for according to the rhythm of work and needs.[99]

While clerks are fairly heterogeneous in terms of the work they do, Crozier maintains that it is this group which perhaps comes closest to the 'traditional image' of the office worker – the ones who form the 'solid base' of the system. Of all the groups we have so far considered, clerks are the ones who are most likely to be drawn from either sex.

While to the outsider the work of the clerk might seem excruciatingly dull, and those who perform it exceedingly unambitious, first-hand experience may cast it in a totally different light. Objectively, it may be low-paid, lacking in prospects and even insecure, but subjectively, it can generate all manner of satisfactions which derive both from the work and from the social life. This is more likely to be the case where she is employed to perform a variety of tasks, few of which are mechanised, and where she interacts with at least the lower levels of management. Moreover promotion, if and when it occurs, is likely to involve the clerk in more responsible work rather than, as in the case of the secretary, the performance of the same kind of work for a higher status employer.

According to Braverman, however, not only are the traditional skills of the clerk being undermined by the growth of office mechanisation and rationalisation, but the clerk herself, like the secretary, represents yet another threatened species of the white-collar environment.[100] In his view, the introduction of computerised accounting systems renders traditional book-keeping skills redundant, with the result that the clerk will be shortly replaced by a person who simply attends a machine. Although one suspects that this development belongs to a more distant future than Braverman implies, there is little doubt that the eclipse of the clerical function would be accompanied by the disappearance of many of the residual satisfactions found in the office environment.

The intention of this section has been to illustrate the tremendous diversity which characterises the world of the female routine office worker. Although certain broad distinctions have been made between the work situation of this group as a whole and that of the secretary, it is quite inappropriate to generalise about this group in terms of job satisfaction. In the first place, attitudes to work are likely to vary according to social background, education and training, position in the life cycle and other factors which are not directly related to the work situation. Secondly, aspects of the job situation – such as the degree of variety and/or interest, location in the office status hierarchy, levels of remuneration, social atmosphere, and opportunities for promotion and/or social mobility inherent in the work – will be an important influence on attitudes.

Yet whilst one is obliged to recognise the many sources of diversity in the outlook of the female office worker, it is possible to distil out from this examination of the more routine grades a particularly insistent theme. It would appear that the most mechanised, repetitive tasks are those which are most likely to promote disaffection. In the first place, this is because these jobs are associated with uncomfortable levels of noise and a variety of unpleasant stresses and strains on the human body. Secondly, the lack of variety entailed in such jobs is likely to induce a sense of boredom. This observation is borne out by the findings of a survey of office machine operators by the Alfred Marks organisation. Nearly half of the respondents 'yearned' for additional variety in their work routine, although a great many were resigned to the inevitability of monotony.[101] Thirdly, these are the jobs which are most likely to be physically segregated and thus to diminish the opportunities for personal contact. The experience of spatial segregation is most likely to be the fate of those involved principally with machines, since the aim of creating such phenomena as typing pools and punching rooms is partly to minimise noise levels in the office proper. Lockwood predicted that the growth of mechanisation coupled with physical segregation would tend to generate a sense of isolation and detachment among those whom it affected, and there is evidence that his expectations were correct. The Alfred Marks study of office machine operators mentioned above found that a lack of involvement with the company was widespread. Of the respondents interviewed, as many as 41 per cent were segregated in a special machine room or typing pool. One-fifth of the respondents claimed that they did not know in detail what their company did, and 17 per cent stated that they did not really understand the nature of their own contribution to their company's operations.[102] Although the development of open planning may perhaps be regarded as conducive to a greater degree of involvement among some members of the office, it is evident that the pressure towards the further subdivision, mechanisation and segregation of office tasks is likely to expand the numbers of those who experience a sense of detachment and marginality, and thus to increase the overall level of work dissatisfaction among the routine grades.

Responses to work dissatisfaction among female office workers

Contrary to the impression given in some earlier studies of female office workers, it appears that many of them, in all grades, are not entirely satisfied with their jobs. The reasons for this vary from grade to grade in much the same way as do the reasons for work satisfaction, but from the highest to the lowest, some aspect of the work situation is often a cause for complaint. This is not to say that the majority of such workers are wholly dissatisfied with their jobs – the evidence is to the contrary – but that many of them do not conform to the stereotyped image of workers who will put up with anything at work because their focus of interest is elsewhere. Even if it were true that all female office workers regarded their principal role as a domestically-based one, this does not preclude their having a desire for an interesting job. Indeed, an Alfred Marks survey of office workers found that 'interesting duties' was the single most important job characteristic sought by respondents.[103] The same survey found that the second most sought-after job attribute was promotion prospects and it was one which was steadily increasing in importance. Yet all the evidence suggests that the hopes of office workers in this respect are likely to be frustrated. A study of clerical workers by Shaw, Elsy and Bowen reveals that the lack of promotion prospects is in fact a major source of dissatisfaction among women in white-collar employment. Sixty-two per cent of their female respondents expressed dissatisfaction with the opportunities for learning new skills as a precondition for promotion. Shaw *et al.* conclude that the desire to get on in clerical work does not 'arise from feelings of relative deprivation in payment levels'. Most of the women were satisfied with their pay and felt better off in this respect than other clerks inside their own firm and with clerks working in other organisations.[104]

Another significant finding of this research is that although their female respondents were more satisfied with their existing jobs than were their male clerical respondents, dissatisfaction was quite widespread among them: 'about a third of all women responding expressed dissatisfaction with the variety and interest of their work, with the opportunities available for them to use their own initiative and with the way in which their work was organised.'[105]

A desire for intrinsic work satisfaction was also reflected in the responses given to questions concerning future occupational choice. In this respect, the authors argue, men and women are no different:

> If we abstract from all the reasons given for choosing either a similar or different job, the need for varied and interesting work was mentioned most frequently by men and women. As a very close second came the demand for better prospects . . . on the whole women were looking for the same job and work characteristics as were the men.[106]

There is a steadily accumulating body of evidence, therefore, which casts considerable doubt on the model of the working woman as largely instrumentally motivated and/or as acquiescent in the structure of opportunities available to her. The next objective, then, is to explore the range and nature of the responses available to female clerical workers when they subjectively experience job dissatisfaction.

Rationalising the situation

One response to the experience of disappointment with one or more attributes of the work situation is to rationalise this away altogether or to minimise its effect by placing importance on another attribute of the job or working environment. Thus a high wage or salary may come to be regarded as ample compensation for a monotonous job, or a pleasant social atmosphere may come to be regarded as compensation for a low pay packet, to the point where these alternative saitsfactions are considered to be the most important attributes of the job and sufficient reason for not doing something positive about the situation.[107] It might be supposed that the tendency to rationalise in this manner is largely a function of a lack of freedom of mobility in the labour market. Although this interpretation may be very useful for an understanding of the work attitudes of those who are limited by their particular skills (or lack of them) or of those who are somewhat constrained by factors arising in their domestic situation, it does not explain why those who are not so restricted fail to take advantage of the favourable labour market for office workers and seek alternative work. Clearly, a secretary who feels that she is being under-utilised is in a very good position to look for a job which will occupy more of her time. Similarly, a typist who does not like the factory-like atmosphere of the typing pool could seek a post in a small firm which does not segregate typists. The state of the labour market is clearly of central importance, but a more comprehensive approach to the question of why many office workers rationalise away their dissatisfactions should include reference to the age of the employees, their reference groups and subjective perceptions of the alternatives. It is possible that older women may be less sure of themselves when it comes to finding jobs, and therefore opt for security even though the current job might leave something to be desired. Reference groups are also likely to be of considerable importance. So long as there are pronounced differences in the work situation of white-collar as opposed to blue-collar employees, even the most tedious of office jobs may be seen to have its compensations over the factory-floor job. Moreover, the office hierarchy itself presents a more immediately visible structure of reference groups, which may shape the individual's perceptions of her own job.

Trade union action

Although female office workers are not as averse to trade unions as folklore would have us believe, there are a number of reasons why most of them would not attempt to resolve their grievances through organised industrial action.

In the case of secretaries, there are a number of factors which militate against the development of a strong union consciousness, or even the will to join a union. First, there is the factor of social background. Silverstone found that only 6 per cent of her respondents came from social classes IV and V, whereas over half of them came from social classes I and II (defined in terms of their fathers' occupations).[108] The significance of this fact, namely that girls from this type of social background are over-represented as compared with their proportions in the female workforce as a whole, has been suggested by Benet. In her opinion, they are more likely to regard unions with disapproval than to perceive them as an acceptable means for improving wages or conditions of work. This might vary according to the type of organisation in which the secretary works, so that antipathy to the unions may be more pronounced amongst business secretaries, but on the whole they are unlikely to favour collective responses to work dissatisfaction.[109] Benet also considers that those secretaries who despite their background have come into contact with orthodox socialism or feminism, and who have accepted it, are likely to quit secretarial work altogether, thus divesting this occupational group of any potentially 'revolutionary' elements.

A second factor which inhibits the unionisation of this sector of the workforce is the peculiar nature of the boss–secretary relationship. Apart from the fact that many secretaries hail from similar backgrounds to those of their bosses, their relationship is itself likely to cement feelings of identification on the part of the woman with her employer. The role of the secretary is largely supportive – she is often characterised as the subordinate member of a *team* even though this concept of a working 'partnership' mystifies the crucial distinctions between employer and employee in terms of power, status and reward. These important differences notwithstanding, a secretary is unlikely to assume an oppositional stance in relation to her boss, since this would effectively make their relationship unworkable. One may assume that if her dissatisfaction reached a very high level of intensity she would be more likely to change jobs, or if her grievances were felt in relation to secretarial work in general rather than to one unfortunate experience of it, she would most probably seek another type of job altogether.

A third inhibiting factor is the low degree of employment concentration among secretaries. As we noted earlier, employment concentration is positively related to the propensity to unionise. It is interesting to note that while this phenomenon may have negative consequences for the pay and working conditions of many secretaries, Silverstone believes that it may sometimes have the reverse effect:

> Many secretaries work in situations where only one or two of them are employed and thus there is no need for any structural arrangement to govern their rates of pay. Partly as a

consequence of this, many secretaries earn salaries far in excess of the norm.[110]

Since most secretaries, therefore, are likely to experience work dissatisfaction, if at all, in isolation rather than in a group, they are more likely to adopt individualised responses. Their background and training all serve to reinforce this preference for personal methods of negotiation. Indeed, Silverstone found that only 6 per cent of her respondents belonged to a union, and nearly all of them worked for newspapers. Moreover only two secretaries out of the total of thirty-three who belonged to a union had joined voluntarily.[111]

This apparent distaste among secretarial staff for trade union organisation is not characteristic of all grades of female office workers, but then few other types of office occupation incorporate a one-to-one relationship with the employer. As we saw earlier, women, especially in the public sector, are just as likely to join white-collar unions as men, where there is a high degree of employment concentration and where there is some precedent for them to do so. However, union membership is one thing, militancy is another, and although one can cite examples of heightened union activity by female-dominated white-collar unions which suggests that women are just as prepared as men to fight when they feel threatened, this is not evidence that union organisation and campaigning is the most typical response to work dissatisfaction.

Professionalisation

There have been several attempts in the past by male and female clerical workers to arrest a perceived decline in their status. Sometimes this has been manifested in the formation of a union, but on other occasions the response has been to assert the professional status of the occupation. For example, in the 1940s a small group of women in the USA formed the National Secretaries Association:

> dedicated to the proposition that secretaries deserved more status, recognition and responsibility. The result was a programme to convince employers that the secretary could be a

professional person as much as the accountant, the draughtsman–engineer or lawyer – if only she were given more responsible tasks than mere typing and dictation.[112]

Similar organisations have sprung up in the UK, the most recent of which is the Executive Secretaries Association, founded in 1970. All of these organisations have been mainly unsuccessful in their attempts to convince employers and the general public that secretaries may be considered on a par with members of the traditional or the new professions. Even though they have instituted all manner of diplomas and qualifications, these represent mere embellishments rather than prerequisites of secretarial status. The major problem appears to be the fact that secretaries cannot claim a monopoly of the body of skills and knowledge upon which their profession is based. As Young has suggested, the degree to which a body of knowledge is socially valued depends on the extent to which there is restricted access to this knowledge and opportunities for those who do have access to it to legitimise its higher status and control its availability.[113] Clearly, while schools continue to equip many of their pupils with basic shorthand and typing skills, and while it is possible to become a secretary at one of thousands of colleges around the country, executive and 'top' secretaries are in no position to assert exclusive rights to a body of marketable expertise. Silverstone maintains that many employers are not acquainted with the secretarial qualifications which are awarded by the associations, and are not particularly impressed when a secretary flourishes her certificates during an interview.[114]

Since one of the expressed aims of these associations is to detach their members' status from that of the rank and file, their numerical strength is likely to be extremely limited, and it is doubtful whether they can be effective in securing the redress of any grievances felt by secretaries in relation to status or promotion prospects.

Alternative occupations

For the women who feel that their present state of dissatisfaction has become intolerable, there is always the possibility of obtaining a totally different kind of job. However, the opportunities in this respect vary according to the type of office job in which one has had experience. Silverstone believes that secretarial work is a bridging occupation – 'one where the potentialities for movement to another type of work are particularly great'.[115] Secretarial work leads in particular to the fields of advertising, publishing and personnel work. Yet the largest single group of ex-secretaries whom she investigated had moved into occupations necessitating a fairly lengthy spell of training, for example, social work, nursing and teaching. A sizeable proportion had become air hostesses, thus moving from one supposedly glamorous job into another. Secretaries are probably much better placed than other types of female office worker when it comes to moving into alternative occupations. Their secretarial experience may open doors to certain professions, and they are more likely to have the academic prerequisites for entry to the training programmes of others. Those employed in the routine grades, however, are more likely to experience only lateral or downward mobility when changing jobs. Their jobs cannot be regarded as bridging occupations, and it may be necessary to attend evening classes at a local college before they can even begin to consider nursing or social work as alternatives. Other non-manual jobs such as working as a waitress, barmaid or shop assistant compare unfavourably with office work in terms of pay, fringe benefits and status. There is the option of manual work but it appears that mobility of this nature is not particularly common.[116]

While the majority of Silverstone's secretarial respondents had given 'serious thought' to moving into alternative occupations, and one assumes that many of those in the routine grades would also think in these terms, there are a number of reasons why this in fact proves to be a minority response to dissatisfaction. In the first place, office work despite all its potential sources of discontent compares very well indeed with all the other traditional female occupations in terms of remuneration, status, working conditions and so on. For secretaries, there are not only these advantages, but it seems that the work itself can be interesting and stimulating given a boss who is willing to delegate and to involve his secretary in his own round of activities. And throughout the office hierarchy there is perhaps always something which can be found to be enjoyable in one's occupation, which may outweigh the desire to move into another. Secondly, those jobs which do not entail downward mobility usually necessitate a period of training and/or non-vocational study. This no doubt represents a major deterrent to those who lack any formal qualifications but who wish to pursue a career.

For most girls, therefore, thoughts of a fresh start in an entirely different occupation will probably never progress beyond the daydreaming stage, except perhaps for a few half-hearted enquiries at a local technical college or a chat with a friend who made the transition successfully.

An alternative office job

A common response to work dissatisfaction is to find an alternative position in the same occupational field. For those who wish to do more than to sublimate their grievances in dreams and rationalisations, this provides the most practical solution. While most female office workers may not be able to move into the occupation of their choice, there is no doubt that until very recently they have been in a sellers' market as far as their skills as clerks, typists, telephonists, secretaries, etc., are concerned. According to Fulop, writing in 1971, the total number of office jobs increases by about 100,000 every year, and the excess of demand over supply to which this gives rise is exacerbated by such factors as the tendency towards earlier marriage and the quantitative increase in the range of occupations open to young girls.[117]

Undoubtedly, the situation is rather less favourable in 1978 when even office staff have felt the pinch of economic recession. Considerable caution should be exercised when interpreting unemployment figures but they do suggest a recent downswing in the demand for clerical workers. According to the DE, in December 1973 in the United Kingdom there were 21,563 women registered as unemployed under the category of clerical and related workers, and 32,888 unfilled vacancies. In December 1975 there were 73,915 registrations and only 9899 unfilled vacancies. In December 1973 a surplus of unemployed over unfilled vacancies was found only in the North-west, North, Wales, Scotland and Northern Ireland. In December 1975 there was no area in the United Kingdom where this surplus did not exist. Since then the numbers of unemployed women in this occupational group have continued to grow.

Most of the unemployed listed under this occupational category are clerks. For example, in Britain in June 1978 they represented 66,832 out of a total of 98,608 unemployed women registered under the clerical and related group. It is possible that these numbers reflect the growth in the number of unemployed school-leavers, some of them perhaps signing on as clerks on the basis of rudimentary office skills acquired at school. However, clerks are by no means the only ones to have suffered the effects of a chill economic wind. In the same month the figures also included 5619 receptionists, 3207 office machine operators, 5318 telephonists, 7083 personal secretaries, shorthand-writers and shorthand-typists, and 6642 other typists. Although much publicity has been devoted to the acute shortage of secretarial labour in the central London area, it is evident that for clerical workers in general the employment situation is much less fortunate. This probably means that there has been a gradual reduction in the choice of alternative jobs available.

In less exceptional times, women are in a favourable position to select the firm which most closely approximates to their expectations and aspirations in relation to pay, benefits, location, general working conditions and bosses. Those who do engage in an interminable round of job-hopping with a view to finding the optimum employment situation are likely, however, to encounter certain drawbacks. First, even though many employers have no doubt become used to high rates of turnover among office staff, they may nevertheless be wary of hiring someone who has an excessive record of job-changing. An occupational history of this nature would certainly be a cause for comment in the interview situation. Indeed, in a guide for employers involved in the hiring of employees, the author instructs her readers to 'look at the REASONS for changing jobs very carefully'.[118] Unless a boss is sensitive to the fact that work dissatisfaction can represent a root cause of job-hopping, he may judge the applicant before him to be basically unstable and liable to leave within a short time, with the result that the interview comes to a swift conclusion. A second drawback is that the interview and accompanying tour of the office rarely afford a genuine insight into either the work situation or the social ambience of the prospective place of employment. It usually takes several weeks before the new employee is in a position to know whether she has found her ideal job. If her judgement turns out to be hastily conceived and she decides to leave, this will only serve to blot her copybook in the eyes of future interviewers.

The only way in which it is possible for a female office worker to overcome these difficulties is to sign on as a temporary worker with one or more employment agencies in the hope of finding a firm which meets with her requirements. According to an Alfred Marks Survey conducted during 1970, 13 per cent of their sample of temporary workers were working in this capacity whilst looking for a permanent job. Of these, over half were hoping that they could find a temporary job where they would like to stay permanently.[119]

The employment agencies do at least provide a means whereby an office worker can search for a satisfying post without the stigma which normally attaches to the frequent changing of jobs. Unlike the situation which obtains when a girl applies direct to an employer, the agencies present the opportunity of a 'trial marriage' which is unusually easy to escape from should the experience prove to be less than attractive.

Becoming a permanent temporary

While some office workers respond to job dissatisfaction by using the agencies as a means of finding a better permanent position, there are others who use the agencies for an altogether different purpose. These are the girls who sign up as temps in the hope of finding the interest and variety which they feel permanent jobs cannot offer. For some girls, life as a 'permanent temporary' is the only way of relieving what is for them the utter boredom and monotony of office work. Tired perhaps of being servile flatterers without any hope of promotion into management, or of promotion out of the typing pool, they respond to the lure of the agencies' advertisements which indirectly promise interest and independence through continual change of environment. All too often there may be a discrepancy between the promise and the practice, but the agencies do at least offer some means of relief from the claustrophobia of the regular nine-to-five job.

The permanent job-hopping phenomenon is not new, but the employment agencies have made it easier. They can sell the temp as an office trouble-shooter, whereas the girl who tries it on her own can become labelled as 'unstable'. Although the permanent temps represent a minority of all temporary office workers, they constitute approximately 20 per cent of single girls who are working in this capacity.[120]

It is possible to regard these girls as those who have become alienated in their permanent work environments but, aware of their favourable position in the labour market, have attempted to reduce the feeling of alienation by exercising some measure of control over the course of their working lives. Blauner's vision of freedom in the work situation tends to fit the position of the temp very closely:

> The non-alienated pole of the powerless dimension is freedom and control. Freedom is the state which allows the person to remove himself from those dominating situations that make him simply a reacting object. Freedom may therefore involve the possibility of movement in a physical or social sense, the ability to walk away from a coercive machine process, or the opportunity of quitting a job because of the existence of alternative employment.[121]

Yet it is a very qualified form of freedom which the temporary experiences. Her degree of manoeuvre is circumscribed by fluctuations in demand for her labour, the conditions laid down by the agency, the nature of each job she undertakes and also by the skills which she has to offer. The freedom is, then, something of an illusion, and perhaps it is not surprising that many of these girls return to the security of a regular job. Temporary work ultimately represents just one more way of coming to terms with the inevitable, another attempt to escape from the deadening rhythms of the enormous file.

Married women in the office

The popular image of the female office worker is that of a single girl in her twenties who is filling in the time between leaving school and getting married. While this may have been the case until the Second World War she is now increasingly likely to be married and aged over thirty. In 1966 married women represented approximately 47 per cent of all female clerical workers.[122] Moreover, a great many of them have children of school age. In a survey conducted by the Alfred Marks Bureau, 27 per cent of their sample of married women had children, and all but two of these had a family aged under fifteen.[123] The situation is rather different, however, in central London where there is a much greater preponderance of young single women in the office population. Silverstone found that only one-third of her respondents in secretarial work were married.[124]

Although married women may not be as willing to undertake office work in the central London area, when one considers the country as a whole we find that clerical work is the second most common source of employment for this group. According to the 1966 census, 22 per cent of economically active married women were employed in this sphere.[125] Owing to the dearth of material relating to women in white-collar work, it is extraordinarily difficult to build up a picture of the characteristics of married women in the office. One has the impression, however, that marriage as such makes little difference to the work situation of the female white-collar worker. This was not always the case it seems, for according to Muriel Wells, who was a shorthand-typist in the 1930s, marriage at that time meant the end of one's career:

About 1930, I was lucky enough to obtain a job . . . in a solicitor's office . . . After a year or two, with much fear and trepidation, I decided to ask whether I could continue working in the office if I got married. Much to my surprise my request was granted, as it was almost unheard of for married women to do this.[126]

Nowadays, it is motherhood rather than marriage which is likely to remove an office worker from the labour force, or at least necessitate some major alterations to her work pattern. Silverstone's research confirms that this is the case among secretaries working in central London.[127]

Contrary to the myth that employers prefer young unattached women as employees, it appears that many actually prefer married women, and only a minority regard those with domestic commitments in the form of young children as unsuitable or undesirable employees.[128] The fact is that older, married women are more likely to remain in a job, and employers are well aware of this. However, this apparent spirit of enlightenment exhibited by employers towards those with families cannot be mentioned without some qualification. First, there has been, until recently at least, a tremendous shortage of labour for an ever-increasing supply of jobs. Therefore employers have been frequently obliged to recruit from this group. Secondly, while employers are willing to hire women with domestic commitments as secretaries, it seems that they expect these women to make adjustments to the prevailing work patterns, particularly in terms of hours. Silverstone found that 35 per cent of the employers she interviewed were willing to hire mothers 'providing that certain conditions were met'. The conditions included the specifications that mothers had to make reliable arrangements for the daytime care of their children, that their children must have attained a certain minimum age and that 'work would not be continually interrupted owing to the demands of the children.'[129] It would appear, therefore, that accommodation is required of married women with children rather than extended towards them. This is also reflected in the very tardy progress towards the introduction of flexitime in British firms.

Indeed, far from employers straining to make it easier for married women to combine employment with their domestic life, there is every indication that they make it very difficult indeed. According to an Alfred Marks Survey of married women in the office, 30 per cent of the respondents said that they often worked overtime, and only 10 per cent said that they never had to stay late: 'However, it's the everyday working pattern which most affects the ease with which a woman can cope with home and office, and some employers are clearly most reluctant to give any concessions.'[130]

In fact one-quarter of the sample said that their bosses were not willing to be flexible over late arrival at the office, extra time off for shopping or time off for domestic commitments. Silverstone also found that the majority of London secretaries worked some kind of overtime on a fairly regular basis.[131] No less than 61 per cent of her respondents occasionally worked late at the office. It is not altogether clear from the various studies whether employers expect employees to work overtime, or whether those who do it on a regular basis are what might be called 'organisation women'. It may be that some women put in long hours, work through their lunchtimes and take work home as a way of ingratiating themselves with their boss, perhaps hoping that promotion will be the ultimate reward. There is no way that one can provide an answer to this question, but it is undoubtedly normal for secretaries to be punctual and to be willing to work overtime. Unfortunately, no systematic figures are available for the routine grades, but one suspects that conformity to the prescribed hours of work is usually expected at these levels also. The conditions of work for such women therefore place considerable demands on those who have young children. It may be suggested, therefore, that inflexibility on the part of employers represents an important variable in the analysis of women's attitudes to work and their occupational distribution.

It is interesting to discover that whereas married women are less numerous than single women in the white-collar workforce as a whole, they represent a majority of all temporary office workers.[132] It seems that because of the inadequacy of state nursery facilities coupled with the inflexibility of employers over such matters as school holiday arrangements, it is only by becoming temps that many women with domestic commitments can continue working or return to work once they have completed their family. According to an Alfred Marks survey in 1970, approximately 13 per cent of all temporary workers are unable to accept permanent work because of personal or domestic commitments.[133] A more recent survey found that 69 per cent of married female temporary office employees in the South-east were working as temps for this reason.[134] Temporary work offers all the flexibility that is lacking in the sphere of permanent work:

> While the office temporary sometimes has to contend with uncertainty, she also knows that, generally speaking, she can arrange her working days and hours so that she can be at home or free for other activities when she really needs to be. Unlike the full-timers, she can take time off when she wants.[135]

All this is true and some agencies love to advertise their role as the saviours of housebound mothers, but it is also true that so long as agencies and temporary workers exist there is no pressure upon employers to adopt more flexible attitudes themselves. An employer who makes a concession to one permanent worker is obliged to extend this facility to all the others – let one married secretary come in at 9.30 and they will all want to. But one temporary working fewer hours is unlikely to have the same effect on the permanent staff. They may grouse and complain but the boss can often point out that she, unlike they, receives no luncheon vouchers, no sick pay and no paid holiday. In the short term, therefore, the employment agencies are of enormous assistance to the woman who wishes to combine work with motherhood or with the care of an aged relative. In the long term, however, their presence siphons off the pressure on employers to rethink their provisions for working hours or to reassess their expectations from female employees in terms of overtime.

There is very little evidence indeed relating to the work attitudes of married women in the office. Clearly any such analysis would have to make a distinction between those who had yet to start a family and those who had returned to the workforce after having completed their family. One study which has investigated the work attitudes of married women in white-collar work unfortunately makes no such distinction.[136] It is interesting to find, however, that 31 per cent of the respondents said that they were working 'because of their dislike of domestic routine'. Although money was a reason for working, it was not regarded as the primary determinant of their decision to return to work. There is therefore at least some basis for the view that many married women return to work because of their domestic circumstances and not in spite of them.

In recent years, it has become fashionable among sociologists to eschew the study of worker attitudes, and in particular the investigation of sources of worker satisfaction and dissatisfaction. The main reason for this, it appears, is that such studies are felt to provide knowledge which enables management to exercise a greater degree of control over their employees. Not only does this position, in my view, represent an over-optimistic view of the extent to which employers consult sociological literature in their efforts to increase efficiency and profitability, but it paves the way for sociologists to interpret the world as it suits them best. What most suits a great many sociologists at the present time is a view of the worker as determined – powerless to resist the economic forces which sweep over him or her in the era of monopoly capital. As Beechey has suggested however, it is essential that one acknowledge the capacity of workers to resist or impede such pressures.[137] If one accepts this proposition, then an analysis of the factors which promote dissatisfaction and which condition responses to dissatisfaction becomes imperative. If the modern worker, whether male or female, is not to be seen as a passive, somewhat mindless being, responding like litmus paper to organisational and technological change, then it becomes essential to examine both attitudes and behaviour more directly. It is quite possible that the realities of the labour market offer very little opportunity for resistance or even for manoeuvre, but the strategies which workers adopt need to be identified and accounted for. It is this premise which has informed the foregoing account of women in clerical employment.

In this chapter I have been concerned to establish a framework of knowledge in terms of which it becomes possible to account for the decision among some women to take up work as temporary clerical employees. White-collar work in the twentieth century is a world in which women largely inhabit the lower-paid, less prestigious territories. Many women find their jobs immensely satisfying, but there are many others for whom office work represents an occupational cul-de-sac. For the latter group, a wide range of responses are available, although it appears that discontent typically finds expression on an individual basis. I have endeavoured to show how 'permanent temping' may be regarded as one of the available strategies. It has also been shown that married women constitute a substantial proportion of the female clerical population, yet circumstances prevailing both inside and beyond the workplace present them with many practical difficulties. These can be negotiated to some extent by entering temporary employment. Having set the supply side of the temporary labour market in context, my next objective is to account for the growth of a demand for temporary clerical labour and to examine the role of the private employment agency in the alignment of supply and demand.

4

Markets for Temporary Clerical Labour and the Role of the Private Employment Agency

The existence of temporary workers in the white-collar sector is almost entirely dependent upon both long-term and short-term labour shortage. This chapter is concerned to identify the conditions under which these shortages arise and to examine the role of private employment agencies in channelling the supply of temporary labour. Both the state of the market for temporary clerical labour and the manner in which agencies align jobs and workers represent important variables in the study of temps' attitudes to work.

Markets for temporary clerical labour

Employers have always been faced with variable workloads, and have depended on casual or temporary labour to help meet seasonal and fluctuating demands for their goods and services. In America, for example, the presence of a large migratory labour force solves the problems of fruit-growers who find it uneconomical to hire fruit-pickers on a year-round basis. In Britain, casual labour was once a common feature of the dockyards.[1] Similarly, in the building industry, the system of labour subcontracting is based upon a supply of workers employed on a casual basis. The hotel and catering industry also employs a large number of temporary workers because of the seasonal nature of its operations. The demand for temporary labour, however, is not confined solely to sectors of the economy which experience uneven demand for their products and services. Approximately two-fifths of all temporary workers are employed in financial, professional, scientific and miscellaneous services.² In the case of both nursing and clerical work, the use of temporaries is partly based upon an acute long-term shortage of labour. The source of the demand for temporary labour thus varies from industry to industry, and for this reason it is doubtful whether the temporary workforce as a whole may usefully be regarded as a unitary phenomenon. It is tempting to try to do so, however, since many temporaries would appear to qualify for membership of the industrial reserve army, or relative surplus population, as defined by Marx: 'Every worker has to be classed in this category when he is unemployed or but partially employed.'³

The concept of the industrial reserve army is of central importance in Marx's analysis of the capitalist mode of production. He argues that its role is two-fold: to act as a flexible pool of labour to meet certain specific manpower requirements as and when they arise, and to act as a competitive force whose presence tends to undermine the material position of other workers. Not only does this army act as a 'lever' which promotes capital accumulation, but its growth is said to be an inevitable consequence of capital expansion, particularly when this entails a change in the organic composition of capital itself towards labour-saving methods of production.

It is very difficult to derive an accurate knowledge of the size of the temporary workforce as a whole, because it is by definition in a perpetual state of flux. Indeed, the task of precise definition itself represents a major problem. One study which set out to ascertain the size of the temporary workforce chose to regard work as temporary when their respondents defined it as such. However, they found that a source of confusion lay in the distinction between part-time and temporary work.⁴ It seems most appropriate, in my view, to define temporary work as a form of employment where the employer/employee relationship is potentially transient, and where both parties acknowledge that tenure is not guaranteed. This definition may perhaps entail its own set of problems, but it does incorporate the important characteristic that such work is recognised as inherently impermanent by both employer and employee from the very outset. Another problem involved in the task of estimating the size of the temporary labour force is the fact that many people employed in this capacity are simply not recorded. Yet whilst it must be recognised that any statistical representation of the temporary labour force is likely to be incomplete, one may derive some idea of its dimensions from a survey conducted by NOP for the Employment Services Agency in 1975. The survey found that 7 per cent of a sample of 4783 people who were working at the time of the interview regarded their present jobs as temporary, and a further 4 per cent had considered their present jobs to be on a temporary basis at some time in the past. A further 14 per cent had been employed in a temporary capacity during the five years prior to the survey.[5] Temporaries, therefore, represent a small but not insignificant part of the labour force and their numbers are expected to increase. As Parker and Sirker have shown, they are located in a wide range of jobs, although there are a number of occupational categories with which they are particularly associated. These include catering and bar work, cleaning and caretaking, sales work, labouring and clerical work.[6]

The development of the market for temps in office employment has been mainly due to the great expansion of white-collar work since the Second World War. The period 1945–70 was one of tremendous growth in the number of office jobs. The demand for labour could not be met even though it was becoming more common for married women to return to work after completing their families. Thus it came about that firms began to hire temporary office staff as a short-term solution to the long-term problem of unfilled vacancies. Although private employment agencies have encouraged firms to use temporary labour as an aid to efficient staff planning, it has been found that they are most commonly hired to fill a vacancy until a permanent worker is recruited or when a permanent member of staff is sick or on holiday.[7]

The view has often been expressed that a rather more sinister intention informs the use of temporary clerical workers. In 1974, NALGO claimed that the hire of temps to fill gaps created by staff shortage obviated the need to pay wages sufficiently high enough to attract and retain permanent staff.[8] Unions in a number of Western countries have claimed that temporaries can be used as strike-breakers and that their presence is generally inimical to the interests of labour. In this way, the unions have given concrete expression to the fears which Marx indicated as likely accompaniments to the presence and growth of a reserve army of labour. However Eric Hurst, Joint Chairman of Brook Street Bureau, one of the largest private employment organisations, has argued that the main role for temps is to supply abnormal and peripheral requirements and not to provide competition with permanent workers.[9] It is extremely difficult to resolve the competing claims and it may be that in those cases where the hire of temps has had a depressing effect on the wages of permanent staff, this was an unintended consequence of the employers' actions.

The widespread use of temps as holiday stand-ins and during peak work periods means that demand for their services fluctuates throughout the year. In December 1967, for example, about 23,000 temporary office staff were working for agencies in the GLC area, whereas the figure for July 1968 was 41,000.[10] More recently, economic recession has led to an overall reduction in the demand for temporary clerical workers throughout the year. It has become more common for firms to try to manage with their existing pool of staff when a vacancy remains unfilled or when an employee is ill or on holiday. In spite of the less favourable economic climate, there is still a large demand for temps, especially in central London.

Although there remains a substantial demand for office temps in some areas of the country, it is important to recognise that both short-term and long-term fluctuations in demand may have important implications for attitudes towards temporary work. For example, the financial insecurity implied not only by seasonal fluctuations but also by a long-term contraction in demand may deter people from entering this mode of employment and encourage temps themselves to return to permanent work. This observation is lent some support by the findings of the NOP survey mentioned earlier. A pilot survey of 1936 people, some of whom were currently working and some of whom were not, asked respondents if they would undertake temporary work in the future. Although 24 per cent replied in the affirmative, the majority did not intend to do so, the main deterrent being the perceived insecurity of the work and the disadvantages with which this was associated.[11]

Thus, while the agencies' advertisements often convey the impression that the temporary clerical market is an Aladdin's cave of wondrous opportunities, the reality may sometimes be rather different. Whilst the fear of insecurity must inform occupational choice and job attitudes among a great many of today's working population, the direct experience of it is an almost inescapable feature of temporary clerical employment. Consequently, the attitudes towards work held by temps in office work must in part be regarded as a function of the vagaries of the market for their labour.

The role of the private employment agency

According to the 1975 NOP survey, private employment agencies play only a very minor role in the temporary labour market considered as a whole. It found that the majority of temps were employed directly by the person or organisation for whom the work was to be performed. Only a small proportion of their respondents had obtained temporary work via a formal intermediary. As few as 10 per cent of the women interviewed had gained their positions through private agencies.[12] However, in certain areas of the country the role of the private employment agencies is greater than this figure suggests. Moreover, whilst agencies are active in the supply of temporary labour in a wide range of occupations, they are particularly prominent in certain fields. A survey of industrial and business companies in France, for example, found that whilst agencies accounted for 71 per cent of the overall temporary market, they accounted for 82 per cent of the temporary office staff market, including 91 per cent of the temp secretary market.[13] In Britain and in the USA the majority of temporary placements made by agencies are in the field of clerical work. The NOP survey found that 24 per cent of temporary clerks and office machine operators and 44 per cent of temporary secretaries had obtained their posts through private agencies. The next objective, therefore, is to examine the way in which the agencies came to play this role in the sphere of white-collar work and to explore the manner in which it is currently performed.

Origins and development

Ever since medieval times there have existed certain organisations closely akin to the modern private employment agency. The earliest example may be seen in the hiring fairs for agricultural workers which prevailed during the middle ages. The concept of the hiring fair developed into permanently established hiring halls where domestic staff were screened and selected for prospective employers. According to Campling, organisations known as registry offices developed in the eighteenth and nineteenth centuries which also specialised mainly in the supply of domestic personnel, although after the middle of the last century they began to supply catering and even nursing staff.[14] Towards the end of the nineteenth century employment agencies specialising in the placement of office staff began to appear. It is interesting to note that agencies dealt mainly in female-dominated sectors of the labour market where there was an excess of demand over supply.

During the first decades of the present century there was a considerable growth in the number of agencies both in Britain and the USA, their main role being to supply permanent workers for the expanding industries at that time. In both countries, charges of unethical practices and exploitation were levelled against the agencies, and laws were passed in America to regulate their activities. Even in Britain, the public health authorities recommended in 1909 that all agencies should be registered, but until very recently only nursing and domestic staff agencies were actually required to do so on ¡a nationwide basis.

Although the agencies mainly dealt in permanent placements, the practice of supplying temporary labour began prior to the First World War in Britain, and according to one spokesman for the industry it was 'well established' by the end of the 1930s.[15] According to Moore, the origins of the temporary help industry in the United States came somewhat later.[16] Whilst there were many individual firms supplying temporary labour before the Second World War, it was not until the 1940s that nationwide organisations began to appear specialising in the supply of certain types of temporary labour. In Britain and in the USA, the 1930s were lean years, and firms which required temporary labour had no problem in finding staff themselves. The permanent side of the agencies' operations was very badly hit by the Depression, and subsequently, by the impact of the Second World War, which made it difficult to operate. During this period, many agencies closed down, never to reopen. Those which survived during the war were those which specialised in temporary placements, since there was an acute shortage of labour and because there were many people who were not able to commit themselves to a permanent job. The agencies brought the employers and those who were seeking work together and many of them flourished on the profits. Brook Street Bureau, now one of the largest office staff employment organisations in Britain, was founded at this time on an overdraft of £50.[17]

Since the Second World War, there has been an enormous expansion in the number of private employment agencies supplying labour on both a temporary and permanent basis. Immediately after the Second World War, the number of agencies was only a fraction of what it is today, although it is impossible to state how many existed at that time due to the absence of a comprehensive system of licensing. In 1977 there were about 5500 agencies, of which the largest single group dealt with office staff.[18] Nobody knows for certain just how many people are employed by agencies in a given year, but the Federation of Personnel Services has estimated that approximately 600,000 temps worked for agencies in 1976. The industry as a whole is characterised by enormous profits and enormous losses. Among the smaller agencies, that is the single-branch firms, it has been reported that almost as many are obliged to go out of business each year as those which enter it.[19] Yet there are rich pickings to be had for the successful agencies. In 1973, for example, Brook Street Bureau reported a pre-tax profits rise of 112 per cent on the previous year, from £849,531 to £1,810,211. During the same period, turnover rose by £5 million to £14 million. In recent years the structure of ownership in the employment agency field has become more international in character. St Paul's, a subsidiary of what was at one time the second largest group of agencies in the country, was bought by Ecco SA, a French temp help company, in 1977. This development occurred shortly after the Alfred Marks organisation, another very large group in the field, was purchased by the Swiss-based Adia Interim group.

The growth of private employment agencies operating in the field of white-collar employment was largely predicated upon the post-war conditions of near full employment and acute labour shortage in the expanding sphere of office work. The demand for labour created by these circumstances rendered it increasingly difficult and costly for firms to conduct their own recruitment for both temporary and permanent vacancies. The private agencies stepped in to fill the breach. Although they could do nothing to remedy the deficiency of supply, they could at least claim to speed up the process whereby employer and employee came together. To some extent it could be argued that the agencies have actually increased the supply of labour. In providing the option of temporary work, they enable many married women to find the flexible conditions of employment which are often lacking in permanent work. The growth of the agencies' activities in the sphere of temporary office work has therefore rested not only upon a growing demand for labour but also on their own ability to mobilise an otherwise redundant pool of labour.

Another factor which has contributed to the proliferation of agencies is the small amount of capital necessary in order to set up in business. As Fulop has pointed out, all that is required is 'a desk, a telephone, and sufficient promotional outlay to make [the firm] known'.[20] However, as many small firms have found to their cost, it is a great deal more difficult to stay in business.

It has been suggested that 'agencies flourish when other channels prove unsatisfactory', and indeed there can be little doubt that agencies are at least partly a response to the inability of the state employment service to provide either an efficient or an attractive channel for the recruitment of both permanent and temporary staff in the office sector.[21] Although the exchanges were originally intended for the purpose of bringing about a more efficient use of labour, their failure in this respect has long been manifest. It was during the period between the wars that they acquired their association with the unemployed rather than with the soon-to-be-employed, and subsequently they gained a reputation for dealing mainly with the placement of unskilled and semi-skilled manual workers. Thus, for many years after the war, their historical associations tended to make them less than attractive to those who were looking for white-collar jobs.[22]

The government has also been aware of this problem for a long time and in recent years has made strenuous attempts to modernise the image of the exchanges. In 1967 the DE opened an office in Manchester which dealt exclusively with the placement of full-time office staff. According to R.M. Jones, its external appearance had much more in common with that of the private employment agency than with the traditional Ministry exchange, and it had achieved a very favourable record of placements as compared with private agencies in the Manchester area.[23] Since the early 1970s, the principle of modernisation has been applied much more extensively. A major effort to exorcise the spectre of the dole queue image began in 1973 with the creation of the first Jobcentre. Jobcentres, which are essentially the modern equivalent of the old labour exchanges, are virtually indistinguishable from private employment agencies in external appearance. By April 1977, 297 Jobcentres had opened and there were plans to open new ones at the rate of approximately 100 per annum during the next five years. By all accounts, they have been very successful in achieving the aims for which they were intended.[24] The institution of the Jobcentre was shortly followed by yet another innovation. In 1976 the government established a temporary help scheme at Canning Town Jobcentre and subsequently at other offices around the country. The government's service, however, differs in one key respect from that provided by the private firms. A temp using the public service automatically becomes the responsibility of the client firm, and is paid and administered by the client. In March 1978 I contacted the ESA in order to find out what kinds of workers were using this facility and to discover whether or not it had proved to be a success. I was informed that the main users of the temp services were women seeking jobs in shops and offices. Since the ESA had not yet attempted systematically to monitor its performance in this field no statistical information concerning its degree of success or failure was available.

The growth of private employment agencies dealing in the supply of labour for both temporary and permanent positions in the office sector is thus the net result of several factors – an excess of jobs over the supply of labour, the growth of married women seeking employment, the failure of the state to provide an efficient, attractive alternative, the inadequacy of direct methods of recruitment, and the relative ease with which it is possible to set up in what can often be a very profitable business. To a much lesser extent, increased manpower planning by firms may have contributed to their expansion but this is more true of the American situation. There is little evidence as yet to suggest that the growth of agencies in Britain has resulted from any systematic attempt by employers to use temps as a means of reducing the number of permanent staff on their payrolls.

The private employment agencies in the UK have been remarkably free from state supervision as compared with those operating in the rest of Western Europe, although in recent years there have been moves to subject them to a much greater degree of control. The employment agencies have always been required in principle to conform to certain minimum standards, however, since the potential for malpractice on their part was recognised almost as soon as they first appeared. In 1921 an act was passed which enabled local authorities in the London area to introduce a licensing system if they so wished. Although this act granted considerable powers to the authorities in theory, it seems that they rarely extended them to the point of actually revoking the licence of a disreputable agency. Moreover, the licensing system did not become established nationwide until 1973.

It was in 1973 that the Employment Agencies Act was passed and it became effective in June 1976. Local authority licensing was abolished and agencies became subject to a centralised system of licensing and control. The Act distinguishes between an employment agency, which is one that introduces a worker to a client for direct employment by the latter, and an employment business, which hires workers employed by the business to a third party. The regulations impose not only the obligation to obtain a licence but also to comply with a number of specified duties and obligations.

In the first year of the Act's operation, 5541 applications for licences were made, and 4685 were granted. Two hundred and forty-seven applications were withdrawn and the remainder were still being considered. DE inspectors made over 6300 visits to agencies and businesses, of which 166 were concerned with the investigation of a complaint. One agency was prosecuted for operating without a licence and other offences under the Act, resulting in fines of £400.[25] The situation at the present time is that the present government is unwilling to take any further action unless very grave abuses are seen to be perpetrated by the agencies.

The theory and practice of the private employment agency

Until recently there has been very little qualitative or even quantitative information available concerning the operations of private employment agencies. Most of the data has been furnished by the agencies themselves, or by their representative organisations, for example, the Federation of Personnel Services and the International Institute of Temporary Work. There have been very few independent enquiries into their activities and only one major investigation by the government. The 1973 Employment Agencies Act should help to remedy this situation since it requires both permanent placement and temporary hire agencies to maintain detailed records of their transactions. In addition, the Manpower Services Commission has agreed to sponsor an enquiry into the private employment services. For the moment, however, it is extremely difficult to construct an adequate picture of the quality of the service which the agencies provide. The bulk of information derives from those who, whether for profit or for the sake of a principle, are anxious to see that private employment agencies survive. Consequently one has to approach material emanating from these sources with some degree of caution. Certain leading figures associated with the industry have expressed the view that independent enquiries are both welcome and necessary. For example Eric Hurst, of Brook Street Bureau, has publicly declared that 'this service has nothing to fear from the most searching investigation of its operation'.[26] Yet one doubts whether this view is shared by all operators in the field. The present writer encountered a degree of resistance on the part of some agency personnel to the prospect of scrutiny by an outsider. Similarly, when R.M. Jones attempted to conduct a study of private agencies in the Manchester area, he found it 'impossible to win the confidence of a majority of the agency operators'.[27] In both cases, this problem led to modifications in the design of the research. Similar problems were encountered by Olesen and Katsuranis in their study of temporary workers in San Francisco.[28] Given the fact of widespread criticism of the agencies, it is perhaps not surprising that some agency personnel have adopted a rather closed attitude. A further reason why the agencies may sometimes be less than willing to become the subjects of close investigation concerns the competitive nature of the business itself. The agencies are anxious to safeguard lucrative contracts and to ensure that their charges compare favourably with those of their competitors. This inevitably means that there is a reluctance to divulge a great deal of information to outsiders.

Very little in the way of systematic data has been furnished by opponents of the agencies, although almost every aspect of their operations has been subject to critical comment during the last decade. A great many of the criticisms are based upon personal experiences and thus do not provide an objective basis from which to assess the agencies' activities. This is not to say that they are lacking in foundation, but only that occupational anecdotes represent an insufficient guide to the performance and conduct of these organisations. For the most part, the case against the agencies rests on matters of principle rather than on hard facts.

However, in spite of the paucity of objective information, one cannot evade the task of examining the nature of the service which they provide. One of the primary objectives of this research is to identify the factors which influence the attitudes to work of female clerical employees working in a temporary capacity. Accordingly, it is necessary to examine the extent to which the agencies are both willing and able to provide women with jobs which match their stated requirements.

The role of an employment agency or business is that of an intermediary in the labour market, bringing supply and demand together so as to achieve placements which are satisfactory to both parties. In theory, this process of selection is effected by interviewers who possess a considerable degree of expertise and knowledge of the local job market, and who are highly skilled in the task of screening and selection. The interview may be supplemented by a range of tests designed to ascertain the level of skill possessed by the applicant in relation to certain tasks. The advantages of this method of recruitment from the point of view of a prospective employer are its speed and effectiveness compared to other methods in a situation where labour is scarce and recruitment costs are high. In theory, an individual agency is able to build up a relationship with its client firms such that the interviewers develop a specific knowledge of their clients' labour requirements, their conditions of work, salary scales, etc., in order to facilitate the selection of appropriate candidates. Furthermore, the interviewer should be able to furnish the client with whatever information may be pertinent to his requirements, such as current salary or wage levels for particular types of staff.

From the point of view of those seeking employment, whether of a permanent or temporary nature, the agencies are potentially able to offer a useful service. One of their main attractions is that they can secure a post for an applicant in rather less time than it would take by individual methods. The agencies are also able to extend the number of jobs from which the applicant may choose. Moreover, they should be able to provide a form of advice and consultancy service to the applicant in order to help her locate the position most suited to her skills and requirements. The service is available during normal working hours and frequently on Saturday mornings, and unlike that provided to the client, it is free.

However, information deriving from a number of sources suggests that agencies do not always provide an optimum service for their clients and applicants. A study of the quality of temporary help services in the United States, for example, found that as many as 43 per cent of users regarded temps as less efficient than regular employees.[29] A survey conducted in France by SOFRES, a government survey unit, found that while companies had a 'fairly positive' image of temporary agencies, the staff supplied were not always considered to be suitably qualified. When asked to comment on the proposition that 'you are sure to have qualified staff', only 34 per cent responded in the affirmative.[30] A number of British surveys have also tapped a reservoir of discontent among employers with regard to the quality of the service provided. The NBPI survey found that only a few of the firms which it investigated were positively satisfied with the service provided, and about half registered dissatisfaction.[31] In her research conducted among London-based employers, Silverstone found that 65 per cent of her respondents were 'unreservedly dissatisfied' with the service offered by the agencies. While the employers were less than satisfied with both the temporary and permanent staff which they had been sent, they were particularly disgruntled about the quality of temporaries. This was felt by the employers to be the fault of the agencies and they assumed that applicants were not being tested, 'otherwise they presumably would not have sent them out, or else they chose to overlook standards.'[32]

A study commissioned by the Department of Employment and conducted by the Institute of Manpower Studies in 1975 investigated the use of temporary staff in eight firms representing a wide range of employment situations. Part of the study was concerned with employers' assessments of the quality of staff provided by employment businesses. The conclusions of the investigation were less than favourable:

> The Employment Businesses are the main source of information concerning the supply of temporary staff; their effectiveness, however, in meeting the needs of firms is not always great. Firms are concerned that staff from this source, particularly for secretarial and clerical jobs, are often not 'screened' and do not always meet the firm's specifications.[33]

A small independent survey conducted by Doran in 1970–1 found evidence of discontent among employers in relation to the permanent staff supplied by agencies. 70 per cent of the employers he interviewed expressed the opinion that applicants were inadequately screened by the agency interviewers. Over half the agencies investigated by Doran did not test applicants.[34] A survey of 30 London employment agencies conducted by the magazine *Top Secretary* in 1974 likewise found that agencies tended not to test permanent applicants. Only two agencies were found to test for speed and accuracy and to conduct their interviews in complete privacy.[35]

Although employers frequently grumble about the cost of the agencies' services, much of the discontent found among client firms appears to be based upon a lack of confidence in the selection techniques used by the agencies. A survey conducted in 1973 by the trade journal *Index to Office Equipment and Supplies* reported an 'overwhelming vote of no confidence in the vetting that the agencies carried out'.[36] To date, there has been little formal pressure on the agencies to institute rigorous testing procedures. Those who are members of the Federation of Personnel Services are obliged to test temporary applicants, but they are not required to test permanent applicants, and some agencies maintain that it would be uneconomical for them to do so. One is inclined to doubt whether the principle of testing is universally applied to temporary applicants, in spite of the importance attached to this procedure by the FPS. Quite apart from the fact that only a minority of agencies belong to this organisation, it is clearly very difficult to enforce a rigorous standard of testing in all agencies and at all times.

The quality of interviewing staff is frequently a cause for complaint among users of the agencies' services, but the latter strenuously deny that staff are inadequately trained. The larger ones insist that their interviewers are very rigorously trained both in selection technique and in company philosophy. There seems to be very little opportunity to test the quality of interviewing staff in general, although if, as ASTMS suggests, there is a high rate of turnover amongst interviewers, one could surmise that it is not always possible for new interviewers to undergo extensive periods of training, nor for agency principals to hire only the most experienced people for the job.[37] It seems most unlikely that the small single-branch firms, which are in the majority throughout the country, offer specialised training courses for their interviewers. In these companies, interviewer skills are probably learnt on the job through a process of trial and error. According to an article by Macpherson in the *Financial Times*, 'there are many examples' of young graduates looking for a short spell of employment who obtain jobs as interviewers after only a couple of days of 'perfunctory training'.[38] In fairness to those agencies who do seek to maintain high standards in this respect, one cannot judge all the operators by the example of those whose inferior quality has achieved publicity. Moreover, it should be noted that the Institute of Employment Consultants was set up in 1963 with the specific intention of raising the standards of qualification and performance of agency personnel.

A common criticism of the agencies is that the system whereby some interviewers earn commission on the basis of the number of placements they make tends to result in hasty and ill-judged placings. This objection has been lodged by ASTMS but again there is no way of knowing whether commissions have this effect or whether they result in higher quality service. One would suppose that it depends very much on the level of basic earnings, the policy of the individual agency and the integrity of the individual interviewer. The agencies themselves are inclined to adopt a defensive posture when confronted with the possible abuses deriving from commission-based systems, and are apt to characterise malpractice in general as a phenomenon confined to a tiny minority of operators. According to Skeels, however, in a review of the activities of employment agencies in America, 'competition forces even the ethical private employment agent toward questionable activity'.[39]

It is obvious that there are points to be made on both sides and that, as Fulop has suggested, both agencies and employers could do more to raise the quality of the service.[40] Employers who make regular use of agencies could increase the degree of interaction and communication of information between themselves and the agencies, and be more willing to make specific complaints which would be susceptible of investigation. The agencies could set much higher standards for their interviewing personnel and be more attentive to the specific needs of employers. They should also be more prepared to take the initiative when employers are persistently vague when detailing their requirements. The regulations prevailing under the 1973 Employment Agencies Act are in fact intended to bring about these kinds of improvement in the standard of the service provided and to eliminate the sorts of abuses and malpractices which have come to light.

However, no matter what attempts are made by agencies, employers and the government to overcome existing problems, it is evident that the quality of the temporary services provided by agencies will always be contingent upon current levels of supply and demand in the labour markets within which the agencies operate. For example, in the spring of 1978 it was reported that there were nine times as many vacancies for temp secretaries as there were girls to fill them.[41] Under such circumstances, agencies are clearly in a difficult position when it comes to supplying firms with only the most highly qualified, experienced temporary personnel.

The service which the agencies provide to the applicants is probably no better and no worse than that extended to employers, although the person looking for a job is able to communicate her specific requirements more directly to the interviewer, and of course the service is free.[42] In the case of permanent placements, there is a very good reason why agencies probably do make serious attempts to find jobs which closely approximate applicants' specifications. If a permanent employee does not remain in her job for a certain length of time, the agencies are obliged to refund the placement fee to the employer. In the case of temporary placements, however, the financial penalties for a bad match between job and applicant are probably much less swingeing. Employers can, and do, withhold payment for unsatisfactory service, and in her survey of London employers, Silverstone encountered cases where firms had successfully sought compensation from agencies.[43] However, the vast majority of temporary placements last less than six weeks and it may be that many employers are willing to lower their expectations when they have an urgent need for staff for a short period. Consequently, temps are much more likely to be required to adapt to the jobs available.

There are other reasons why temps may not always find themselves in the type of jobs they wish, and indeed, why they may sometimes find themselves unemployed. The ease with which an agency is able to match a girl to a suitable job is of course very much a function of the existing demand for her skills. There are both seasonal and regional variations in the demand for temporary labour, and the industry as a whole is characterised by booms and slumps. Whereas the highly-qualified secretary in London can probably find suitable temp jobs in abundance throughout the year, even at a time of economic recession, the filing clerk looking for a temporary post in Newcastle during the winter is likely to be presented with Hobson's choice. During the course of my research, I interviewed five agency principals in the North-east of England. All of them agreed that it was virtually impossible to keep a temp employed all year round, unless she was very highly qualified. One of these told me that the majority of his recruits were married women seeking permanent jobs. There were single girls, but they too were anxious to gain a permanent job rather than to find year-round temporary positions. However, he felt that many of the girls would have preferred temporary jobs as an antidote to boredom, but that, given an adverse employment situation in the area, it would be impossible to find continuous work. Such temporary placements as he did make were a feature of the summer season, when students in particular were sent to replace staff on holiday at various firms. The residue of temporary staff were either married women who were content to take employment when and where it became available, or else those who were filling in between permanent jobs.

The threat of insecurity, then, is the chief occupational hazard of the 'permanent' temp. In recent years, the vulnerability of the temp to periodic unemployment has been exacerbated by the flagging fortunes of the British economy. In the mid-1970s, all the major agencies reported a marked drop in demand for temporary staff, and as a result, many firms began to diversify their activities into other fields of employment.[44] According to one estimate, the unfavourable market situation was reflected by a 40 per cent drop in the number of temporaries.[45] Although some agencies predicted that the maternity provisions of the Employment Protection Act would stimulate a new market for temps, the level of demand in 1977 was still well below that prevailing in the peak year of 1973.[46] However, in the spring of 1978, the FPS reported a regeneration of the market – a trend which was regarded as indicative of a more prosperous economic climate generally.

That there are variations in demand in different parts of the country, at different times of year, and for different skills, and that there are periodic recessions in the industry as a whole cannot be directly attributed to the agencies. However, it is not always clear from the agencies' promotional literature and advertising that the service which they provide to applicants is thus qualified. The job-hunter is informed in many advertisements that the agency can find her interesting work in abundance, not that the prevailing economic wind may make it necessary for her to wait for a few weeks until it can be located. Moreover, it is seldom intimated that the agency may be unable to provide continuity of employment:

BONUS FOR WORKING 37½ HOURS PLUS PAID WAITING TIME. TAX FREE FOR STUDENTS. PAID SAME WEEK YOU WORK. NO SELF EMPLOYED PROBLEMS. Most important, we pay high rates and we will keep you in work for as long as you want.[47]

WE REQUIRE . . . Top Temp Staff (all grades) NOW. WE OFFER constant work, individual attention, bonus . . . [48]

Today or Monday. S/T D/T C/T. Guaranteed jobs with full hours – Pay each week for hours worked . . . [49]

ARE YOU FREE! Exp legal temps & Sh/Audio 100/60 £2 ph. Guaranteed employment, W.1.[50]

It must be emphasised that the above examples are atypical of the advertisements which one normally encounters in the evening papers or interspersed between pictures of scantily clad men and women on the escalators of the London tube system. However, they do exemplify the occasional representation of temporary office work as a secure form of employment. Most agencies do not explicitly guarantee continuous work since it might be difficult for them to honour such claims, especially in the case of the more routine grades of office worker. Yet it would be difficult to avoid the conclusion, from a perusal of even the more carefully worded advertisements, that the agencies represent anything other than a direct means of access to an occupational horn of plenty. It could be argued, in defence of the agencies, that while their advertising displays a tendency towards hyperbole, it does not differ markedly from any other form of advertising in this respect, and that therefore few people are likely to accept the claims at face value. Certainly, it seems likely that an over-optimistic impression of the advantages and opportunities afforded by temporary employment would be modified by first-hand experience.

It may well be that among those people who take up temping because they do not require continuous employment, or because they are unable to find permanent employment, a potential lack of jobs which closely approximate to their interests and capacities may be experienced as less of a problem. The majority of temps are married women, and for many of them, working for an agency represents an alternative to not working at all. This does not mean that they are invariably content with the jobs they get, nor, indeed, that they are quite happy to stay at home when the agency cannot find work for them. However, they may tolerate these difficulties at certain times because at other times the agencies are able to meet their broad requirements, and more importantly perhaps, because temporary work, when it is available, offers all the flexibility that is lacking in the sphere of permanent work. This latter advantage, from the point of view of the would-be employee, is well illustrated by the experience of one of my respondents:

I would like to go as a permanent with the insurance company where I temp, but they do not employ part-time staff, and I can only work until 3.30 p.m., so I have to stay working for the agency. It seems a short-sighted policy for the firm to take as they must have wasted hundreds of pounds during the past three years paying the agency for my services, but they won't bend the rules on part-timers.

No matter what the quality of the service provided, there can be little doubt that the agencies provide a solution for the married woman whose desire to work is thwarted by intractable attitudes among employers. Now clearly, one's evaluation of the role of the agencies in this respect is bound to depend on how one comprehends this 'desire to work' among married women. If it is perceived as a purely economic motivation, as the expression of an acquisitive urge imposed upon them by the imperatives of capitalist commodity production, then one is likely to regard these firms as agents of a wider process of exploitation. If, on the other hand, one perceives the desire to work as a flight from domesticity, the agency is more likely to be regarded as providing an escape route for the prisoners of patriarchy, albeit an unintended consequence of what is primarily a commercial activity. It is evident, then, that a close attention to the reasons which women themselves give for their resort to temporary work is of considerable relevance to the continuing debate concerning the role of the private employment agency.

The main opponents of the agencies, of course, are the trade unions. Their attack on the agencies has been sustained and unequivocal, and at one time, public denouncements were *de rigueur* at the annual Trades Union Congress. The precise nature of their objections is exemplified in the following extract from a NALGO discussion document:

> Because temporaries do not receive sick pay and holiday pay their rates are higher than permanent staff and they are consequently a source of friction. The agencies charge a substantial commission on top of the normal rates of pay, and thus employers become involved in unnecessary costs. The use of agency staff who are temporary, and lack job security also undermines trade union organisation. Most important, however, temporary staff from agencies obscure the problem of low pay among permanent staff. Because employers can obtain temporaries to fill gaps caused by staff shortages, they are not obliged to pay sufficiently high wages to attract and retain permanent staff.[51]

Opinions of this nature have been widely expressed by a number of unions, and there have been some instances of industrial action in support of the demand to outlaw the agencies, or to reduce the number of temps hired within particular sectors of industry. The unions have presented a forceful case for abolition and their interpretation of the role of the agencies provides a useful corrective to the idea that they are merely benevolent organisations – something akin to a dose of salts being injected into an otherwise sluggish labour market. However, there is little evidence that they have contemplated the implications of abolition from the point of view of women themselves. The unions express a firm confidence in the ability of the government to provide an alternative to the private service. As presently conceived, however, the state scheme delivers the temp into the direct control of the employer. Yet as I shall show, many women enjoy the degree of autonomy afforded by the system operated by the private agencies. In the case of the agency temp, the employer is situated at a distance from the place of work and the client firm is vested with very limited powers of control. Thus, the substitution of a public service for that operated by the agencies would greatly diminish the autonomy of the temp. The strategies proposed by the unions, therefore, would represent a qualitative transformation in the character of temporary work from the point of view of the employee. In the case of the woman who turns to temporary work as a means of escape from an oppressive or unsatisfying domestic environment, it is possible that the abolition of the private service would not entail any reduction in the number of opportunities to do so. However, there is little evidence that the unions are concerned to ensure that the state service would replicate the flexibility encountered in the private service. Indeed, it could be argued that in postulating a state alternative to the private temporary schemes the unions are in effect accepting the idea that women should fit in with employers' expectations. Irrespective of whether married women work as temps out of choice or out of necessity, there can be little doubt that this entails a considerable degree of accommodation on their part. To the extent that the unions do not couple their demands with a call for measures which would diminish this burden of accommodation, the abolition of private employment agencies would represent something of a hollow victory.

In this chapter we have seen that temporary work is relatively unusual in the field of clerical employment. This is readily explained in terms of the principal disadvantage attaching to temporary employment, namely its insecurity. Under the most favourable market conditions there may be an occasional hiatus in the supply of jobs, and during periods of economic gloom, the experience of unemployment is likely to become more frequent and more protracted. Apart from this, it is doubtful whether temporary work carries any financial advantages in the long term. In 1968, the NBPI found that the higher rates of pay for agency temps were offset by the loss of many benefits such as paid holidays, sick leave, superannuation, bonuses and redundancy pay. Since then, many agencies, under pressure of competition, have introduced benefits for employees such as holiday pay and luncheon vouchers, but they are by no means universal and it may be necessary for a temp to work for several months with a single agency before she is entitled to them. Furthermore, the earnings of temps do not always keep pace with those of permanent staff. In 1968, for example, the NBPI report found that the earnings of permanent staff had increased more than those of temporary staff during the three-year period in which the survey was carried out. Again in the winter of 1974, it was reported that temporary remuneration was not keeping pace with the levels obtaining in the permanent sector.[52]

It is not difficult, therefore, to comprehend why few clerks forsake the relative security of permanent employment in order to become permanent temps. It is also not difficult to understand why many of those who do become permanent temps eventually quit. Apart from the disadvantages so far identified, there is the additional problem that temping may fail to live up to expectations. The agency, in its capacity as occupational gatekeeper, may be unable or unwilling to effect a perfect correspondence between the employee's skills or requirements, and the nature of the assignments to which she is sent. Thus, while a dissatisfaction with permanent clerical work may cause a girl to take up 'permanent' temping, a dissatisfaction with the kinds of jobs she then obtains may cause her to abandon it.

The fact that the majority of women in clerical employment are consequently to be found in permanent jobs cannot be taken to mean, therefore, that there is a universal contentment with the conditions and character of permanent office work. As with any other occupational 'choice', a decision to enter, to remain in or to return to permanent employment must be considered in relation to the rewards and penalties attaching to alternative courses of action.

The study of occupational choice also requires that one take account of the factors which sets limits to the practical possibilities of realising a desired course of action. This observation is particularly relevant for an understanding of the strong representation of married women in temporary office work. The fact that the majority of temps are married women cannot be taken to mean that such women regard work merely as a fringe activity because they are seemingly prepared to risk unemployment. As we have seen, it is equally possible to interpret their involvement in temporary office work as an index of the difficulties they encounter when trying to locate permanent positions. Thus, patterns of occupational choice and occupational mobility cannot be regarded as the expression of free-floating and unrestrained work aspirations. As this analysis of the role of the private employment agency has shown, it is essential that one examine the constraints upon action imposed by the vagaries of the market for labour, and by the expectations and practices of occupational gatekeepers.

5

Office Temps

The phenomenon of temporary work is where a great many historical and contemporary themes concerning women converge. It represents the net result of the discrimination, dissatisfaction and inflexibility which a great many women experience because they *are* women in a man's world – the world of white-collar masters and white-blouse subordinates. It is an escape route for the girls who have become trapped in the female ghetto of the office by their socialisation, education and training, by the limited range of occupations available to them, and by the unfulfilled promises of the recruiting advertisements. It is also a solution for the women who want to escape from suburban monotony but who cannot find an employer who is willing to meet their needs half way.

The phenomenon of temporary work highlights the fact that women must make all the adjustments if they wish to work in the office – adjustments to its hours, its overtime, its opportunity structure, its mechanisation, its boredom and its traditional structure of relationships. Temping is an alternative to self-effacement.

To a considerable extent, therefore, temping may be regarded as symptomatic of the presence of patriarchy, both within the labour market and beyond. However, many writers consider that it is erroneous to perceive the occupational circumstances of women purely in terms of processes of male domination.[1] This note of caution is particularly apposite in the case of female temporary office workers. Neither the supply of nor the demand for such employees can be accounted for simply in terms of attempts by men to maintain a position of relative advantage, in the labour market, or in terms of discriminatory attitudes among employers. The resort to temporary work is at least partly explained in terms of the objective conditions of clerical work itself. Once this is recognised, it becomes necessary to look for the wider economic processes which structure the contemporary nature of white-collar employment. Similarly, the demand for temporary clerical labour has very little to do with 'male chauvinism', whereas it has a great deal to do with labour shortage in the permanent sector, and to a lesser extent with the efforts of employers to effect economies in their full-time permanent staff requirements.

It may be readily conceded, therefore, that it is necessary to take account of the contributions of both patriarchy and the wider economic system if one is to comprehend the phenomenon of temporary clerical labour. However, this observation brings us no nearer to an appreciation of the factors which women themselves consider to have impelled them towards temporary employment. Indeed, it is only too easy to lose sight altogether of women's own perceptions of their work situation and to suppose that an acceptance of the popular stereotypes of the female temp represents a satisfactory substitute for a more direct investigation of their attitudes. In this chapter, then, I am concerned to examine temporary clerical work from the employee's point of view. By studying directly the experiences and attitudes of those who work in this capacity, it is possible to dismantle the mythological versions of the woman at work. It is these myths – that women are invariably passive, that their aspirations are consistently attenuated, that the home or the opposite sex is their central life interest and that they always adjust to limited opportunities at work – which represent the ideological justifications for the exploitative systems of both capitalism and patriarchy.

In the popular imagination, the temp is often perceived in terms of all the favourite stereotypes of contemporary womanhood. Although fewer marriages are made in offices than are made in heaven, there is a belief that temps are primarily motivated by the desire for a husband. The mass media have done much to promote an image of the temp as a man-hunting good-time girl, short on skill and high on unreliability. A recent example of the tendency to present a somewhat tarnished image of the temp was provided in a centre-page article in the *Observer*. In this article, entitled

'Everybody Loves Temps', Bernard Hollowood introduces us to 'Dorcas', who is presumably supposed to be representative of the temp workforce in general:

> Her qualifications are not too impressive. Her shorthand is rudimentary and her typing slow. But she is an attractive brunette and she would like to marry within two years, before she is 23. 'If you must know,' she said, when I questioned her, 'I'm ready to fall in love and for preference I'd like to fall for an affluent bloke. And being a temp gives me a chance of meeting more boss types. So far I've met nobody who really matters. Oh, there's always someone who wants to take me out to dinner and afters, but nobody sufficiently interesting. Young Mr Pollock was my last date and he was hopeless – wanted payment in kindness at the first opportunity – so I shall move on next week.'[2]

The promotional material of the agencies too, must surely have bolstered the notion that temps are just so many rolling stones, primarily motivated by the pleasure principle. Another favourite image of the temp is that of the clerical mercenary, which corresponds to the stereotype of the acquisitive female so beloved of investigators of women at work in the 1950s and 1960s. This image is popular with the unions, who have continuously characterised temps as self-interested enemies of the working class, single-mindedly bent upon the maximisation of their own wage-packets. This view of the temp remains firmly entrenched, in spite of the weight of evidence which suggests that temporary employment is less financially rewarding in the long term.

The next objective, then, is to investigate the background, experiences and attitudes to work of female temporary office employees in order to derive a more informed understanding than is provided by the popular stereotypes. The following account is based upon the responses to a postal questionnaire which I sent to a group of female office temps via the employment agencies for whom they worked. The questionnaire was distributed in 1971–72 in three areas of the country – London, Birmingham and the North-east. I received 139 replies and the regional composition of the group was as follows: London 32 per cent, North-east 36 per cent, Birmingham 32 per cent. The account presented in this chapter also incorporates the findings of a three-month period of participant observation as a temporary filing clerk which I undertook at a company in the Midlands.

Characteristics of office temps

The female office temp is typically much younger than the average woman in employment. The relative youth of women in temporary clerical work is evident from the comparison of my results with figures compiled by the Department of Employment shown in Table 5.1.

The relative youth of women office temps, a finding confirmed by surveys conducted by the FPS and by the Alfred Marks organisation, is perhaps less remarkable when one considers that the proportion of women working in routine white-collar jobs in general decreases with age.[3] In a recent survey of female office workers, just under half the sample were aged between twenty-one and thirty, and only 7 per cent were aged forty-one or over.[4] To some extent, therefore, the reasons for the preponderance of young women in temporary office work are similar to those which account for the relative youth of women in clerical work generally. These include, for example, the increasing popularity of office work as an occupational choice among girl school-leavers. How-

TABLE 5.1. *Age structure of female office temps compared with the age structure of the total female workforce*

Age group	Temps %	Total female workforce, 1971 %
15–19	11.5	12.8
20–29	55.4	22.7
30–39	18.7	16.1
40–49	11.5	21.7
50–59	2.2	19.4
60+	–	7.2
No answer	0.7	–

($N = 139$)

SOURCE For total female workforce, *Women and Work: A Statistical Survey*, Department of Employment Manpower Paper no. 9 (London: HMSO, 1974) table 9, p. 47. Reprinted by permission of the Controller of Her Majesty's Stationery Office.

ever, it is possible that the tone of the agencies advertising copy plays some part in attracting younger girls into temporary employment:

Baby, are you hot enough for Manpower?

'My granny ran off with my granny shoes,
my mum wants to borrow my midi,
my brother keeps pinching my maxi raincoat,
and my big sister wants to get a job from Brook Street Bureau.'
'Fashion mad your lot.'

TEMPS. Young, attractive and enthusiastic. Available min. 6 weeks. For immediate interview, phone now.[5]

SECRETARY £1.70! No s/h required! 45 wpm! Long booking! West London! Young company![6]

Many of the larger agencies often supplement the youthful orientation of their recruitment literature with photographs of smart, bright-eyed young women in their twenties. Magazine advertisements of this nature are more typically found in such products as *Honey* and *19* which have a young readership than in those magazines such as *Woman* and *Woman's Own* which are read by somewhat older women.

The age profile of office temps varied between the three regions covered by my study. Although the majority of temps in all three areas were aged under thirty, there was a much greater proportion of women aged thirty to thirty-nine in the North-east than elsewhere. In London and Birmingham, the proportion of temps in this age group was 13 per cent and 14 per cent respectively, whereas in the North-east the proportion was 28 per cent. The FPS survey of office temps similarly found that women in this age range were more preponderant in this area than in both London and the Midlands.[7]

Just over half the sample were married (53 per cent), and this degree of representation is slightly more than is found among women in clerical work generally (47 per cent of whom are married), but rather less than the figure of 60 per cent generated by an FPS survey of office temporaries.[8] As might be expected from the regional variations in age distribution, married women formed a much greater proportion of office temps in the North-east – 68 per cent, as compared with 44 per cent of temps in London and 46 per cent of those in Birmingham. Thirty per cent of respondents were responsible for children of school age or under, and once again, such women were more common in the North-East – 40 per cent, as compared with 27 per cent in London and 21 per cent in Birmingham. Of those women responsible for children, 39 per cent had one child, 49 per cent had two children, 10 per cent had three and 2 per cent had four or more. The proportion of women responsible for children of school age or under is about the same as the proportion in the female routine white-collar workforce as a whole. As compared with women in *full-time* office jobs, however, temps are much more likely to be responsible for children under sixteen. Hunt found that only 1.7 per cent of full-time women in this occupational category had children under five and 9.8 per cent had children aged five to fifteen.[9] The corresponding figures for temps were 8.6 per cent and 23.7 per cent respectively. Whilst the degree of responsibility for young children among temps is not as great as that found among women in part-time office jobs, this finding does highlight the importance of temporary work as a method of obtaining employment among those who would otherwise find it very difficult to do so.

Female temps originate from a wide diversity of social backgrounds, although a relatively high proportion are drawn from the middle classes (see Table 5.2[10]). Similarly, a high proportion of married temps were the spouses of men in middle-class occupations. Thirty per cent were married to men in manual occupations; 5 per cent to men in intermediate occupations; 58 per cent to men in white-collar occupations; and 7 per cent gave no answer or insufficient information. The single largest group were married to men in intermediate white-collar occupations (38 per cent).

Although the daughters of the middle classes and the wives of middle-class husbands are greatly over-represented among my respondents as compared with the pattern found among the general female working population, it has proved impossible to ascertain whether they are more numerous among temps than among the permanent female office population. Silverstone's study of office staff did reveal a very strong over-representation of women from middle-class backgrounds, but her results related only to women in secretarial jobs.

TABLE 5.2 *The social class background of office temps*

Father's occupation	Temps %
White-collar	
Higher professional, managerial and other white-collar employees; large industrial or commercial employers, landed proprietors	6
Intermediate professional, managerial and other white-collar employees; medium industrial or commercial employers, substantial farmers	20
Lower professional, managerial and other white-collar employees; small industrial or commercial employers, small proprietors, small farmers	20
Intermediate	
Supervisory, inspectional, minor officials and service employees; minor self-employed	11
Manual	
Skilled manual	29
Semi-skilled manual	8
Unskilled manual	3
No answer or insufficient information	4

(*N* = 139)

Having considered some of the broad social characteristics of office temps, I shall now turn to an examination of their educational background and degree of training. On the basis of a study of temporary workers employed by a New York private employment agency, Gannon and Brainin have proposed that the type of individual who is attracted into this industry is one with few marketable skills. They suggest that 'the temporary help industry may be providing a haven for those less attractive workers who would find difficulty in successfully negotiating the rigorous hiring procedure of established firms seeking a permanent workforce'.[11] The results of my own survey do not provide support for this perception of temporary workers, at least in the field of clerical employment. In terms of both education and training, temporary office workers compare very favourably with other women in white-collar work.

Bearing in mind the fact that at the time of my study the school leaving age had not yet been raised to sixteen, it is instructive to consider the findings relating to patterns of school leaving among temps. Just over two-thirds had left at the age of sixteen or above and as many as 8 per cent had left at the age of eighteen. This pattern is consistent with Hunt's finding that women in non-manual occupations form a much greater proportion of those who left school at sixteen or over.[12] In terms of this dimension of educational experience, then, temps resemble other women in white-collar employment. Terminal education age was significantly cor-related both with social class background and type of school attended.[13]

The school examination record of office temps compares well with that of the female clerical population in general. Hunt found that amongst women employed in skilled non-manual work (a category she uses which includes most forms of routine clerical work) 20 per cent had obtained GCE 'O' level or its equivalent, 1.4 per cent had obtained GCE 'A' or 'S' level or equivalent, and 14 per cent had passed other exams, including CSE.[14]

It is interesting to note from Table 5.3 that one-fifth of the group had already received some preparation for a future in clerical work whilst still at school. The likelihood of this destiny for many of my respondents was increased by the educational choices they made after leaving school. Over half (53 per cent) had not pursued any full-time course of education or training since leaving school, but of those who had, no less than 87 per cent had undertaken a training in clerical work. Over one-third of my respondents (37 per cent) had passed a secretarial course. Very few had undertaken a course in higher education. Only two women (1 per cent) had successfully completed an academic course at degree level or its equivalent.

There was a strong relationship between employment status and the extent of vocational training after school. Whereas the majority of secretaries and shorthand-typists had taken a course relevant to their occupations, the majority of those in other categories had not. Thus while the secretaries and shorthand-typists in my survey were relatively well qualified, a majority of the rest had entered clerical employment without any

TABLE 5.3   *Examinations passed at school*

Examinations passed	Temps %
GCE 'O' level or equivalent	
None passed	52
1 – 3	14
4 – 6	21
7+	13
GCE 'A' level or equivalent	
None passed	89
1 – 2	7
3 – 4+	4
CSE	
None passed	89
1 – 3	4
4 – 6	6
7+	1
Other school exams	
None passed	71
Commercial	19
Academic	10

(N = 139)

form of relevant training. This observation would initially seem to support the view that temps are justly characterised as the flotsam and jetsam of the labour force. However, the findings of a recent Alfred Marks survey enable one to dispense with this idea. In an investigation of women employed in office jobs having some degree of mechanisation, it was found that only 58 per cent had received any formal training for the machines on which they were currently employed. Of those who had received some training, 60 per cent had acquired this whilst actually at work, and less than one-third had received training at school or college.[15] It seems then that temps are not unusual in having a lack of relevant training prior to entry into the labour market. With the exception of secretaries and shorthand-typists, temps, like many other women in routine white-collar employment, tend to have acquired their skills once they are actually working. A minority learn outside the workplace by attending evening classes, but the great majority achieve competence on the job.

It is inappropriate therefore to regard temps as some kind of pariah group within the white-collar labour force.[16] Neither their educational background nor their vocational training suggests that they are unusually deficient in marketable skills and capacities. In terms of formal academic qualifications they compare extremely favourably with women in clerical work generally. A lack of formal training for clerical work prior to entry into the labour market is commonplace among female office workers. Indeed, if it is the case that without the option of temporary work many of my respondents would have been unemployed, the reason for this lies not so much in the nature of their education and training as in their responses and those of others to their domestic circumstances.

The occupational composition of my respondents is shown in Table 5.4. In this context it is relevant to point out that both the FPS survey and an Alfred Marks survey conducted in 1973 also found that secretaries and typists of various kinds tend to predominate among the temporary clerical population.[17] Since I found no significant relationship between employment status and the reasons for taking up temporary work, it may be suggested that

TABLE 5.4. *The occupational distribution of temps**

Job category	Temps %
Secretary	23
Shorthand-typist	19
Copy/audio typist	23
Clerk-typist	6
Book-keeper/skilled clerk	7
Junior clerk/filing clerk	11
Machine operator	4
Telephonist	4
Receptionist	4

(N = 139)
*Classified according to the type of job in which registered with the agency

this distribution is a function of the higher demand for temps with these particular job skills.

A majority of my respondents had been employed in a permanent capacity at some time during the five years prior to the survey. Of the 20 per cent who had not, most were married and two-thirds were responsible for children of school age or under. Sixty-eight per cent of my respondents were asked to supply more detailed information of their working lives during the five years up to and including the time of the survey. The information supplied by this smaller group suggests a fairly low level of job stability. The average length of time spent in one job varied from less than one month to over three years, but as many as 50 per cent reported an average length of service of less than one year.

Temps are not characteristically mobile between agencies. Nearly two-thirds of all respondents had worked for only one agency. Twenty-five per cent had worked for two agencies, 9 per cent for three and 4 per cent for four or more. Mobility was much more likely to have taken the form of movement between temporary and permanent jobs. The widespread pattern of attachment to a single agency probably results from the fact that certain advantages follow from the development of a good relationship with a particular firm. A temp having a history of company loyalty is not only more likely than others to be given jobs when these are scarce, but she is also in a better position to negotiate for jobs having the conditions she requires.

At the time of my survey, almost half my respondents had been working for their present agency for less than six months. As one would expect amongst a group of temporary workers, length of service in the present job is typically much shorter than that found among the female workforce generally. Hunt found that 50 per cent of working women had been in their present job for more than three years.[18] However, as with the female labour force in general, length of service amongst temps is related to age as Table 5.5 shows.

These findings, in conjunction with those produced by other surveys of temporary office workers, suggest that very few women become established as 'permanent' temps. A survey conducted by the Alfred Marks Bureau in 1970 found that the average period of total annual employment for a temp was six weeks.[19] The FPS informed me that this was still the case in 1978. In the USA

TABLE 5.5 *The length of time spent working for the present agency amo*
different age groups

Length of service	All temps N = 138* %	15–19 16 %	20–29 77 %	30–39 26 %	40–49 16 %	50–5 3 %
Less than 6 months	49	88	52	42	19	–
6 months up to 1 year	18	6	19	27	13	–
1 year up to 2 years	13	–	14	19	6	33
2 years up to 5 years	14	6	9	12	44	67
5 years and over	2	–	–	–	13	–
No answer	4	–	5	–	6	–

*One respondent did not give her age

Gannon and Brainin found that the median number of days worked by a temporary clerical employee before termination was only nineteen days, although the range was from 1 to 192 days.[20] It is possible that these figures underestimate the average duration of employment as a temp. Both surveys relate only to the length of service with a single agency, and thus their findings obscure the possibility that a more lengthy involvement in temp work is achieved by movement from agency to agency. At least two American studies of temporary employment have claimed that many temporaries register with more than one agency.[21] However, neither study furnishes precise information concerning the extent of this practice, nor do they state whether multiple registration actually leads to a more protracted involvement in temporary work. My own findings indicate that this practice of occupational polygamy is atypical, and the weight of evidence suggests that temping is usually a short-term mode of employment.

Yet there are grounds for supposing that a substantial minority of temps begin this type of work with the intention of remaining in it. The Alfred Marks survey mentioned above found that in the winter of 1970, whilst 32 per cent of temps intended to work for only a few weeks, 27 per cent said that they would be working for several months and as many as 41 per cent intended to work as temps on a regular basis with breaks.[22] Those intending to work on a very short-term basis were somewhat more preponderant in the summer months of 1970, but those defining themselves as long-term temps still represented 38 per cent of the total. Given the discrepancy between intention and practice, one must conclude that the circumstances of temporary work are such as to sway a considerable number of women from their original intentions.

Reasons for doing temporary work

'Look, Kathy, everyone of us is looking for a way to beat the nine to five routine, the TGIF and Blue Monday drill. Right?' I nodded. 'OK. Lots of girls become stewardesses because of that. And models, and lots of other things. Well, working as a temp secretary gives you the same freedom. If Monday morning bugs you, don't work on Monday mornings. Maybe that's what it's all about. *No more Mondays!*'[23]

The role of temporary work as a solution to certain difficulties and problems encountered by women both inside and beyond the workplace is very much apparent when one analyses the reasons why females become temporary clerical employees. Table 5.6 sets out the responses to an open-ended question concerning the decision to enter temporary employment. Those who responded often gave several reasons for becoming temps. Consequently, Table 5.6 shows the proportions responding under different categories of motivation.

Although there is a great diversity of reasons for doing temporary work, they may be grouped into three broad categories. First, it has been chosen in preference to permanent work because it is expected to provide greater rewards in terms of such criteria as job satisfaction, pay and the opportunity to meet people. Secondly, it is a strategy adopted by those who do not require or who cannot accept employment on a continuous or full-time basis. Thirdly, it has been chosen as an interim measure by those looking for a permanent job or who are passing the time before taking up a permanent job that they have already been offered. Of the three major categories of motivation, it is the second which is most frequently cited. The same finding has emerged from other surveys of temporary office workers.[24]

First, then, there are certain aspects of temporary employment which in themselves represent major reasons for entering this type of work. There are some respondents for whom a real choice exists

TABLE 5.6   *Reasons for becoming a temporary office worker (responses given by all temps and also according to variations in domestic circumstances)*

Reasons for becoming a temp	All temps N = 139 %	Single temps 65 %	Married temps 74 %	Temps without dependent children 98 %	Temps with dependent children 41 %
Prefer the varied routine of temping	27	34	20	31	17
Do not require or cannot accept permanent work due to personal or domestic commitments	18	2	32	5	49
Doing temporary work while looking for permanent job	17	23	11	21	5
Temping provides opportunity to work when you want	17	12	20	21	5
About to move or go abroad	9	20	0	13	0
Pay reasons	9	11	8	10	7
To meet people	7	11	4	10	0
To gain experience	7	11	4	8	5
Difficulty obtaining permanent work because of need for special hours	6	0	11	0	20
Difficulty obtaining ideal permanent job	5	6	4	6	2
Filling in between employment in other fields	3	6	0	4	0
On working holiday from abroad or elsewhere in the U.K.	2	5	0	3	0
No answer	1	2	1	1	2

between temporary and permanent employment, but they have chosen the former because they consider it more desirable. In fact the single most common reason for doing temping among my respondents was the desire for a more varied routine of work. The following comments exemplify the way in which temping is perceived as a preferred alternative to permanent office work:

> Working in a permanent job can often cause a girl to get in a rut, unless the job is absolutely super with opportunities to be promoted.

> I get restless in one place too long because the work gets very monotonous.

> I get claustrophobia in permanent jobs.

> It is more varied and interesting. You meet new people, you don't get stuck in a rut and it's therefore less inclined to become boring.

Thus, for many women, temping is expected to be a panacea for all the ills found in permanent employment. No matter how misplaced their expectations may turn out to be, they sign on with the agencies in the hope of finding the interest and variety which eludes them in secure but predictable permanent jobs. Although single women and women without dependent children were much more likely to cite this factor, it was also an important secondary motivation amongst those with more pressing domestic and personal circumstances.

It is interesting to note the relative insignificance of a desire for better pay as a reason for doing temporary work. As compared with the desire for greater variety in work, the pecuniary motive plays little part in propelling women towards this mode of employment. Women do not on the whole perceive temping as a means towards the enhancement of wages. The theme of excellent pay prospects is very common in the agencies' advertising, but potential temps often recognise that the benefits of good hourly rates are likely to be offset by the lack of fringe benefits, holiday pay and so forth. Consequently, those intending to work as temps on a regular basis are unlikely to be motivated by purely financial considerations. However, in spite of the financial disadvantages, temping can sometimes offer better levels of remuneration for younger women. Since the rates offered by agencies are frequently paid according to skill rather than to age, there are obvious attractions in temping for those who would otherwise be paid according to their junior status:

> I'm only nineteen, but I'm separated from my husband and I've got a child of two. I left school without any qualifications in order to be a wife and mother but now I'm going out to work because he left me suddenly without any offer of financial assistance. I've had three permanent jobs since he went but not only were they boring but they paid peanuts. I became a temp mainly because this sort of job is paid by the hour, not by age. At 19 a clerical job without typing involved pays only £10 gross. After deductions, rent, nursery fee, electricity bills, this would leave only £1 a week for food and clothes.

It is also interesting to find that a desire to meet people does not figure prominently as a motivation for entering temporary employment. This reason is somewhat more common amongst single women and those having no dependent children, but the findings here do not suggest that temps are unduly concerned to extend their range of acquaintances.

Secondly, temporary work has been chosen by many women because they require flexible conditions of employment. Eighteen per cent of my respondents specifically stated that this was because of the pressure of certain domestic or other personal commitments:

> I have two children and do not like to leave them to fend for themselves during holidays, after school hours or through illness. Being a temp I can choose my own hours.

> The hours I work are more convenient for the children and my husband. I do not work during school holidays.

> Because I have children – they can be ill at any time, one needs time off for dental appointments, etc., and I only want to work during school hours.

> It enables me to take time off during school holiday periods when I have no one to look after the children.

Whereas the importance of the desire for variety in work highlights the significance of previous work experience as a factor governing occupational choice, these comments illustrate the influence of domestic commitments on decisions about jobs. In fact half of all the respondents with dependent children gave this as a reason for becoming a temp.

Seventeen per cent of my respondents said that they had become temps because of the opportunities it afforded to work when they wanted. A few of the single temps qualified this point by saying that they were thereby enabled to have longer holidays and/or holidays whenever they felt like it. The majority of those mentioning this reason, however, did not give any very clear indication as to why they sought either short hours or only intermittent spells of employment. Since many of them were married women, although not typically responsible for dependent children, it may be surmised that domestic circumstances were often of central relevance.

Despite the fact that many temps appear to have chosen this type of work because they consider it to be in harmony with the pressure of circumstances beyond the workplace, it is important to consider whether or not their decision is really just a matter of personal preference. To put it another way, is it possible to make sense of their responses *simply* in terms of their domestic circumstances? It could be argued that this 'choice' results not simply from personal convictions about the relationship between marriage, motherhood and work, but also from the unwillingness of many employers to provide flexible conditions in the sphere of permanent work. My respondents made repeated reference to the importance of flexible working hours as a reason for their resort to temporary employment. They wanted to be able to take time off for school holidays, when their children were ill or had to visit the dentist, and they wanted to work school hours. They took it for granted that their needs in these and other respects were incompatible with the normal requirements of the office. In saying that they had chosen to work in a temporary capacity because of their domestic circumstances, they implicitly acknowledged the fact of inflexibility in the organisation of contemporary office work.

Thus, it may be said that many women prefer to do temporary office work because many employers prefer not to accommodate them on any other basis. On the whole, however, my respondents tended not to characterise their decision in these terms. Temping was seen as something which suited them – as a convenient way of reconciling the dual demands of home and workplace. To the extent that they felt in any way constrained into this type of work, the constraints were seen to derive from their domestic circumstances. Such a perception of the situation is of course perfectly consistent with the cultural maxim that the nature of a woman's work participation should be contingent upon the requirements of her family. These observations might seem to add fuel to the argument that women are essentially acquiescent creatures when it comes to the structure of work opportunities. It should not be forgotten, however, that many women felt that in becoming temps they had taken positive action to extricate themselves from an unsatisfying domestic environment: 'As the children were all at school I became bored at home and felt I could relieve this by doing something useful – temp work is convenient for school holidays and for getting home in time for school to be out.' The mere fact of going out to work was for many women a form of escape, even though circumstances prevailing both within and beyond the workplace restricted their range of occupational choice. The same observation is made by Olesen and Katsuranis in their survey of office temps in California: 'Temporary work relieved them of the drudgery, dehumanisation and alienating features of housework.'[25]

Generally speaking, when temporary work had been chosen because continuous, full-time employment was not required, this was mainly because of the implications of certain domestic commitments. A small number of respondents, however, did not want permanent jobs because they were about to move or go abroad (9 per cent) or because they were on a working holiday from overseas or elsewhere in the UK (2 per cent). All of the women mentioning these reasons were single.

Finally, temporary work can be regarded as a purely transitional mode of employment for women who are seeking, or who are shortly to take up a permanent position. Seventeen per cent of my respondents said that they were doing temporary work whilst looking for a permanent post:

It's the easiest way of looking for permanent employment while still being employed.

Temporary work for me was just a fill-in between jobs.

I'm doing it until I can find suitable permanent employment.

While some women made it clear that they were merely filling in time, others stated that they hoped that temporary work would provide direct access to a desirable permanent position. A small number of temps expressly stated that they had experienced difficulty in finding the kind of office job they wanted and had therefore taken up temping (5 per cent). Three per cent were filling in between permanent posts in other fields, such as acting or nursing.

Yet another group claimed that they had been unable to find permanent jobs because of their need for special hours. This group consisted entirely of women who were married and who had responsibility for dependent children. For these women, temping was not something to be preferred, but a mode of employment imposed upon them by inflexible attitudes in the workplace. Unlike those who tended to characterise their reasons for temping as determined purely by domestic constraints, these women were acutely aware that the assumptions of employers and personnel officers imposed severe limitations to their freedom of manoeuvre. They had been obliged to accept, if somewhat reluctantly, the fact that temping might be the only alternative to unemployment. It may be suggested that while some women with domestic commitments maintain that they have voluntarily chosen temporary work and others with similar domestic circumstances claim that they have been forced into it, their different reasons represent varying subjective interpretations of the same objective situation. Some women feel that the demands of the home dictate what is possible, while others consider that expectations in the world of work set limits to their freedom. At the very root of all their motivations, however, is the inescapable fact that employers are insufficiently willing to introduce flexibility into their terms of employment.

Seven per cent of my respondents were temping in order to gain experience before looking for a permanent job. One married respondent stated:

I'm doing temporary work to get a return to office work and up-date experience as at interviews prospective employers think one is deficient in some way because I've been away from the relevant type of work for some time.

The reasons that women gave for becoming temps clearly varied according to their domestic circumstances. Age was another source of variation in the reasons mentioned. The desire for certain specific rewards from temporary work was more common among younger women. Both financial considerations and the desire to meet people were mentioned more frequently by those under thirty. The most important reason for temping among women of this age was the desire for a more varied work routine.

Among women of all ages, temporary work was often chosen because it enabled them to work when it suited them. In the case of older women, however, this flexibility was usually sought because of the pressure of domestic commitments, whereas younger women, especially those aged 15–19, were planning to take long holidays abroad and/or more days off work than would be possible in a permanent job.

The resort to temporary work as a purely interim measure between permanent jobs was also more common among younger women. Women aged 20–29 were rather more likely to be just filling in the time between office jobs or hoping for direct access to a permanent job, whilst those aged 15–19 were more likely to be attempting to gain experience or filling in time between employment in a different field altogether.

Thus far, it can be seen that the age and domestic circumstances of my respondents were related to the reasons given for doing temporary work. However, since location was yet another source of variation it cannot be supposed that differences in the reasons mentioned are adequately accounted for simply in terms of the female life cycle. Women in the North-east were more likely than those elsewhere to be temping because domestic commitments prevented them from accepting permanent work or deterred them from seeking it. Conversely, they were much less likely to be temping because of a desire for a more varied routine of work. Only 14 per cent mentioned this factor, whereas 24 per cent of those in London and as many as 43 per cent of those in Birmingham cited this aspect. The relatively greater importance of temping as a solution to the home/work dilemma among women in the North-east does, of course, reflect the fact that women in this area were dissimilar from women elsewhere in terms of age, marital status and degree of responsibility for children. However, this observation begs the question of why women who were older, married and responsible for children were disproportionately represented in this region. It may be suggested that the nature of local employment opportunities provides the answer. Job scarcity in the North-east renders the opportunity to work all year round as a temp in preference to permanent employment extremely limited. The proportion of young, single temps in this region is correspondingly diminished. Job scarcity also means that there is little or no pressure on employers to provide flexible working conditions for women with young children. Keen competition for the available pool of jobs may render it very difficult for women with domestic commitments to find work. The option of temporary work thus assumes a particular importance for such women in the North-east. In sum, local employment conditions mean that temping is much more a matter of simple expediency than elsewhere. The proposition that the state of the local labour market has a strong bearing on occupational choice is further supported by my finding that women in this region were more likely than elsewhere to be doing temporary work as a purely interim measure. Twenty-four per cent were temping whilst looking for a permanent office job, as compared with 16 per cent of those in Birmingham and 9 per cent of those in London. They were also more likely to have experienced difficulty in obtaining the type of office job they most desired. Thus, an awareness of regional variations in employment opportunities would seem to be of central relevance for an understanding of the reasons why women enter different types of jobs, and indeed, for an understanding of why they work or do not work at all. As a 1974 government survey has stated:

> Part of the variation [in activity rates] between regions is the result of differences in the structure of the regional populations by age, marital status and employment status, but a detailed study by J. K. Bowers concluded that variations in female activity rates by region were more closely connected with differences in industrial structure and employment opportunities.[26]

Educational background was yet another source of variation in the reasons for doing temporary work. Although the reasons mentioned were not associated with school leaving age, they did vary according to levels of educational achievement. For example, of those who had not passed any 'O' levels or equivalent examinations, only 18 per cent mentioned the desire for a more varied work routine. Conversely, this reason was cited by 36 per cent of those who had passed one or more 'O' levels. Amongst this latter group, this was by far the most important motivation. Amongst those lacking this level of educational attainment, the main reason for temping was the desire for flexible conditions of employment, either due to domestic circumstances or because of some other unspecified reason. However, this finding should not be taken to mean that educational achievement is the ultimate determinant of women's attitudes towards work. The desire for greater work satisfaction was by no means exclusive to those with 'O' levels.

   This account of the reasons why women enter temporary clerical employment underlines the importance of an eclectic approach to the analysis of occupational choice. In particular, it testifies to the inadequacy of any attempt to account for variations in job choice purely in terms of the life cycle. Whilst age and domestic circumstances are evidently related to the reasons for temping, it is clear that previous work experience plays an important role. A disenchantment with permanent office work has led many women into temporary work, in the hope that greater interest may be found in a succession of different jobs. It is also clear that local employment conditions have some bearing on occupational choice. Where these are unfavourable, women are forced into a position of compromise such that preferences about the nature of work may have to be suspended or suppressed. The decision to do temporary work is also a function of intransigency on the part of employers. No matter how women choose to represent the circumstances leading to their entry into this type of work, it is essential to recognise that the widespread unwillingness of firms to provide flexible conditions of employment renders temping Hobson's choice for many married women.

The experience of temporary work

A general survey

Attitudes towards work are inextricably bound up with the experience of work. They are not fixed, like some quantum of energy, but capable of modification by the circumstances of a single job or by the accumulated experience of a succession of jobs. The priorities which a woman possesses when looking for a job may be reinforced when she actually obtains a position, but they may also be amended, suppressed or forgotten. My next concern, therefore, is to give an account of the views which women express about their experiences as temporary workers.

From Table 5.7, it can be seen that the majority of temps are prepared to nominate at least one aspect of temping which appealed to them. It is evident that among temps as a whole, the most appealing aspect of this type of employment is felt to be the opportunity which it affords for varied work. Variety is encountered in two principal ways, and a high premium is placed on both. First, it derives from the continuous change of workplace. The temp inevitably finds herself working in a great diversity of organisations. The firms to which she is sent are differentiated in terms of size, ownership and function and this means that there is infinite variety in the context, if not the substance of her work:

I do get much more variety of jobs, from architects' offices to record companies.

I like the opportunity to work in different types of office.

. . . the opportunity of seeing the different kinds of work firms do.

Secondly, variety derives from the fact that the temp may be required to perform a succession of different kinds of work tasks. The degree to which this is the case is to some extent a function of agency policy and the flexibility of the temp herself, but in the normal course of events the nature of the work at hand is subject to some variation. The differences between one job and another are often very subtle but real enough to allay the feeling of boredom which may arise when one performs the same routine in the same workplace for an extended period:

I like the fact that I keep changing jobs and so don't get bored with the usual routine.

It's varied work. You don't get a chance of being bored with one subject.

TABLE 5.7 *What do you like most about being a temp? (Responses for all temps and for temps with varying domestic circumstances)*

Aspect of temporary work mentioned	All temps N = 139 %	Single temps 65 %	Married temps 74 %	Temps without dependent children 98 %	Temps with dependent children 41 %
Variety of work	42	51	34	48	27
Flexible hours/opportunity to work when desired	28	22	34	21	44
Sense of freedom/being own boss/no ties	24	32	15	28	15
Meeting people	13	14	12	16	5
Pay	6	2	9	5	7
You are appreciated more	2	2	3	2	2
Opportunity to earn money while looking for a permanent job	1	2	1	2	–
It gives you confidence	1	2	1	1	2
Jobs are found for you	1	–	3	2	–
Nothing	4	3	3	3	5
No answer	5	8	3	6	2

> You meet different people and do different types of work and you don't get a chance to become bored.

> I like the challenge of learning a new job each time.

Variety, both of job content and of workplace is inherent in temping, and if circumstances are favourable, it is possible to accelerate the rate of change simply by requesting a transfer. Herein lies one of its main sources of satisfaction, and one of its principal advantages over permanent work.

The second most attractive feature of temporary work was the flexibility of working conditions. A particularly appealing aspect of temping was felt to be the opportunity which it afforded to determine for oneself the number of hours, weeks or months worked. The importance attached to this characteristic of temporary employment clearly varied according to domestic circumstances, but it is interesting to note that it was given high priority by those who were single and those who had no dependent children. The appeal of flexible working conditions to those whose domestic situation does not render them absolutely necessary is not surprising when one takes stock of the implications of regular nine-to-five employment. A sudden impulse to take a day off cannot be freely indulged, the claims of family, friends and lovers must be subordinated to the obligation to adhere to office hours, and annual holidays begin to assume the status of a trip to Mecca. For the single girl with a gypsy in her soul, temp work can be a godsend, as one ex-temp whom I interviewed more recently explained:

> I liked the casualness of temp work. I used to love travelling and if I'd got the travelling bug, the next day I'd phone the agency and say, 'I'm off now. I'll see you again soon.' And I'd just go. And I've often done that – just make up my mind in one day, put a back-pack on, and go.'

This girl also pointed out that taking time off according to one's inclinations does not entail the same negative consequences for the temp as are likely to be encountered by the permanent worker:

> I know people who've been at companies for seven years as a temp. They prefer to be temps because they can take time off

when they like. You see, there's different rules for temps. When you're permanent you can get fired and that's not a good reference when you go for another job. You know, 'what happened at your last employment?' 'Oh. I gót fired.' But if you're a temp, 'Oh, I've been temping all the time.' It doesn't go against your character you see. Whether you're a good temp or a bad temp doesn't come into it at all.

The third most attractive feature of temporary office work is felt to be the peculiar sense of freedom and control which it generates. Movement from job to job means that the temp can remain aloof from the pressure to conform to prevailing norms concerning output and behaviour. Failure to conform to existing standards in any work situation carries no swingeing penalties for the temp, since her immediate boss is not vested with the normal prerogative of hiring and firing. The more subtle pressures towards conformity which often prevail in the office, such as gossip, or ostracism by co-workers, lose their potency when applied to someone who is only a temporary member of the group. Temping thus affords a much greater degree of freedom from the traditional sanctions of the office environment:

> Not having to please people above me and remember that I'm to obey orders as I would in a permanent position.

> Freedom. Being able to 'hold your own' against unscrupulous bosses.

> The independent feeling that you can ask for a transfer if you aren't happy.

> Peculiar sense of freedom. Not being tied down by regulations.

The extent to which temporary employment affords a heightened sense of control is an important theme in Olesen and Katsuranis' analysis of American temporary employees. In their view, temps experience a heightened sense of autonomy and control not simply because of their marginality at the place of work but because they are able to influence the assignments offered to them:

> The fact that they could and did say no to certain assignments gave them a feeling of greater control than many other workers

have. Permanent employees who refuse work assignments risk dismissal, censure, or at least their supervisor's displeasure. Temporaries could say no with less risk.[27]

Olesen and Katsuranis point out, however, that the degree of autonomy and control is heavily circumscribed. First, a persistent refusal to accept undesirable assignments on the part of the temp may result in agency displeasure and a consequent hiatus in the supply of jobs. Secondly, the temp often lacks the knowledge necessary for an informed appraisal of an assignment prior to its commencement. Thirdly, where a job proves to be less than satisfying, the temp is obliged to enter into negotiations with the agency for a transfer, and there is no guarantee that the request will be accommodated. Fourthly, temps may sometimes feel constrained to accept undesirable jobs in order that they can refuse jobs or demand ones more suited to them at other times. The opportunities to bargain for favourable assignments are also subject to the prevailing demand for temporary labour. Thus, the temp is not so much in control of her situation as in a relatively well-placed position to negotiate for the conditions of work which she most desires. Notwithstanding these qualifications, Olesen and Katsuranis are moved to comment: 'In our·analysis these women emerged not as creatures adrift in a rapacious business world, but as individuals exercising critical judgments for themselves and for the industry they made possible.[28]

On the basis of my own research I am inclined to support these conclusions. As Table 5.8 shows, my respondents were by no means mistresses of their own destinies, but they evidently felt able to influence the course of their working lives.

In comparison to the importance attached to the three factors so far considered – namely, variety, flexibility, and freedom and control – the weight given to other characteristics of temporary work pales into insignificance. The opportunity to meet people holds some residual appeal, but apart from this such factors as pay and the feeling of being appreciated carry minimal importance. This may be taken to mean, on the one hand, that the range of gratifications provided by temporary employment is fairly narrow, but on the other hand, that there is considerable agreement as to what these gratifications actually are. The importance placed on these three characteristics is undoubtedly related to domestic

TABLE 5.8   *When it comes to being sent out on a new assignment, which of the following best describes your position in the matter?*

Response	Temps %
I have no choice at all and have to go where I'm sent	7
I go where I'm sent, but if I really didn't like the job the agency would probably find me something better	48
The agency knows me well and tries to find jobs that suit me and that I would like	44
No answer	2

(N = 139)

circumstances but it would be unwise to neglect the fact that variety constitutes an important secondary attraction for women with dependent children and ranks equally with flexible conditions among married women.

The aspects of a job which generate satisfaction are not necessarily the same as those which govern occupational choice. My findings suggest that variety looms larger as a source of gratification than as a reason for becoming a temp. This underlines the multidimensional nature of work attitudes and also their susceptibility to modification.

Turning next to the unattractive aspects of temporary employment, it is evident from the data presented in Table 5.9 that there is less agreement than one finds in relation to its attractions.

The single most common source of dissatisfaction is job insecurity. The uncertainty of regular employment constitutes the chief occupational hazard of this type of work, and it is likely to be particularly acute during the winter months. I asked my respondents whether they had ever been out of work for longer than a week because the agency was unable to find work for them. Exactly one-third said that this had happened to them.

Of course, insecurity is not only an objective condition but a state of mind. One does not need to have experienced it in the former sense before it is felt to be a threat. Indeed, my own experience leads me to suppose that it is fear of insecurity rather

TABLE 5.9 *What do you like least as a temp? (Responses for all temps and for temps with varying domestic circumstances)*

Aspect of temporary work mentioned	All temps	Single temps	Married temps	Temps without dependent children	Temps with dependent children
N =	139	65	74	98	41
	%	%	%	%	%
Insecurity	27	22	31	27	27
Negative aspects of change	19	15	22	14	29
Boring jobs/lack of responsibility	18	29	8	20	12
Temps don't fit in	18	18	18	17	20
Lack of fringe benefits	18	25	12	20	12
Low pay	10	11	9	12	5
Travel problems	4	3	5	3	7
Nothing disliked	3	–	5	3	2
Method of pay	2	5	–	3	–
Treatment by the agency	1	2	1	1	2
No answer	6	5	7	5	7

than the direct experience of involuntary unemployment which colours the attitudes of temporary workers. More often than not, one cannot be sure that there will be a continuous supply of jobs from week to week. Normally details of one's next assignment are not available until only a couple of days before it is due to begin. In many cases, such details are sent by post. A postal delay can greatly exacerbate anxieties and what is worse, it can mean that a whole morning's pay may be lost due to the necessity to wait until the requisite information can be obtained. It is this kind of experience and the ever-present fear of unemployment, especially for the less well-qualified, which renders temping less than attractive for many women:

> The insecurity. There is no guarantee that there will be work from one week to the next.

> The insecurity of the lack of work in winter.

> Having to wait before knowing if and where I am working next week.

> You could be out of work when you need the money most.

The feeling of insecurity is not only promoted by the uncertain state of the market, but also by the possible implications of ill-health:

> You've got to be an optimist that you're going to get work the following week. You've got to be very optimistic and very healthy because if you suffer – if you're going to be ill every month – don't be a temp. Because you're going to lose all that money and eventually you'll step out of the job and someone else is going to be in there the next day.

It is ironic to find that whereas the variety encountered in temporary work constitutes one of its major attractions, a substantial minority of temps cite change as a source of dissatisfaction. The following comments illustrate this point of view:

> It has an unsettling effect in that it is almost impossible to organise yourself or your life properly as you never really know

where you will be from one week's end to the next and how long it is going to take you to get to and from work, etc. It encourages irresponsibility and a 'don't care' attitude.

Monday morning – arriving at a new place and feeling slightly nervous, wondering if you can manage the work satisfactorily.

Not knowing from one week to the next where one will be working and, more important, not being able to get involved in one's work.

The continuous change of working environment, and possibly work task as well, does place unusual strains on even the most adaptable of employees. The temp is constantly obliged to familiarise herself with the prevailing office procedure, and to establish some sort of relationship with co-workers and employers – in short, to display an unusually high degree of personal flexibility. What at first seems to be an enjoyable way of working may prove in the long term to be highly disagreeable. It is useful to cite in this context the conclusions reached by Gannon and Brainin concerning the outcome of frequent job change:

> If the changes in assignment are so quick that the individual is unable to cope with the environment, it is probable that he will quit . . . Although further research in this area is needed, the present analysis suggests that job rotation is associated with positive outcomes only when the method of implementation does not create an uncertain environment in which the individual employee cannot function effectively.[29]

Another source of dissatisfaction was the nature of work temps are required to do. Eighteen per cent of my respondents said that the aspect of temping which they liked least was the fact that jobs were often boring and/or lacked responsibility:

Being asked to do inferior jobs with no responsibility.

Bosses keep the interesting jobs for permanent staff and don't like to show you anything new.

The jobs like typing long lists or just envelopes – a 'nothing' job, that, although important, doesn't take much ability.

Some establishments take on the involved duties themselves, thinking that really a half-week stay by the temp is not worth explaining the 'ins and outs' to, and therefore you are left with the telephone calls and simple correspondence.

Indeed, as Table 5.10 shows, over half of my respondents considered that their skills were not being fully utilised.

My respondents did not feel, on the whole, that they were being underutilised in the sense of having insufficient work to occupy one's time, as Table 5.11 shows. The experience of having too little work to occupy the time available emerges as unusual. However, being busy is by no means an insurance against monotony. Many of my respondents found that even a rapid succession of jobs was insufficient to prevent a strong sense of boredom from surfacing.

This finding may seem surprising since many of my respondents had chosen temping in order to escape from boredom in the permanent job and since so many felt that variety had proved to be one of the most appealing aspects of temporary work. Yet these comments draw attention to what is possibly the chief irony of temporary employment, namely, that it is more rather than less likely to consist of jobs which are highly routine and repetitive and which require little specialist knowledge. The essence of the temp's market value is that her skills are immediately transferable. She is rarely required to stay at any one firm for a lengthy period and she is frequently sent to jobs that cannot be filled by any other means. Taken together, these circumstances militate against the

TABLE 5.10   *In general, how would you say that the jobs you get as a ter match your skills? (fixed-choice question)*

Response	Temps %
The jobs I get are too specialised for my skills	–
The jobs I get are right for my skills	44
The jobs I get do not require me to use my skills fully	54
No answer	2

(*N* = 139)

TABLE 5.11 *How do you feel about the amount of work you have to do on temporary jobs? (fixed-choice question)*

Response	Temps %
I am often given little or nothing to do, and am told to work slowly or look busy	11
Working at a reasonable rate, I usually find I am kept occupied most of the time	78
Bosses seem to have little idea of the amount of work that one person can do, and I am very often overworked	9
No answer	2

($N = 139$)

possibility that individual assignments will be skilled, varied or responsible.

A substantial minority of my respondents mentioned the feeling of 'not fitting in' or of 'not belonging' as a cause for dissatisfaction:

Sometimes feeling left out because I am in strange surroundings.

Not belonging, and knowing that you are regarded as temporary only.

Some people will not accept strangers, especially temps.

The feeling of detachment mentioned by many of my respondents is inherent in a mode of employment which is characterised by continuous change of location, and indeed, some agencies have turned it into a selling point:

It is frequently more economical for a company to use —— temporary help services than to call back former employees . . . His or her skills are at maximum level. He or she is familiar with the new equipment currently in use in an office, and does not become a part of the social organization of the office.[30]

Whether or not the claims of agencies are justified, it is evident that some temps at least are not happy with this situation. Olesen

and Katsuranis found a sense of isolation to be a common experience among their temporary respondents:

> Many interviewees reported that they found their work sites
> isolating and lonely. They were not welcomed into groups of
> permanent employees, and the attitudes of those employees
> were sometimes corrosive of the temporary's self-esteem.[31]

Olesen and Katsuranis point out that these negative feelings
may be balanced by a sense of pride in one's capabilities – a
definition of self as an occupational troubleshooter – but they
argue that the temp is nevertheless highly vulnerable to feelings of
inferiority, not least because permanent staff distance themselves
from and devalue temps as a way of enhancing their own sense of
worth.

Although this may well be true in certain instances, my own
results do not suggest that temps are invariably met by a hostile
reaction from an 'in-group' of permanent staff. As Table 5.12
shows, it is often the permanent staff who make friendly overtures.
Again, the majority of my respondents reported an accommodative
posture on the part of permanent staff with regard to the execution
of the work itself – see Table 5.13.

Undoubtedly there are a great many temps who are made to feel
like outcasts, but even in their case the passage of time may soften
the negative attitudes of permanent staff towards them. The
response of permanent staff to the temporary is not standardised

TABLE 5.12   *In getting to know the permanent people you
work with, do you find . . . ? (fixed-choice question)*

Response	Temps %
The permanents are friendly and make the approach to you	63
You have to make most of the effort in getting to know them	32
Neither you nor they are particularly interested in getting to know each other	5
No answer	1

(*N* = 139)

TABLE 5.13   *Which of the following best describes your experiences when you first begin a new temporary assignment?* (*fixed-choice question*)

Response	Temps %
You are expected to get on with the job and work things out for yourself	7
You are expected to be able to do the job, but if you need advice, people will help you out	54
Employers and co-workers are very helpful in showing you how the work is done	38
No answer	1

(*N* = 139)

but is likely to be coloured by such factors as previous experience of temporary workers, the numbers of temps employed, the reasons why temps are hired by the employer, and the level of pay that the temp receives.

Equally dissatisfying was the lack of fringe benefits. In relation to this aspect, my own findings are at odds with those of a survey of temps conducted in 1970 by the Alfred Marks organisation.[32] According to this survey, this was by far the greatest cause for dissatisfaction amongst temps. No less than 66 per cent of the Marks' respondents cited this as the greatest single disadvantage attaching to temporary work. Insecurity was mentioned by only 18 per cent. I feel that it is worth mentioning this point, since the Marks survey is the only one I have been able to locate which actually asked office temps what they disliked about their work, and it is the area in which our findings differ most. It is very difficult indeed to account for this discrepancy, and given the general lack of information in this field, one is reluctant to claim that one's own findings represent a closer approximation to reality. However, there is one body of data which would seem to lend greater support to the findings of the present research. Parker and Sirker asked a sample of persons to state what they considered to be the disadvantages attaching to temporary employment. The sample consisted of people who had had a temporary job, or had seriously considered taking one, or who considered that they might take one in the future, and the question related to all forms of temporary work. They found that the most frequently cited disadvantage was the lack of security. The second disadvantage, which came 'a long way behind', was not enough money. However, the lack of fringe benefits was felt to be a disadvantage by only a small minority.[33] These findings are, of course, not strictly comparable with data relating to agency temps in office work, but they certainly conflict with the findings produced by the Marks survey. Whilst my own data suggests that the lack of fringe benefits is undoubtedly a prominent source of grievance among office temps, I consider that the Marks findings present a somewhat exaggerated impression of the extent to which financial considerations inform women's assessments of this method of employment.

Having said this, it is only fair to point out that 10 per cent of my respondents cited low pay as a cause for complaint. If one considers this finding in conjunction with the previous one, then it is apparent that extrinsic characteristics of the job are perceived as important. One can even argue that the fear of insecurity is at base the fear of loss of earnings. However, it is important to recognise that certain intrinsic characteristics of temporary work are as much a cause for dissatisfaction as those which may be considered extrinsic.

As with the sources of satisfaction, an examination of the causes for dissatisfaction reveals certain variations according to domestic circumstances. Single women were much more likely to cite boredom and lack of responsibility as a cause for complaint than married women and women with dependent children. This is consistent with the earlier findings that single women are more likely to have entered temping precisely in order to escape these problems. To the extent that this expectation is not met we would expect this consideration to loom large in their catalogue of complaints. Married women and those with dependent children appear to be more concerned about the problems of insecurity and the negative consequences of continuous change. This finding is consistent with the fact that these women are more likely to have entered temporary employment simply because they want to work. Temping has not been chosen mainly because of its special characteristic of continuous job rotation, but because it is a solution to the problem of reconciling home and work demands. The setback to one's intentions to escape the home environment represented by a hiatus in the supply of jobs must surely be experienced as something of a disappointment by these women.

Finally, it is appropriate to examine the impact of the experience of temping on my respondents' preferred mode of employment. As Table 5.14 shows, there was a fairly even split between those who preferred temporary work and those who preferred permanent work, although once again, some variation is evident according to domestic circumstances.

Among those who said that they preferred permanent work, the three most frequently cited reasons for their choice were as follows: greater job security and a regular pay packet, mentioned by 37 per cent; a preference for being more involved with one's work and being able to progress, 37 per cent; and a desire to be settled, 31 per cent. No other single reason came anywhere near to approaching these factors in importance. The importance of fringe benefits in fourth position, mentioned by 13 per cent, was very much an also-ran in the hierarchy of preference.

Among those who said that they preferred temporary work, the three main reasons were as follows: variety and change, 57 per cent; flexible conditions, 45 per cent; the opportunity to meet more people, 37 per cent. Again, these three reasons far outweighed any others in importance. A preference for having no ties and a feeling of freedom was mentioned by 18 per cent. It is interesting to note that the feature of meeting people appears in this context despite the fact that it does not constitute an important reason for going into temporary work, nor does it rank as a major satisfaction. It does appear to have a fairly strong bearing, however, on one's assessment of the relative advantages of the two modes of employment. This finding draws attention once again to the fact that the priorities attached to work should not be regarded either as static or unidimensional.

Participant observation

In the following section I am concerned to illustrate and elaborate some of the general findings noted above by offering an account of my own experiences of temporary work during a three-month period of participant observation. I am confident that the particular assignment that I undertook was more representative of the disadvantages of temping than the advantages. Having had a great deal of experience as a temp, albeit in a student capacity, I am very much aware of the potential for satisfaction in temporary work. One hopes that this side of the coin has been fairly represented in

TABLE 5.14 *On the whole which do you prefer – permanent work or temporary work?*

Response	All temps	Single temps	Married temps	Temps without dependent children	Temps with dependent children
	N = 139	65	74	98	41
	%	%	%	%	%
Permanent	49	46	51	44	61
Temporary	47	46	47	52	34
Like both	3	5	1	3	2
No answer	2	3	–	1	2

the foregoing discussion. In fairness to myself, I should point out that it was not my original intention to spend the whole period in one firm. Unfortunately, my proposed strategy to spend some time in several jobs was thwarted by the agency's refusal to move me, in spite of the fact that co-operation had earlier been promised. Consequently, I was obliged to make the best of the opportunities available, which meant spending the entire time in one location. What follows, therefore, should not be regarded necessarily as a typical experience, but rather as one person's encounter with some of the experiences which promote discontent and, most probably, a decision to return to permanent work.

Three days after I enrolled at the agency, an assistant telephoned to say that they had found me work as a clerk. Thus it was that I found myself at the offices of the XYZ Credit Company, located a short distance from the centre of Middletown, one of the largest cities in the country. Since the office was situated very conveniently on the main bus route to Middletown from my home, I assumed that the agency had attempted to accommodate me with respect to travelling. However, I was obliged to question this assumption later, when several temps grumbled to me about the impossible journeys which they had to make from *their* homes, some of them having to get up at 6.30 a.m. in order to arrive at work by 9.00 a.m. Perhaps I had just been lucky.

The firm occupied eight floors of a large, modern office block. The resemblance between one floor and another, however, extended only to the shape. The locus of higher management was adorned by wall-to-wall carpets and elegant furnishings, that of lower management by fairly stylish fittings and bright paintwork, whereas the filing department, where I was to be employed, was a barren wasteland of rickety chairs and tables, with not so much as a calendar to grace the fading, dirty walls. This enormous room was dominated by tall, musty filing cabinets which effectively prevented the sunshine from entering. Although much recent sociology has discredited the view held by early occupational psychologists that work environment plays an important part in determining work attitudes, it is hard in retrospect to dismiss that drab, dingy office as an irrelevance.

I arrived in this department after having been given directions by the receptionist, and was quite surprised to find that my presence went completely unacknowledged. After standing about in front of the supervisor's desk for several minutes without being able to attract her attention, I finally decided to take the initiative and informed one of the clerks that I had arrived. At last I was introduced to the supervisor, who gave me a very brief description of the work, which was to sort pieces of paper (correspondence) into some kind of order ready for filing into 'bays' or open filing cabinets. The filing system was in fact highly complicated, and unknown to myself at the time I proceeded to sort the correspondence quite incorrectly. Being used to a measure of explanation when first beginning a temporary job, I was very surprised at the whole attitude – a total lack of interest in who I was, and an equally noticeable lack of interest in showing me how to do the work. When employers fail to give temporary employees an adequate understanding of the work routine, it may be because they assume familiarity with the type of work. They do not expect to have to give lengthy training programmes, and in any case instruction is an expensive commodity. In this case, it eventually became clear to me that the indifferent attitude had arisen because of the massive turnover of temps in the office, and all had grown weary of explaining the office system over and over again. For the same reason, a new face in the workplace was no source of interest but a commonplace. At this stage I was unable to distinguish between temps and permanents, but all were equally uninterested in my presence. Whilst it is easy and indeed only fair to sympathise with this attitude, it was then very hard to settle down during those first few days, when nobody spoke to you or even acknowledged your presence with a blank stare. Even the sociologist, in her capacity as a participant-observer, is not immune to the chill and loneliness of an indifferent environment.

Since the element of socialising was completely absent from my first week in the office, there was little else to do but concentrate on the work in hand. Rather than consider the nature of this particular work in isolation, I feel it is necessary to mention some aspects of filing in general, lest the reader feel that I am painting an unduly depressing picture of this one situation. Filing can be thought of as the office equivalent of unskilled manual labour. Apart from literacy and a degree of numeracy, no qualification is necessary for the post of filing clerk. Usually, however, filing is one part of a wider field of activity in an office, so that the personal secretary may be found filing away the boss's correspondence before arranging his appointments, or the clerk-typist may file invoices in a small cabinet before typing orders. Presumably the degree to which filing is the sole occupation of an employee is a function of the size of the organisation. In the case of a small or medium-sized office, filing is one of many tasks, and frequently affords the opportunity to inject a little of one's own personality into the system, but in the case of the large, complex organisation such as the one where I now found myself, the division of labour is such that filing becomes a total occupation, and time-and-motion experts have rigidly excluded the possibility of personalising the system. From the employer's point of view, the latter situation is ideal for the employment of temporary staff, since the work is standardised and requires no special knowledge, nor any idea of how the firm works as a whole.

In the small office, even though it means spending some time in getting to know the complexities of the firm as a total system, and in finding out who its personnel are, at least the clerk may ultimately gain a conception of how her work fits into the whole. In the case under study, however, I am tempted to use the term 'alienation' to describe a situation where the worker was but a cog in a wheel, performing a standardised task and lacking any understanding of how that task meshed with the rest of the organisation.

Thus, with minimal understanding of the filing system, and no idea whatsoever of the nature or functioning of the company, I struggled to master the process of filing into bays. This bleak situation was not helped by the fact that the filing system contained many anomalies which led to a great deal of misfiling and consequently made the task even more difficult. Physically, the work was very tiring since it involved reaching up to very high shelves and crouching very low in order to reach the bottom ones. Had I not been very tall it could have been much worse, for many girls had to make use of the solitary stool in order to file in the top shelves. Sitting on the floor proved to be one of the least tedious ways of performing the job, though at great peril to one's tights, and on one occasion resulted in my having to have a number of large splinters removed from my bottom by a nurse. It would be hard to overstate the dreadful conditions of the work – dirt, splinters, laddered tights, aching backs and feet – all were part and parcel of this tedious occupation. On top of all this, there was not even the customary satisfaction of getting through the work because not only was there no end to the backlog of filing, but in addition it was impossible to file a great deal of it on account of the chaos and disorder in the bays.

In view of the picture painted above, it is perhaps not surprising that most of the other temps with whom I worked were anxious to find alternative employment with the agency. Of the total of seven temps who were employed by this firm when I began the period of participant observation, only two made no attempt to secure a transfer, and both were students. While both of them did not think that the job was very interesting and would have preferred to move, they told me that they were more concerned to have a job for the duration of the summer in order to save some money. Among the other temps, however, there was a general desire for a different assignment. The degree of consensus regarding the unsatisfying nature of the work in hand is particularly interesting when one considers that these temps were highly diversified in terms of social background, domestic circumstances and previous work experience.

Pat, for example, was the most outgoing of all the temps. She was twenty-two, single, and had worked for the agency for four months. She had obtained RSA qualifications at school and had subsequently undertaken training as a GPO telephonist. She told me that she was very disillusioned with temporary work. She had given up a permanent job as a telephonist/receptionist in the hope of finding, as she put it, 'a more fulfilling job', and one which provided the chance to meet a greater variety of people. As it turned out, she had been placed in what she considered to be very boring jobs, none of which matched her qualifications. She had had four placements altogether, three of which involved routine clerical work, and on one occasion she had even been sent to man the turnstiles at the city zoo. It had also been impossible to form lasting friendships. Consequently, she had requested a transfer from the agency on each assignment. As far as the present job was concerned, Pat was extremely dissatisfied, but thought that she might as well stay there since she had made arrangements to emigrate in three months' time. Twice, however, out of desperation, she rang the agency in the hope that she might find work as a telephonist.

Susan, who was twenty-one and single, had been doing temporary work for only one week. She had become a temp so that she could look around for a more interesting permanent job than she had formerly been used to. One of her difficulties was that she had no formal qualifications and so the field was 'rather limited'. She believed that temp work might prove to be rather interesting since it implied a variety of places to work, but apart from this she could see no real advantages. Permanent work, she felt, was far more secure, and there was the additional benefit of paid holidays. She thought that the present job was very boring but expressed the view that it might improve. As the time passed, however, this was not to be, and she grew increasingly concerned to find an alternative assignment.

Jean, who was nineteen, was married with a very young child. She had abandoned a permanent job because it had been so boring and monotonous, and hoped that temping would offer greater variety and a larger pay packet. In addition, her child was going to a day nursery, and she told me that temporary work meant that she could work to suit her domestic commitments. The only disadvantage she could think of was the insecurity. Notwithstanding the premium placed on secure employment, she too asked the agency to move her.

Although the temps had very diverse pre-histories before coming to this company, as well as differing expectations from temporary work, a common attitude prevailed. This was a profoundly negative orientation to this particular job, which found expression in numerous calls to the agency requesting a transfer. In every case, it was not so much the nature of the social relationships at work (or rather, the lack of them) which prompted this action, but the nature of the actual work.

During the first month of the study, I learnt for certain of at least seven individuals who had sought alternative employment from the agency. Transfers, however, were not forthcoming. All those who applied for a different job were initially told that it was impossible and that they should try again after a week. Of those who asked for a transfer, two had no success at all, two had to wait three weeks, and three found their own means of escape. In this workplace, therefore, the 'freedom' of the temp was very much attenuated. As the temp season (which runs from early May to late September, coinciding with the holiday period) drew to a close, the hopes of a transfer grew slimmer and slimmer, and the agency informed us that the only alternative to remaining there was unemployment.

However bad the actual market situation might really have

been, all were united in the belief that there *were* jobs, but that the agency was not really interested in our 'welfare'. Several commented that when they had first enrolled they had been impressed by the warm reception and the optimistic forecasts of interesting work, but that this apparent concern had seemed to disappear very rapidly.

It was mainly the common discontent with the work and with the agency that brought the temps together. It was at least food for conversation in a situation which otherwise hindered our chances of communication. We came together at last mainly through the efforts of Pat to promote conversation about our misfortunes. Having once identified with each other in our mutual loathing of the work, we gradually became more friendly, but we nevertheless continued to pursue escape strategies on an individual basis.

It might seem from the above account that the temporary office worker, at least in the lower grades of this type of employment, is easily dissatisfied and unwilling to give a job a chance. Apart from the fact that the present study is far too limited to warrant generalisations of this kind, such a judgement would be unsatisfactory on the grounds that it bordered on the psychologistic. It seems more likely that the total preoccupation with obtaining a transfer among these girls was due to the particularly unpleasant nature of the work at this company. For even those who were merely filling in before going abroad or before taking up a permanent position made some attempt to escape. It is hard to avoid the conclusion that their discontent was the product of frustrated expectations from temporary work as the key to freedom, interest and variety, and indeed, from office work in general. The discrepancy between what a girl is sometimes led to expect from her education and what she may actually find in the way of employment opportunities was all too clearly highlighted in the dusty environs of the XYZ company's filing department.

The fifteen permanent staff who were employed in the filing department were a much more homogeneous collectivity than the temporary staff. The average age was approximately eighteen, and for many this had been their only job since leaving school. Within this group, however, it was possible to identify one clear-cut division. Although everyone performed more or less the same tasks, namely sorting and filing, some girls had been charged with the responsibility of filing correspondence relating to particular customers. These girls sat at their own desk while most of the others sat at another desk a few feet away. The permanent staff, therefore, fell into two work groupings and it was apparent that this division extended beyond the mere arrangement of work duties and seating facilities. For, throughout my period of observation, it was clear that the girls were very friendly towards those sitting at their own table and somewhat hostile towards those sitting elsewhere. This social division was curiously demonstrated when two of the girls got married in the same week, one from each group. It is normal practice in offices of this kind for a number of festivities to be held on the afternoon preceding the great event, which include festooning the future bride's coat with toilet rolls and newspaper cuttings selected for their relevance to post-nuptial activities; giving cards and presents; and seeing the week out with a glass or two of sherry. These various celebrations were held as usual in this office, but although one might have supposed that all the permanent staff would get together and toast the two brides-to-be as one collectivity, this was not to be. Separated by a distance of only six feet, the two groups sat resolutely at their respective tables and held two different 'stag parties'. The only occasion on which a sense of unity was generated amongst the permanent staff was when news was received one morning that one of their number had sustained some minor injuries in a car accident and had been detained in hospital. Great concern was expressed by all the girls, irrespective of where they sat.

All the permanent girls were united in their expressed dislike of their work and frequently complained aloud with such comments as 'I'm screaming with boredom' and 'Why do I do it?'. At the end of the day there was always a stampede towards the lifts and they very seldom worked overtime. On one occasion, the supervisor announced that she required volunteers for overtime on Saturday mornings. The response was a loud chorus of groans, and one girl shouted out to the supervisor: 'If you spent seven hours at this all day, would you want to do any more?'

Given this widespread dissatisfaction with the job, it was quite puzzling to me that they nevertheless remained with the firm and did not make any serious attempts to find alternative employment. When it is considered that many of them had been with the firm for a number of years – one, indeed, having been there for nine years – one is obliged to consider what it was that kept them there, especially since they were unequivocal in the dislike of the work. One of the reasons appeared to be that they had some interest in maintaining their social relationships at work. Whereas the temps were bound together by nothing more than a mutual distaste for the job, the permanent staff had clearly formed friendships amongst themselves, and lest it should be supposed that I am merely imposing categories upon the relationships which I observed, it should be pointed out that this was the reason which they themselves gave for remaining with the firm. One of the permanent staff told me that she 'didn't think you would find a friendlier place'. Although this attitude could be regarded as a rationalisation, a product of an inability to obtain alternative work, the importance of the social ambience of the workplace, albeit bifurcated, did appear to be quite marked. Nearly all the girls went out with others from the office in the evenings either to discotheques, parties or pubs, whereas none of the temps mingled after hours. The permanent staff wore all their new clothes to the office, despite the hazards of dirt and sharp edges on the filing cabinets. Since there were no men in the office, it was only possible to conclude that either the permanent staff were exceptionally concerned about their appearance, or that they were seeking the approbation of those who constituted the focus of their work and social life.

Whereas for most of the permanent girls, social life *was* the office, the temporaries, with the exception of the young girl who had to care for a small child, all led active social lives beyond and divorced from the workplace. To some extent, work was viewed rather instrumentally as a means of financing a full social calendar. Social life at work was regarded as little more than a fringe benefit. Given this attitude, and the fact that in any case, friendships formed at work tend to be highly transitory for the temp due to the constant change of workplace, it is perhaps not surprising that the nature of the work tended to assume a more central importance in the minds of the temps at the XYZ company.

Apart from the apparent concern to maintain their friendships, another reason for staying among permanents was the limited field of opportunities available to them. None of the girls had typing or secretarial qualifications, and none had any 'O' levels. Consequently, the only jobs for which they could apply were likely to be much the same as the present one, and possibly lacking the 'friendly atmosphere'. One girl who made the loudest noises when it came to criticising the work told me that she would like to change but that there were never any jobs in the paper.

A comparison of the attitudes among the permanent and temporary staff suggests that a lack of marketable skills is decisive in governing responses to an unsatisfying work situation. In contrast to the permanent staff, all but two of the temps had some educational qualifications, ranging from CSE to 'A' level. In addition, they had had more experience of different types of office work. In objective terms, then, and also in terms of their own subjective assessments, the temps were not trapped by circumstance. Their immediate concern was to extricate themselves from this situation. In contrast, the permanent staff had resigned themselves to their lot and looked towards their companions to provide interest and enjoyment.

Over the course of several weeks, those temporaries who had not sought or who had failed to secure a transfer became something of a clique within the office, setting themselves apart from the permanent staff and to some extent from newly-arrived temps. In fact, the arrival of a new temp was not greeted with any enthusiasm or even comment. Whereas I had once felt so badly about this very indifference, I now found that I was displaying it myself. The news of a transfer was received with a mixture of jealousy and that type of cautious congratulation that must have accompanied an escapee from a POW camp during the war. Out of the frying pan . . . ?

The detachment from the permanents was to a large extent a product of the hostility which they expressed towards us. Not only were individual temps the butt of contemptuous and often bitchy remarks made by the permanents, but the whole group of us were sometimes subject to generalised insults and cool behaviour. Temps were often discussed by the permanent staff. This usually happened when all the temps had left at 4.30 p.m. I alone always stayed on until 5.00 p.m. as this suited me better than working a half-hour lunch and leaving early. On one occasion a discussion centred on the issue of temps' ability to enjoy flexible hours, and considerable disapproval was expressed. On another occasion, the view was put forward that temps did not bother to clear up their desks, and that they, the permanent staff, got all the blame.

I do not consider that antagonism is a necessary feature of the relationships between permanent staff and temporaries, and indeed the results of my survey suggest that mutual adjustment is more typical. In the XYZ filing department, however, the expression of ill-feeling towards temps most probably acted as a safety valve for the accumulated discontent among the permanents. I found however that hostility towards oneself as an individual tended to diminish with the passage of time. In my early relations with the permanent staff I had to make practically all the effort in engineering any communication. Only one or two initiated conversations with me, while most of them confined their communications with me to suspicious stares. By the time I left, however, I felt that I knew them almost as well as the temps – the distinction having been considerably blurred by time and familiarity. However, it took many weeks before the ice began to thaw in our communications, and in the normal course of events time is not on the side of the temp. She is usually despatched to another assignment before the process of adjustment can begin.

A description of the office would not be complete without reference to the supervisor. Her authoritative manner only served to exacerbate our discontent with the work. She was particularly displeased with the temps' level of productivity. All work had to be recorded on work-sheets – not only the number of files removed or replaced, or the pieces of paper filed away, but even the number of times one answered the telephone, in addition to a host of other minor duties. Most of the permanent staff admitted to me that they misrepresented their entries by anything up to 200 per cent. This was possible because there was no way of actually checking the returns. The temps, however, either did not bother to misrepresent their productivity, or the thought had not occurred to them. Consequently, our productivity appeared to fall far short of that of the permanent staff. The supervisor did not fail to bring this to our attention. This circumstance exemplifies the problems temps experience in negotiating the prevailing work norms of the office. Although, as we have seen, the opportunity to remain relatively detached from existing work routines appeals to many temps, this lack of integration can lead to confusion and ill-feeling.

To summarise, the filing department of the XYZ company affords some insight into the nature of temporary work and, in particular, its less appealing characteristics. The intolerable nature of the work was made worse by the unpleasant relationships with the permanent staff. The constantly changing composition of the temporary group prevented lasting relationships among them from developing, and thus sociability was at a minimum. Only those temps who had remained at the office for a period of over four weeks or so could be described as relatively 'integrated'. This meant that in spite of the interpretation placed upon the work-sheet returns, the productivity of the temps was high – there being no social life to distract one from the work at hand. High turnover among temps was the inevitable consequence of this nexus of circumstances, and this in turn only served to promote ill-feeling towards the temps and a marked reluctance to spend time in familiarising them with either the routines of the office or its personnel. My observations also throw some light on the reasons why some girls seek to escape from an oppressive work situation and others become resigned. In this case, an important determinant of attitudes was one's actual or believed capacity to obtain something better.

Attitudes towards future employment

In the previous two sections I have endeavoured to present an insight into the characteristics of temporary office workers, their reasons for entering this type of employment and the experience of temping. Finally, I shall present some of the findings concerning my respondents' priorities for the future. I am unable to give any account of the future path taken by my respondents since I did not follow up the original questionnaire. However, I am able to show that a desire for interesting and varied work remains a most important consideration.

I asked my respondents to state the relative importance of a number of job characteristics in governing decisions about future employment. Table 5.15 shows the pattern of responses. The responses have to be looked at as a whole because there are a number of job characteristics which, although ranking low in terms of being very important, nevertheless emerge as important secondary considerations. This applies in particular to pay, holidays and general working conditions. It is interesting to find that the nature of work relationships both with colleagues and with bosses was considered to be important by almost everyone who was prepared to comment. However, since I found no significant

TABLE 5.15   *If you were looking for a job, how important would the following to you?*

Job characteristic	Very important %	Important %	Not important %	N
Varied and interesting work	70	25	2	
Pleasant people to work with	56	41	–	
Good bosses	54	41	3	
Personal freedom	39	45	12	
Pay	35	58	4	
Being given responsibility	33	42	23	
General working conditions	26	65	6	
Meeting people through work	24	40	35	
Good holidays	22	56	18	
Chances of promotion	22	36	39	
Secure employment	21	35	40	
Being part of a team	15	32	49	

(N = 139)

relation between marital status and the importance attached to relationships at work, this finding discredits the idea that married women differ from other female workers in the emphasis placed on sociability. In fact, married women differed very little from other respondents in terms of their attitudes towards future employment. There *was* a significant difference between married and single women in their evaluation of varied and interesting work. Whereas 80 per cent of the latter rated this as very important, only 61 per cent of the former did so. Nevertheless, for both groups this characteristic was the one most frequently named as very important. Married and single women also differed significantly in terms of the importance placed on personal freedom and chances of promotion. In relation to both factors, a higher proportion of single women than married women named these as important or very important. Just over half of the married women considered that chances of promotion were not important, whilst only a quarter of single women shared this view. Personal freedom was rated not important by only 3 per cent of single temps, but by 19 per cent of married temps. The overall picture, however, does more to confirm the similarities rather than the dissimilarities of attitudes between married and single women.

Such differences as did exist were ones of degree rather than of sharp polarisation.

An interesting finding is the relatively low importance placed on secure employment especially in view of the fact that this consideration weighed so heavily in my respondents' assessment of temporary work. It may be suggested that this factor is not a major determinant of job choice since it can normally be taken for granted in the field of office work. It is only temporary office work which renders women vulnerable to periodic unemployment and thus more aware of the problem of insecurity. Conversely, such factors as varied and interesting work, pleasant workmates and good employers and pay cannot be assumed to characterise any future job. Consequently, these characteristics emerge as the principal criteria according to which women discriminate between the jobs available.

Apart from the differences of emphasis between married and single women noted above, there were very few items in relation to which a woman's social circumstances were predictive of attitudes. Neither age nor responsibility for dependent children were significantly correlated with the importance attached to the various job attributes. Women in the North-east were less inclined than those elsewhere to place importance on personal freedom, but this probably reflects the fact that they were more likely to be married and perhaps that this would be considered something of a luxury in the more unfavourable economic situation of this area.

The finding which does deserve special emphasis, in my opinion, is the remarkable consensus about the importance of varied and interesting work. Although a woman may be obliged to compromise her preferences because of the nature of her domestic circumstances and the intransigency of employers, there can be little doubt that a desire for intrinsic job satisfaction informs the attitudes of a great many women, irrespective of their out-of-work circumstances.

Finally, it remains to be said that the vast majority of my respondents declared a preference for a working life rather than a purely domestic existence. I asked them to state what they would do if they inherited an income which was sufficiently large to enable them to stop working altogether. Table 5.16 shows the pattern of replies.

A number of writers have asserted that women do not regard

TABLE 5.16   *If you inherited some money and had enough to live on with-
             out working, would you want to work anyway?*

Response	All temps %
Yes, because I would be dissatisfied/bored otherwise	68
Yes, but I would do voluntary work	8
Yes – no reason given	3
No, I would travel/spend my money	9
No, I would enjoy my leisure	5
No, because I would prefer to be at home with my family	2
No – no reason given	4

(*N* = 139)

work as an important focus of their existence. In their view, single
women tolerate it until they have achieved their main ambition of
securing a marriage partner, while married women return to work
mainly in order materially to enhance their domestic environment.
In view of the dispiriting nature of the broad range of economic
opportunities available to women, such responses are certainly
credible. However, the findings shown above demonstrate that
such attitudes are neither universal nor inevitable. It should also
be noted that marital status was not predictive of the anticipated
response to an inheritance. The responses of women with
dependent children did differ significantly from those of other
women, but this was mainly in terms of the likelihood of doing
voluntary work. They were no more likely to cease work
altogether than women without dependent children.

From the replies given to my question it was evident that the
majority of married women and single women alike viewed a
purely domestic existence as unsatisfying:

> Having been at home with two children for some years one gets
> rather closed in, and your life tends to revolve round home and
> children. Going out to work helps your outlook on things to
> broaden, as well as the financial gains. So anything that helps
> your life brighten can only be passed on to your immediate
> family.

> Life would be so boring just sitting or even doing the household
> chores and you would miss the company terribly.

As I am a widow and my two children are away at boarding school for 36 weeks of the year, I need a job to give life some purpose and in order to get out and meet people.

Work relieves boredom – keeps one on their toes with regard to things going on around the world and keeps your brain active.

Most of those who stated that they would give up work intended to make full use of the opportunities afforded by a combination of wealth and leisure:

I'd much rather travel the world, learn as much as possible about other cultures, and perhaps even write a book. I have already done a bit of travelling and the 'bug' has bitten deep.

There are so many things I want to do and I begrudge any time spent at work.

Those who stated that they would give up work in order to concentrate on a more conventional domestic life-style were very few and far between:

Having achieved quite a good position with a very good salary, my only ambition now is to be a full-time wife and mother.

I prefer being home, looking after my husband and baby.

Since this question was of course entirely hypothetical, perhaps one should be cautious in attaching too much significance to the replies. Moreover, one must remember that the group included a large number of women who had sought work in spite of certain domestic commitments. To this extent, the majority preference for a continuing working life is not altogether surprising. At the same time, one is obliged to recognise that financial considerations do not appear to be the most fundamental determinant of whether or not a woman seeks gainful employment. A more important consideration is the relative satisfactions thought to derive from domesticity or from work.

The findings deriving from my questionnaire and participant observation enable one to form a picture of the type of person who enters temporary office employment, the reasons for doing so and the nature of temporary employment itself. It is evident that the popular assumptions about office temps bear little relation to the facts. There is no reason to suppose that they are mainly women who, because of sheer incompetence, would be unable to find work by any other means. In the case of my respondents, problems in finding alternative employment were more clearly related to difficulties associated with domestic responsibilities than to any discernible lack of skill. Nor are temps primarily motivated by a desire for wage maximisation. In the long term the economic situation of the temp is likely to be worse than that of the permanent office worker. Even in the short term the advantage of high hourly rates may be offset by short spells of unemployment. In view of these circumstances, plus the fact that few temps state that the desire for better pay is of major significance, it seems quite legitimate to discard the notion that the temp is simply a woman possessed by the demon of avarice. Nor is there any support here for the idea that temping attracts women who wish to increase the number of their acquaintances, male or otherwise. My respondents placed importance on good working relationships and some felt that temporary work was to be preferred to permanent work because of the greater opportunities to meet people, but on the whole, the social spin-off from temporary work is at most only a secondary consideration.

I have also shown that the work situation of the temp is characterised by many paradoxes. First, while the work is likely to offer more variety than permanent employment, it is likely to consist of tasks which are more repetitive. Secondly, while the temp is less bound by prevailing work norms in the place of employment, this very detachment may promote an uncomfortable sense of isolation. Thirdly, while the opportunities for mobility foster a heightened sense of control over the work situation, the unpredictable character of these opportunities and the possibility of unemployment promote feelings of insecurity and vulnerability. Thus while in certain respects the temp appears to have broken free from the constraints encountered in the permanent sector, her own work situation presents an alternative set of limiting features.

My results also suggest that the image of temporary work propagated by agency advertising does not always conform to the reality of temping. Whilst the themes of varied and interesting work; work matched to the skills of the temp; and a constant supply of suitable and attractive jobs are those most frequently found in the advertisements, many of my respondents' expectations in these respects had not been fulfilled. Even when some expectations had been met, there remained residual sources of grievance.

It is a matter for conjecture as to whether or not the agencies themselves could take steps to remove the many sources of dissatisfaction, thus reducing the numbers of women who quit temping in favour of permanent work. Certainly, they would appear to have little control over the major source of dissatisfaction, insecurity. This derives in the main from fluctuations in the demand for temporary office workers and to a lesser extent from the sheer number of agencies. Agencies could of course alleviate this problem by the provision of compensation for unemployment, but few choose to do so. The rarity of such provision is quite easily explained. The cost of compensation would almost certainly have to be passed on to the client firm in the form of higher rates for temp hire. This provision would thus render the temp a very expensive commodity indeed and in all probability would lead to a major reduction in demand. However, some firms in this country do provide compensation for unemployment, usually after a qualifying period of thirteen weeks or thereabouts. Compensation is actually obligatory in a number of European countries, including France. In some countries, financial security is effected through an assurance scheme to which both temps and temporary hire firms contribute. Yet even if it were possible to guarantee financial security, it is doubtful whether this would be sufficient to eliminate the feelings of uncertainty experienced by many temporary workers. For those who view work as something more than a source of income, the knowledge that one is financially secure is unlikely to compensate for the uncertainty of employment itself. It is this latter attribute of temporary work which is likely to remain, irrespective of the steps taken by agencies to improve the material situation of their employees. The agencies can also do little to remove the dissatisfaction which is sometimes felt as a result of continuous change. This and the widespread discontentment with the job content of temporary assignments derive from the inherent characteristics of temporary employment rather than from any action or lack of it on the part of the agencies. It may be surmised, however, that the frequent shortfall between expectations from temporary work and the actual experience of temporary work could be reduced if the agencies were less prone to over-advertise and over-glamourise the options available.

Finally, I wish to identify some of the more general issues arising from this account of women in temporary clerical employment. First, it is evident that domestic circumstances represent only part of the explanation for a woman's occupational choice and responses to her work situation. Given the current lack of state nursery facilities, crèches at the workplace, and the slow introduction of flexitime, a woman's domestic responsibilities inevitably set limits to the range of jobs to which she may reasonably aspire. Similarly, it is also evident that a great many women accept that their involvement in the world of gainful employment should be geared to the needs of children and husbands. Consequently, it would be quite erroneous to dismiss domestic circumstances as irrelevant to the study of women's attitudes to employment. However, while out-of-work circumstances do have a bearing on occupational choice, and while they may continue to colour responses to the experience of work itself, it must be recognised that the objective conditions of the work in hand represent an autonomous influence on job attitudes. This is suggested by the lack of any sharp discontinuities between married and single women in their assessment of both the advantages and disadvantages of temporary office employment. Secondly, it is evident that the study of women's occupational choices and responses to work must take into account the market situation of the women concerned. The totality of one's marketable skills, including education, training and experience, plus the demand for those skills, have an important bearing on whether or not an occupational choice is merely a compromise or represents a positive attempt to indulge one's preferences. The issue of market situation is also relevant for an understanding of the way women respond to their jobs. As we have seen, whilst a buoyant demand for white-collar labour makes temporary employment possible, fluctuations in that demand render it inherently insecure. The fear of periodic unemployment may be so great that women feel obliged to leave an otherwise enjoyable mode of work. In this way, shifts in the priorities attached to work may be necessitated by an unfavourable market situation.

Taken together, these two propositions suggest that the study of women's attitudes towards work should be both eclectic and longitudinal. The present study has endeavoured to meet the first criterion, although it falls short of the second requirement since changes in my respondents' attitudes were only ascertained by the device of retrospective questions included in the questionnaire. Ideally, the sociologist should investigate and chart shifts in the priorities attached to work as they actually occur. Nevertheless, the use of the more limited technique has served to illustrate the importance of a diachronic approach.

The empirical foundations upon which my conclusions are based are unlikely to satisfy those who believe that scientific rigour should be the guiding principle for sociological research. However, it is not always the case that the most interesting areas for investigation are amenable to the application of this principle. Furthermore, it may happen that unexpected contingencies can oblige the sociologist to compromise his or her research strategies, no matter how rigorous in their initial design. The present research was beset by a great many procedural problems, one of which was the inaccessibility of the type of worker being studied, and another was the difficulty of securing the unqualified co-operation of certain agencies. These circumstances meant that the methods adopted were ones which depended on the operation of chance, expediency and the goodwill of temps and their employers. However, in my view, the value of much sociological research to date lies not so much in its methodological precision as in the challenge which it has presented to contemporary prejudices, myths and ignorance. One hopes that the findings presented in this chapter will generate a more questioning approach to popular conceptions about women's attitudes towards work.

Conclusions

The original stimulus for this research was a deep sense of personal dissatisfaction with the way in which women had been represented in the literature of industrial sociology. I was dissatisfied not only with the evident neglect of female participation in the labour market, but also with the simplistic way in which it was customary to interpret their work behaviour. The area of study in which both weaknesses were particularly manifest was the sociology of clerical occupations. First, women clerical workers appeared as a residual category in the relevant literature, despite the fact that they constituted a numerical majority of clerical employees. Secondly, their inferior rewards and status were held to be the inevitable outcome of an attenuated ambition, imposed by socialisation and later reinforced by domesticity. This assumption seemed highly questionable since one was informed elsewhere that depressed levels of pay and prestige among male workers should be examined in relation to prevailing structures of power. It also seemed to be at odds with the important principle, established by studies of orientations to work among male employees, that work attitudes should be regarded as mutable. It seemed appropriate, therefore, that one should attempt to redress the balance in favour of those who constituted the majority of persons working in this sector of the labour force, and that in so doing one should utilise those theoretical frameworks which had proved to be useful in the study of male employment.

Since my research was partly designed to compensate for the prevailing neglect of a particular group of female workers, it is appropriate to begin this concluding section with a discussion of the sources of this sociological myopia. In my view, the neglect of women in clerical occupations cannot usefully be accounted for simply in terms of a sexist orientation among male industrial sociologists. This is a seductive explanation, but it overlooks the existence of a lack of interest in routine white-collar workers more generally. If sociologists have not shown much interest in women clerks, then it must be said that they have not been particularly intrigued by their male counterparts either. It is only possible to speculate upon the reasons for this general neglect, however, since members of the discipline rarely offer any insight into those factors which attract them towards particular fields of study and which divert them from others.

In my opinion, the neglect derives in part from a tendency to prejudge clerical work as a bastion of monotony and mediocrity. The Dickensian caricature of the clerk as a plodding, humble servant, experiencing neither disaster nor excitement, appears to have impressed itself upon the minds of sociologists and caused them to divert their attention elsewhere. Their imaginations have been more readily captured by those occupations which are thought to be more bizarre, more colourful, more degraded and more privileged, and which lend themselves more readily to the conceptual clichés which form the stock-in-trade of industrial sociology. To the extent that women inhabit what are felt to be the most mediocre of these mediocre occupations, they have accordingly received the minimum of an already minimal attention. The tendency to shun the office as a field for investigation has probably been reinforced by the view that its inhabitants represent a major buttress of capitalist society. For those sociologists who are interested in locating the vanguard of revolutionary change, the office must have been regarded as unfruitful territory.

It is of course possible that a soupçon of male chauvinism has played its part in rendering female clerks an under-researched group, and it is also plausible that the limited representation of women in research posts has not been conducive to the development of research in this area. However, the invisibility of the female office worker is at least partly a consequence of the failure of this entire occupational category to capture the hearts and minds of contemporary investigators.

It is evident that any research which is prompted by a concern to remedy absences in the literature does not necessarily make a theoretical contribution. Feminist research of this kind may certainly increase the total stock of information in a particular field of enquiry. There is no guarantee, however, that it will lead to a more sophisticated level of understanding in the area of study concerned. On the other hand, it is possible that by widening the field of enquiry in this way one may discover information which challenges the adequacy of existing models, concepts and theories. The study of women in particular situations may generate data which cannot readily be accommodated within the prevailing sociological terms of reference. This observation leads me to a discussion of the implications of the material presented in Chapter 3 for the sociology of clerical occupations.

My analysis of women in routine white-collar work suggests that there is a dimension to office life which has been greatly overlooked by sociological studies of this mode of employment, namely, sexual interaction. Once it is recognised that employers and employees are typically differentiated by gender, it becomes necessary to question whether their relationships can be adequately accounted for purely in terms of such factors as size of workplace, the organisation of work, levels of pay and job security, and status consciousness. Once one has discovered the existence of women in the office, so to speak, it becomes possible to conceive of employer/employee relationships as forms of interaction which are influenced by assumptions about appropriate gender behaviour. Thus, from the point of view of an employer, a secretary may come to be regarded as unsatisfactory not simply because she fails to achieve a certain level of output, or because of bad timekeeping, but because she fails to conform to expectations concerning appropriate female behaviour. Similarly, it is at least possible that some women derive job satisfaction not simply from levels of remuneration, or from the character of work itself, but also from the rewards which may attach to a conspicuous deference to masculine authority. A woman's femininity is frequently exploited by employers in the office environment, but it can also represent an important power resource with which to manipulate the boss. His superordinate status, after all, depends partly on the woman's willingness to adopt a posture of submissiveness. In this way, whilst one's femininity may impose the necessity for a public display of subordination, it may promote the private feeling that one is actually the power behind the throne.

The opportunity to deploy one's femininity to material or psychological advantage is not equally available to all categories of female clerical workers, but it is most certainly unavailable to their male counterparts. For this reason, a sociology of clerical occupations which concentrates solely on the male workforce leads to a neglect of an important source of differentiation within the workforce as a whole. Furthermore, if one ignores gender-based interaction in the office, one is likely to overlook the possible significance of sexual liaisons. There can be little doubt that members of the office do enter into sexual relationships with each other, ranging from mild flirtations to alliances of a more adulterous nature. My analysis has barely touched upon this dimension of office dynamics but I am nevertheless convinced that it is of considerable relevance for an understanding of many of the antipathies, frustrations and commitments that are found there. It is also possible that sexuality is an important component of other occupational environments. However, sociologists have tended to assume that we inhabit a world where sex is something which only occurs in bedrooms. It may be that an attention to heterosexual and even homosexual liaisons in the world of work would constitute a useful point of reference in future studies of occupations.

My argument therefore is not that gender is the principal or sole determinant of social interaction in the office, but only that a failure to recognise its possible significance may lead to a misrepresentation of the factors governing employee attitudes and behaviour, patterns of promotion and demotion, and relationships between employers and employees. To this extent, it is hoped that the present research exemplifies the need for further empirical research of a feminist nature in the field of industrial sociology. Such studies are required not simply in order to compensate for the long-standing neglect of working women, but in order that we may re-appraise the adequacy of the traditional terms of reference in the sociology of occupations.

The principal concern of this research, however, was to develop a more satisfactory understanding of the factors governing women's work attitudes than had been provided by sociologists in the 1950s and 1960s. My particular interest lay in the field of female clerical employment, and it was within this context that I hoped to demonstrate the utility of an eclectic approach to the study of work attitudes, as had already been exemplified in studies of male employment in industry and in the white-collar world. My next objective, therefore, is to rehearse some of the original problems in the literature and to consider the implications of the present study for the sociology of women in white-collar work and of women in employment more generally.

When I began this research in 1970 there was a widespread predilection for untested assumptions about women as a basis for discussion of their work attitudes. In spite of the growth of economic activity rates among women, especially married women, since the second World War, there was still a tendency to view economic activity amongst all but the poorest women as a social aberration. The attempt to breach the gap of understanding led some sociologists to dust off the oldest remnants of early industrial sociology and to apply them to the sphere of women's employment. The growth in activity rates was held to be symptomatic of post-war consumerism, and women were assumed to be primarily motivated by a desire for the means with which to purchase little extras for the home. Others chose to base their explanations on the Parsonian distinction between expressive and instrumental sex-role orientations. While the primary preoccupations of the male worker were held to be money , power and status, the woman worker was held to be drawn to the workplace by a quest for congenial social relationships. This model was also used as a basis for discussion of the economic behaviour of single women. More than one writer suggested that the attenuated ambitions of young, unattached females reflected a preoccupation with social intercourse.[1] It was these assumptions, plus the notion that a woman's chief attachment was unreservedly to the home, which one felt to be unsatisfactory, partly because they *were* assumptions and partly because they were gradually being challenged by feminist writers.

Another source of dissatisfaction with the prevailing literature was the deterministic view of women as economic actors, and relatedly, the widespread disregard for the dimension of meaning in the study of women's work behaviour. This perspective was in marked contrast to that adopted by Goldthorpe *et al,* and advocated especially by Silverman in his book *The Theory of Organisations*.[2] In addition, there was little attention paid to the impact of work experience upon work attitudes, in spite of the fact that elsewhere one found a particular stress placed upon the contingent character of attitudes to work. The prevailing emphasis therefore on subjective perceptions of work and the factors which modified or sustained those perceptions conflicted sharply with the ready acceptance of the idea that women's attitudes were unproblematic, determined by non-work circumstances, and fixed for life in a state of uncomplaining acquiescence. Those who were prepared to concede that there might be more than one standardised attitude to work among female employees nevertheless tended to concentrate implicitly or explicitly on the impact of a single variable, such as the life-cycle or employment status.

The present study, therefore, has been concerned to substitute investigation for assumption, and to explore the interaction between work attitudes and work experience in the sphere of white-collar employment. The choice of temporary workers for these purposes was dictated partly by a curiosity based on personal experience, but more importantly by a belief that the attitudes of women employed in this capacity presented a serious challenge to the conventional wisdom of sociological literature. Furthermore, since I was concerned to highlight the contingent nature of work attitudes and to identify the factors governing changes in perceptions of work, it seemed appropriate to investigate a group of people whose work situation was characterised by continuous change.

My analysis of women in temporary clerical employment suggests that women's occupational choices and responses to work are influenced by a very wide range of variables. These variables may be divided into three groups. First, there are a number of what may be termed non-work factors. These include age, marital status, responsibility for dependants, educational history, location, responses to domesticity, the occupational mobility of the spouse and the cumulative impact of primary and secondary socialisation. This is not an exhaustive list, but it does incorporate some of the principal factors impinging upon work attitudes which may be said to derive 'beyond the factory gates'. Secondly, there are a number of influences which derive more directly from the work situation itself. These include the objective character of work-tasks, levels of pay and prospects for promotion, relationships with co-workers and employers, the policies of employers with regard to recruitment and conditions of work, the activities of occupational gatekeepers such as private or public employment agents, previous work experience, and the level of information concerning occupational alternatives. Again, the list is not comprehensive, but it does serve to illustrate the very considerable range of factors which may have a bearing upon both occupational choice and responses to work. The third group of variables concern the character of the market for labour. Job choice and job mobility are likely to be influenced by temporal changes in the demand for one's own skills and for labour more generally. They are also likely to be influenced by regional variations in labour demand. Although it is possible to distinguish the three clusters of variables in this way, it is evident that they are interconnected. For example, a firm's recruitment policies towards married women are likely to be influenced by the character of local labour markets and by assumptions about the impact of domestic commitments upon employee reliability.

The observation that female attitudes to work are contingent upon such an enormous range of circumstances is unlikely to provide much comfort to those who would wish to establish an all-embracing theory of the determinants of worker attitudes. Indeed one suspects that it is the very impossibility of constructing such a theory which has prompted a heightened interest in other aspects of the sociology of work, such as patterns of accommodation and conflict in industrial relations. Yet while my research does not resolve the problem of identifying the key determinants of employee attitudes, it does serve to illustrate the redundancy of monocausal approaches to the study of women's orientations towards work.

My analysis of women in temporary clerical employment also suggests that it is wrong to suppose that women consistently display a passive orientation to the situation in which they currently find themselves. Temporary workers exemplify *par excellence* women's capacity actively to negotiate the limiting structures which confront them. The vast majority of female temps are engaged in strategies which enable them to counter or to overcome a wide range of constraints. In some cases, these strategies involve a flight from the oppressive features of domesticity. In other cases, they involve an attempt to establish a sense of control over the work situation. It cannot be denied that these strategies frequently end in frustration or resignation, but they do at least remind us of the lesson learnt from history, that women are capable of resisting structures of oppression.

This observation leads me to register certain reservations concerning current orientations in feminist writing. It is perhaps appropriate to conclude with a discussion of the recent contribution of feminist literature since it is likely to have a considerable impact upon the future direction of research into female employment. Yet there are grounds for supposing that it is likely to reproduce some of the deficiencies which characterised the sociology of female employment in the 1950s and 1960s.

After the initial discovery that women had been ill-served by sociologists in the past, there arose a major preoccupation with the development of a Marxist interpretation of the structural location of women in capitalist society. At first, the analysis turned mainly upon a discussion of the articulation between domestic labour and capitalism, but more recently there has been a heightened interest in the role of female wage labour as a variant of the industrial reserve army. Contributors to both fields have urged that it is necessary to examine the inter-relationships between patriarchy and capitalism if one is to develop an adequate theory of the sources of female subordination.

While this theoretical spring-cleaning has represented a most welcome and important corrective to the traditional perceptions of women held by sociologists, it has generated a far more deterministic model of women at work. Since it involves an effort to locate female wage labour in terms of an overarching theory of the imperatives of monopoly capitalism, there is a tendency to represent women as passively fulfilling the 'needs' of a particular economic system. Thus, the growth of female economic activity rates in the post-war period is seen not so much as a collective escape from the confines of domesticity but as a development necessitated by the expansion and diversification of capitalist commodity production. According to this view, capitalism initiates the process of determination, and patriarchy cements it:

In these jobs where women are not doing 'women's work' as such (although it comes to be defined as that) women still, inevitably, live within their femininity at work. It is in the way

they are treated by men at work (particular sexist incidents: for
flirting with; as strike breakers and/or as workers not to be
supported over equal pay strikes); the way they themselves see
their work and its role in their lives (secondary to home, its
convenience to home in terms of travel, little attention to the
interest of the work, temporary, 'nice people', etc.).[3]

My objection to statements such as these is not that they are
necessarily invalid, but rather that they present an over-socialised
or over-determined view of woman. Morgan has identified the
same problem in the literature concerning the role of women as
domestic labourers. He points out that the Marxist–feminist
approach is extraordinarily reminiscent of functionalism in so far
as it seeks to account for social phenomena in terms of a relatively
fixed wider economic and social system, and glosses over the
possibilities for change, experimentation and manipulation.[4] It
may be suggested that this is because these feminists, like so many
writers of the 1950s and 1960s, have ignored the dimension of
subjective meaning. The concept of false consciousness can all too
easily provide a handy justification for the neglect of this
dimension, just as a firm belief in the utility of popular stereotypes
promoted a similar neglect among an earlier generation of
sociologists. If one subscribes to the view that workers are unable
to comprehend the true nature of their exploitation, then it follows
that there is no real need to examine subjective attitudes towards
work. Instead, one is obliged to concentrate on the structural
determinants of worker behaviour. As a result, one may overlook
the extent to which these forces are countered or resisted. Since it
is possible, therefore, that a continuing neglect of women's own
attitudes is likely to follow from the current orientation of feminist
thought, one is inclined to greet this writing with qualified
approval.

I would like to conclude by suggesting that future research concerning women's employment might usefully be guided by Rowbotham's proposition that 'human beings are more than the services they perform for capital'.[5] A perspective which ignores the
way in which women perceive and respond to their work situation
is one which treats women as occupational robots. It is also a
perspective which is more rather than less likely to perpetuate the
belief that women are indifferent to the character of their work,

and that they passively accept the fact of limited occupational alternatives. If we are to overcome these conservative assumptions, we must address ourselves more wholeheartedly to the concrete experiences of working women. Furthermore, if we are genuinely concerned to advance the cause of women's liberation, then we must point towards the ways in which they rattle the chains of their captivity and seek to throw off the shackles imposed by the cultural assumption of female passivity. Unless such potentialities are demonstrated, sociologists will continue to bolster, by default, the fetters of female subjugation.

Appendix

Research Methods

Almost every independent researcher of private employment agencies has commented on the many procedural problems encountered. The principal problem concerns the difficulty of gaining access to temporary workers for the purposes of investigation. The most expedient method of establishing contact with a group of temps is to secure the co-operation of one or more private employment agencies, but this is not always easy, and it may generate certain constraints upon the way in which the research is conducted. Moreover, whilst some agencies may prove willing to collaborate in a questionnaire survey or programme of interviews, there may be some reluctance to hire the researcher herself in order that she can undertake participant observation. Understandably, an agency is likely to agree to this strategy only if the researcher meets certain standards of clerical competence. The agency, after all, has to take account of the requirements of a third party – the client firm. In this field of study, therefore, the problems of access are particularly great, not only because of the physical dispersal of the relevant population but also because of the need to evolve research strategies which are acceptable to the agencies, and which are in harmony with their normal commercial operations.

The questionnaire

The main questionnaire survey was preceded by a small pilot survey which I conducted among both permanent and temporary staff in three firms in the Midlands. A pilot questionnaire was issued directly to 17 employees, and was designed to yield experience of questionnaire construction and distribution as much as to test the viability of certain questions for the schedule proper.

It was decided that a postal questionnaire survey should be conducted in two areas of the country – Birmingham and the North-east. Accordingly I approached a number of agencies in both areas in order to secure agreement in principle to the distribution of a questionnaire among their employees. The schedule contained a mixture of open-ended and fixed-choice questions and provided the opportunity for respondents to comment on any aspects of temporary work which had not been covered.

As a result of an approach to one of the largest employment businesses in the country, it became possible to widen the geographical scope of the survey to include the London area. All of the agencies who offered their co-operation vetted the questionnaire, and only one asked for a modification to be made. This involved the excision of questions relating to trade unions. It was agreed that the schedules should be returned directly to me rather than to the agency, as I felt that this would be more conducive to the free expression of views. The schedules were then distributed via a total of five organisations in Birmingham, the North-east and London.

In view of the geographical spread of the survey, it proved impossible to exercise direct control over the distribution of the schedules. Consequently I am unable to furnish precise information concerning the response rate. Approximately 415 questionnaires were distributed and 145 were returned. Of these, five were from male temps and one was from a student, and because of my primary interest in women who were normally available for full-time or part-time employment, all six were eliminated from the results.

The disadvantages of the postal questionnaire have been widely documented. The main problems concern the notoriously low response rate, and the possibility of self-selection among respondents. On the other hand, the impersonal character of this method may be said to constitute its principal advantage over other research techniques. With regard to the present research, the problem of low response evidently arose, although the extent to which the resultant sample reflects a process of self-selection remains a matter for speculation. Both negative and positive views were equally represented, not only between respondents but often within an individual questionnaire.

Participant observation

Despite all the best will in the world, it is often very difficult for the sociologist undertaking participant observation to identify with her subjects, and really come to terms with their point of view. Those who are working within the constraints of small budgets and limited time-scales may never be able to achieve the protracted and total immersion in a field of study which is necessary for this purpose. Even without these constraints, it is naïve to suppose that one's identity as a sociologist can be so easily discarded. As far as the present research was concerned, this problem was reversed. Since I had had considerable experience of temporary employment before I began the project, the problem was not so much one of coming to terms with my subjects' world, but rather one of how to reappraise this world sociologically.

Admittedly, as a student doing vacation work I had never really experienced the full impact of periodic unemployment, or the lack of fringe benefits. In addition, it was perhaps easier to tolerate the more unpleasant assignments since money was the primary objective for working, and since one could anticipate a return to the more congenial surroundings of the student campus. In spite of these qualifications, however, the point remains that when I began my observation I was not now entering an unfamiliar world.

When I returned to office work in the capacity of a research worker a certain modification of my outlook did take place. This took the form of a greater interest in, and awareness of, the attitudes and behaviour of co-workers, as opposed to my former preoccupation with making money, doing the work and trying to get on with other people in the office. However, it must be stressed that the balancing of roles was weighted towards that of being a temp, since the self-consciousness which often accompanies the researcher in her pose as part of the field of observation was in my case dissolved by habituation to the occupation. This had important consequences for my relationships with other temps. For although I made no secret of the fact that I was studying them, and was therefore regarded to some extent as a student, there was a greater tendency to regard me as one of their number. This was because my lengthy association with the agency had equipped me with a detailed knowledge of the history of the agency, its personnel, and methods of negotiation. Consequently, not only was I able to exchange occupational anecdotes with other long-serving members of the agency, but I was also able to offer practical advice to those who had joined more recently.

The conduct of my participant observation is best described as 'low-profile'. As an employee I had certain obligations not only towards my agency but also towards the client firm. Consequently my interviews with both permanent and temporary staff were held during breaks, and my notes were compiled after the day's work was over. The interviews, especially with permanent staff, were as informal as possible, and were mainly intended to elicit information about previous working experience, attitudes towards the present job, and leisure patterns. Ideally I would have liked to conduct a series of more formal, highly-structured interviews, but it was clear that this would have proved unacceptable to the agency. The collection of data, therefore, tended to take second place to the main business of performing the work in hand. For this reason it is doubtful whether my presence as a research worker had much impact upon the field of study. The unobtrusive character of the research, plus the fact of my long involvement with temporary work, tended to diminish my colleagues' awareness of, and interest in, my specific sociological aims.

Interviews

During the last eight years I have held a considerable number of interviews with people who are in some way related to my field of study. First, I have held extensive discussions with agency principals in the three areas reflected in the research. These included interviews with the heads of two of the largest groups of agencies in the country. In addition, I visited the head of the agencies' representative organisation, the Federation of Personnel Services, on three separate occasions, the most recent of which was in the spring of 1978. Secondly, in order to obtain the views of the agencies' chief protagonists, I visited the head offices of one of the main white-collar unions. This information was supplemented by written replies to my enquiries from another leading white-collar union and from the TUC headquarters. Thirdly, in order to obtain the views of the agencies' chief competitors, I interviewed officials working for the Department of Employment in the North-east and in Birmingham. Finally, I have held many discussions with women who have had direct experience of temporary employment. Taken together, these diverse sources of data represented the final pieces in what has proved to be a very complicated sociological jigsaw.

Notes and References

Introduction

1 M. Shaw, V. Elsy and P. Bowen, *Office Girls: Education and Job Choice*, paper given to the Durham University Industrial Sociology Seminar, 1975, p. 3.
2 S. Rowbotham, *Woman's Consciousness, Man's World* (Harmondsworth: Penguin, 1973) p. 84.
3 S. Cotgrove, *The Science of Society* (London: Allen and Unwin, 1967) p. 54.

Chapter 1

1 J. Long Laws, 'Work Aspiration of Women: False Leads and New Starts', in *Women and the Workplace*, ed. M. Blaxall and B. Reagan (Chicago, London: University of Chicago Press, 1976).
2 Ibid., p. 34.
3 Schools Council Sixth Form Enquiry, *Sixth Form Pupils and Teachers*, 1970.
4 D. Hutchings and J. Clowsley, 'Why Do Girls Settle for Less?', *Further Education*, vol. 11, no. 1 (Autumn 1970).
5 N. Seear, V. Roberts and J. Brock, *A Career for Women in Industry?* (London: Oliver and Boyd, 1964).
6 Cited in *Women and Work — A Review*, DE Manpower Paper no. 11 (London: HMSO, 1975) p. 14.
7 See, for example, S. Sharpe, *Just Like a Girl* (Harmondsworth: Penguin, 1976).
8 J. Long Laws, 'Work Aspiration of Women: False Leads and New Starts', p. 37; J. Acker, 'Issues in the Sociological Study of Women's Work', in *Women Working*, ed. A. H. Stromberg and S. Harkess (Palo Alto, California: Mayfield, 1978) p. 149.
9 The following have all advocated the use of longitudinal research in the investigation of women's attitudes towards work: J. Long Laws, 'Work Aspiration of Women', p. 37; R. Smith, 'Sex and Occupational Role on Fleet Street', and R. Brown, 'Women as Employees', both in *Dependence and Exploitation in Work and Marriage* ed. D. Barker and S. Allen (London: Longman, 1976).
10 D. Lockwood, *The Blackcoated Worker* (London: Allen and Unwin, 1966) p. 125.

11   E. Mumford and O. Banks, *The Computer and the Clerk* (London: Routledge and Kegan Paul, 1967) p. 21.

12   A. Hunt, *A Survey of Women's Employment*, vol. I (London: HMSO, 1968) p. 52.

13   Ibid., p. 51.

14   R. Wild and A. B. Hill, *Women in the Factory* (London: Institute of Personnel Management, 1970), p. 22.

15   Hunt, *Survey of Women's Employment*, p. 194.

16   V. Klein, *Britain's Married Women Workers* (London: Routledge and Kegan Paul, 1965) p. 36.

17   Ibid., pp. 38–9.

18   F. Zweig, *Women's Life and Labour* (London: Gollancz, 1952); Hunt, *Survey of Women's Employment*.

19   Hunt, *Survey of Women's Employment*, p. 181.

20   Ibid., vol. II, p. 101.

21   A. Oakley, *The Sociology of Housework* (Bath: Martin Robertson, 1974) p. 87.

22   M. Young and P. Willmott, *Family and Kinship in East London* (Harmondsworth: Penguin, 1957, 1962) p. 149.

23   Oakley, *Sociology of Housework*, p. 91.

24   Ibid., p. 20.

25   J. Gardiner, 'Women's Employment Since the Sixties', *Spare Rib*, no. 27, p. 19.

26   F. Cairncross, 'No Time for Big Families', *Guardian*, 1975.

27   K. Piepmeier and T. Adkins, 'The Status of Women and Fertility', *Journal of Biosocial Science*, 5 (October) 1973, p. 516.

28   For an abbreviated version of this debate, see R. Brown, 'Sources of Objectives in Work and Employment', in *Man and Organisation,* ed. J. Child (London: Allen and Unwin, 1973) pp. 17–38.

29   W. W. Daniel, 'Productivity Bargaining and Orientation to Work – A Rejoinder to Goldthorpe', *Journal of Management Studies*, vol.8, no.3 (October 1971) pp. 329–35.

30   R. Brown, 'Sources of Objectives', p. 29.

31   W. Baldamus, *Efficiency and Effort* (London: Tavistock, 1961) p. 124.

32   R. Brown, 'Women as Employees' in *Dependence and Exploitation in Work and Marriage*, ed. D. Barker and S. Allen (London: Longmans, 1976) pp. 33–4.

Chapter 2

1.   M. Crozier, *The World of the Office Worker* (Chicago, London: University of Chicago Press, 1971) p. 1.

2   G. S. Bain, *The Growth of White-collar Unionism* (Oxford University Press, 1970) p. 11.

3   Ibid., p. 11.

4   R. F. Elliott, 'The Growth of White-collar Employment in Great Britain 1951–1971', *British Journal of Industrial Relations,* vol. XV, no. 1, p. 39.

5   R. Lumley, *White-collar Unionism in Britain* (London: Methuen, 1973) pp. 16–20.

6   David Lockwood has suggested the term 'white-bloused' worker as a more precise title: *The Blackcoated Worker* (London: Allen & Unwin, 1958) p. 36.

7   M. K. Benet, *Secretary* (London: Sidgwick and Jackson, 1972) p. 34.

8   Lockwood, *Blackcoated Worker,* p. 29.

9   C. Wright Mills, *White Collar* (New York: Oxford University Press, 1951) p. 191.

10.   H. Braverman, *Labor and Monopoly Capital* (New York: Monthly Review Press, 1974) pp. 293–5.

11   Ibid., p. 302.

12   Lockwood, *Blackcoated Worker*, p. 36.

13   Taken from E. Sullerot, *Woman, Society and Change* (London: Weidenfeld and Nicolson, 1971) p. 147.

14   Lockwood, *Blackcoated Worker*, pp. 122–5.

15   Benet, *Secretary*, p. 39; M. Davies, 'Woman's Place is at the Typewriter', *Radical America*, vol. 8, no. 4 (July–August 1974) pp. 7–9.

16   Lockwood, *Blackcoated Worker*, p. 125.

17   J. B. Priestley, *Angel Pavement* (London: Heinemann, 1930).

18   C. Morley, *Kitty Foyle* (London: Faber and Faber, 1940).

19   Benet, *Secretary*, p. 46.

20   Ibid., pp. 53–4.

21   H. A. Rhee, *Office Automation in Social Perspective* (Oxford: Blackwell, 1968) p. 25.

22   Mary Benet notes that the sexes had separate clerical unions until 1939.

23   Wright Mills, *White Collar*, p. 204.

24   Lockwood, *Blackcoated Worker*, pp. 72–81.

25   Crozier, *World of The Office Worker*, p. 87.

26   *The Times*, 'Special Report on Office Efficiency', 13–17 September 1976; and 'A Guide to Productivity in the Office', 12–16 September 1977.

27   *Guardian*, 28 March 1974.

28   *Observer*, 8 May 1977, p. 17.

29   Lockwood, *Blackcoated Worker*, p. 93.

30   Braverman, *Labour and Monopoly Capital*, pp. 326–48.

31   Ministry of Labour, *Computers in Offices* (London: HMSO, 1965).

32   J. R. Dale, *The Clerk in Industry* (Liverpool University Press, 1962), p. 88.

33   R. Price and G. S. Bain, 'Union Growth Revisited: 1948-1974 in Perspective', *British Journal of Industrial Relations*, vol. XIV, no. 3, p. 345; G. S. Bain and R. Price, 'Union Growth and Employment Trends in the UK 1964–1970', *British Journal of Industrial Relations,* November 1972, p. 379.

34   R. Lumley, *White-collar Unionism*, p. 25.

35   J. Westergaard and H. Resler, *Class in a Capitalist Society* (Harmondsworth: Penguin, 1976), p. 76.

36   Lumley, *White-collar Unionism*, pp. 48–51.

37   K. Scott and M. Deere, *Office Staff: Holidays, Turnover and Other Procedures* (London: Institute of Administrative Management, 1975) pp. 9–10.

38   Lumley, *White-collar Unionism,* p.50.

39   G. Bain, *The Growth of White-Collar Unionism* pp. 71, 183.

40   R. Crompton, 'Approaches to the Study of White-Collar Unionism', *Sociology*, vol. 10, no. 3 (September 1976) p. 423.

41   D. Silverman, 'Clerical Ideologies: A Research Note', *British Journal of Sociology*, vol. 19 (1968) pp. 326–33.

42   J. H. Goldthorpe, D. Lockwood, F. Bechhofer, and J. Platt, *The Affluent Worker in the Class Structure* (Cambridge University Press, 1969) ch. 3.

43   Crozier, *World of the Office Worker*, p. 33.

44   Ibid., p. 95.

45   Ibid., pp. 104–5.

46   D. E. Mercer and D. T. H. Weir, 'Attitudes to Work and Trade Unionism Among White-collar Workers', *Industrial Relations Journal*, vol. 3, no. 2 (Summer 1972) pp. 49–60.

47   N. Morse, *Satisfactions in the White-Collar Job* (University of Michigan Survey Research Center, 1953) pp. 66–7.

48   Dale, *The Clerk in Industry,* p. 21.

49   M. Crozier, *The Bureaucratic Phenomenon* (University of Chicago Press, 1964).

Chapter 3

1   M. Korda, *Male Chauvinism: How It Works* (London: Barrie and Jenkins 1974) pp. 19–20.

2   Here, the term 'white-collar work' is used in its broadest sense.

3   D. Lockwood, *The Blackcoated Worker* (London: Allen and Unwin, 1958).

4   M. Crozier, *The World of the Office Worker* (Chicago, London: University of Chicago Press, 1971).

5   For example, S. Rowbotham, *Woman's Consciousness, Man's World* (Harmondsworth: Penguin, 1973); G. Greer, *The Female Eunuch* (London: Paladin, 1971).

6   M. K. Benet, *Secretary* (London: Sidgwick and Jackson, 1972).

7   Korda, *Male Chauvinism*.

8   C. Wright Mills, *White Collar* (New York: Oxford University Press, 1951).

9   Department of Employment, *Women and Work: A Statistical Survey* (London: HMSO, 1974) p. 56.

10   Department of Education and Science, *Commercial Studies in Schools* (London: HMSO, 1970).

11   *DE Gazette*, May 1974: *Young Persons Entering Employment, 1973.*

12   Census of Population 1971: Great Britain. Summary Tables (1 per cent sample) (London: HMSO, 1973).

13   R. Blackburn, *Union Character and Social Class* (London: Batsford, 1967) p. 71.

14   Ibid., p. 72.

15   E. Sullerot, *Woman, Society and Change* (London: Weidenfeld and Nicholson, 1971) p. 147.

16   M. Fogarty, A. J. Allen, I. Allen and P. Walters, *Women in Top Jobs* (London: Allen and Unwin, 1971) p. 25.

17   A. Stassinopoulos, *The Female Woman* (London: Davis–Poynter, 1973) p. 97.

18   *Department of Employment Gazette*, October 1977, pp. 1062–5.

19   M. Shaw, V. Elsy and P. Bowen, *Office Girls: Education and Job Choice*, paper given to the Durham University Industrial Sociology Seminar, 1975, p. 13.

20   Incomes Data Services. *Women's Pay and Employment* (London: IDS, 1975).

21   Department of Employment, *New Earnings Survey 1970* (London: HMSO, 1970) p. 198.

22   Department of Employment, *Annual Abstract of Statistics 1974* (London: HMSO, 1974) p. 183.

23   Benet, *Secretary*, pp. 65–6.

24   R. Lumley, *White-collar Unionism in Britain* (London: Methuen, 1973) p. 36.

25   G. S. Bain, *The Growth of White-collar Unionism* (Oxford University Press, 1970) pp. 40–43.

26   Lockwood, *Blackcoated Worker*, p. 151.

27   L. Mackie and P. Pattullo, *Women at Work* (London: Tavistock, 1977) p. 173.

28 *Spare Rib*, March 1972, p. 1.

29 Lumley, *White-collar Unionism*, p. 36.

30 M. Fuge (ed.), *Careers and Vocational Training* (London: Arlington, 1971)
p. 443.

31 M. Dunn, 'Graduate Secretaries' in *Top Secretary*, October 1972, p. 57.

32 R. Silverstone, 'Just a Sec?', *Personnel Management*, vol. 7, no. 6 (June
1975) p. 35.

33 Ibid., p. 34.

34 B. Rowe, *The Private Secretary* (London: Museum Press, 1958, 1967) pp.
14–15.

35 Silverstone, 'Just a Sec?' p. 35.

36 Advertisement placed by the Department of Environment in *Top Secretary,*
October 1972, p. 91.

37 H. and J. Whitcomb *Strictly for Secretaries* (London: Hurst and Blackett,
1959) p. 9.

38 R. Williams and M. Root, 'Has Your Company Got Secretary Appeal?',
Personnel Management, November 1971, p. 35.

39 Sir Gerald Nabarro, MP. in *Top Secretary*.

40 Rowe, *Private Secretary*, p. 13.

41 Benet, *Secretary*, p. 73.

42 S. Lewis-Smith, *But Will She Be a Good Secretary?* (London: Harrap, 1974)
p. 63.

43 Ibid., p. 68.

44 Greer, *Female Eunuch*, p. 123.

45 H. and J. Whitcomb, *Strictly for Secretaries*, p. 82.

46 Ibid., pp. 49–50.

47 Ibid., p. 44.

48 M. Korda, *Male Chauvinism: How it Works*, p. 42.

49 H. and J. Whitcomb, *Strictly for Secretaries*, p. 90.

50 B. O. Pettman, 'Some Factors Influencing Labour Turnover: A Review of
Research Literature', *Industrial Relations Journal*, vol. 4, no. 3 (1973) p. 53.

51 R. Wild and A. B. Hill, *Women in the Factory* (London: Institute of Personnel Management, 1970) p. 14.

52 A. Harris and R. Clausen, *Labour Mobility in Britain 1953—63* (London:
Government Social Survey, HMSO, 1966).

53 Silverstone, 'Just a Sec?', p. 34.

54 Alfred Marks Bureau, *The Boss Speaks Out* (London, July 1972).

55 Korda, *Male Chauvinism*, p. 39.

56 Benet, *Secretary*, p. 135.

57 Shaw, Elsy and Bowen, *Office Girls*, p. 15.

58 From an article in *Top Secretary*, October 1972, p. 10.

59 Silverstone, 'Just a Sec?', p. 36.

60 Ibid., p. 36.

61 Benet, *Secretary*, p. 19.

62 Reported in the *Sunday Times*, 22 January 1978, p. 13.

63 Benet, *Secretary*, p. 51.

64 M. C. Elmer, *A Study of Women in Clerical and Secretarial Work in Minneapolis, Minnesota* (University of Minnesota, 1925).

65 Alfred Marks Bureau, *Right Hand Women* (London, January 1974).

66 Silverstone, 'Just a Sec?', p. 36.

67 Silverstone's research is very illuminating in this respect. According to her,
'the greatest proportion of London secretaries were the daughters of men in social
class II, and if these are taken together with those who were from social class I
backgrounds, they account for more than half of the London secretaries'. ('The

Office Secretary', unpublished PhD thesis, City University, London 1974, p. 82.)
88 per cent of her respondents had a non-vocational qualification, 67 per cent had
GCE 'O' levels, or their equivalent, 19 per cent had 'A' levels or their equivalent
(for example HSC) and 3 per cent had a university degree ('The Office Secretary',
p. 91).

68   Benet, *Secretary*, p. 88.
69   From the correspondence column of the *Guardian*, 27 August 1974.
70   From the correspondence column of the *Guardian*, 29 August 1974.
71   Donna Zack, former editor of *Secretary Today*, quoted in J. Thackray, 'The
Secret of Secretaries', *Management Today*, April 1972, p. 134.
72   Silverstone, 'Just a Sec?', p. 34.
73   Alfred Marks Bureau, *Right Hand Women*.
74   Silverstone, 'Just a Sec?', p. 34.
75   Carol Blaymire quoted in an article by P. Toynbee in *Cosmopolitan*,
December 1974, p. 89.
76   R, Silverstone, 'The Office Secretary' (unpublished PhD thesis, City University, London) pp. 430–31.
77   Reported in the *Daily Express*, 1977 (exact date unknown).
78   B. Marks, quoted in an article in the *Listener*, 19 and 26 December 1974, p.
815.
79   From an article in *The Times*, 'Neglected Skills of the Top Secretary', by
Shona Crawford-Poole, 29 January 1974.
80   In an article in the *Listener*, 19 and 26 December 1974, p. 815.
81   Silverstone found that 22 per cent of her respondents could think of nothing
about their jobs which they disliked. On the whole, the sources of satisfaction and
dissatisfaction centred on the work itself rather than on levels of pay, type of boss
or type of social environment, although the latter aspects were not unimportant.
82   J. Thackray, 'The Secret of Secretaries', *Management Today*, April 1972, p.
136.
83   S. Hardcastle, 'Past, Present . . . and What of the Future', in *Top Secretary*,
October 1972, p. 42.
84   H. Braverman, *Labor and Monopoly Capital* (New York: Monthly Review
Press, 1974) pp. 341–7.
85   O. Standingford, *Office* (London: BBC Publications, 1972), p. 124.
86   J. Thackray, 'Secret of Secretaries', p. 136.
87   Earlier in this chapter it was pointed out that over half of Silverstone's
secretaries in London had worked their way up from the more routine grades.
However, this is less likely for those who do not possess shorthand. 33 per cent of
the secretaries began as shorthand-typists, but only 11 per cent began as typists or
clerk-typists, 7 per cent as clerks and 3 per cent began as general office workers.
She also discovered that during the period 1940–69 the proportion of secretaries
who had begun their working lives as secretaries rather than as clerks, typists, etc.,
increased significantly. In other words, mobility into the secretarial ranks from the
lower grades is becoming increasingly rare. ('The Office Secretary', pp. 302–5.)
88   An Alfred Marks survey of office machine operators (*Machine Age Girls*,
October 1974), found that 46 per cent of their respondents experienced headaches,
38 per cent backaches, 33 per cent eye strain, and 15 per cent wristache. According
to Love, technological advances in recent years have increased the health hazards
of the office environment. (M. Love, *The Health Hazards of Office Work*, pamphlet
produced for a conference of women office workers, New York City, October
1973, pp. 2–3). In comparison with factory accidents, of which about 500,000 were
reported in 1975, the number of accidents in offices is small. There were,
nevertheless, over 5000 reported in 1975, of which just under half were accounted
for by falls.

88   Braverman, *Labor and Monopoly Capital*, pp. 293–358.

90   Crozier, *The World of the Office Worker*, p. 86.

91   T. Wardle, 'Mastering Management by Machine Age', *Guardian*, 25 March 1974, p. 15.

92   Benet, *Secretary*, p. 146.

93   Ibid., p. 146.

94   Ibid., p. 137.

95   See for example, L. Harris International, *Secretaries & Typists in London*, 1973.

96   N. Bromage and D. Graves, 'What Secretaries and Typists Like About Their Jobs', *Industrial and Commercial Training*, vol. 8, no. 9 (September 1976).

97   R. G. Stansfield, 'Typing Pools: A Study in Satisfaction in Work', unpublished manuscript, 1948. Cited in R. Silverstone, 'The Office Secretary', (unpublished PhD thesis, City University, London, 1974) p. 271.

98   Alfred Marks Bureau, *The Battery Birds* (London, April 1971) p. 20.

99   Crozier, *The World of the Office Worker*, p. 84.

100   Braverman, *Labor and Monopoly Capital* p. 338.

101   Alfred Marks Bureau, *Machine Age Girls* (London, October 1974) p. 23.

102   Ibid., p. 21.

103   Alfred Marks Bureau, *The Ideal Job* (London, April 1976) p. 27.

104   Shaw, Elsy and Bowen, *Office Girls*, p. 13.

105   Ibid., p. 17.

106   Ibid., p. 19.

107   A. Fox, *A Sociology of Work in Industry* (London: Collier–Macmillan, 1971) p. 14.

108   Silverstone, 'The Office Secretary', p. 82.

109   Benet, *Secretary*, pp. 91–2.

110   Silverstone, 'The Office Secretary', p. 186.

111   Ibid., pp. 395–6.

112   Thackray, 'The Secret of Secretaries', p. 96.

113   M. Young, 'An Approach to the Study of Curricula as Socially Organised Knowledge', in *Knowledge and Control*, ed. M. Young (London: Collier–Macmillan, 1971) p. 33.

114   Silverstone, 'The Office Secretary', pp. 382–94.

115   Ibid., p. 320.

116   R. D. Barron and G. M. Norris, *Sexual Divisions and the Dual-Labour Market*, paper to the BSA annual conference, Aberdeen 1974, p. 31.

117   C. Fulop, *Markets for Employment* (London: Institute of Economic Affairs, 1971) p. 87.

118   S. Lewis-Smith, *But Will She Be a Good Secretary?* (London: Harrap, 1974) pp. 53–6.

119   Alfred Marks Bureau, *A Profile of the Office Temp* (January 1971) p. 23.

120   According to a national survey of temporary office workers, *The Temporary*, prepared by the Federation of Personnel Services of Great Britain: London, 1975, p. 18.

121   R. Blauner, *Alienation and Freedom* (University of Chicago Press, 1964) p. 16.

122   Figure derived from table in Department of Employment, *Women and Work: a Statistical Survey* (London: HMSO, 1974) p. 55.

123   Alfred Marks Bureau, *Married Women in the Office* (January 1972).

124   Silverstone, 'The Office Secretary', p. 78.

125   Department of Employment, *Women and Work: A Statistical Survey*, p. 55.

126   M. Wells, 'Life in the Office', *Spare Rib*, no. 24, June 1974.

127   Silverstone, 'Office Secretary', p. 436.

128   Ibid., pp. 438–41.
129   Ibid., p. 440.
130   Alfred Marks Bureau, *Married Women in the Office*, p. 20.
131   Silverstone, 'Office Secretary', p. 201.
132   Federation of Personnel Services of Great Britain, *The Temporary* (London: FPS, 1975) p. 6.
133   Alfred Marks Bureau, *A Profile of the Office Temp*, p.22.
134   Federation of Personnel Services of Great Britain, *The Temporary*, p. viii.
135   E. L. Winter, *Your Future as a Temporary Office Worker* (New York: Richards Rosen Press, 1968) p. 21.
136   Alfred Marks Bureau, *Married Women in the Office*.
137   V. Beechey, 'Some Notes on Female Wage Labour in Capitalist Production', *Capital and Class,* Autumn 1977, pp. 54–5.

Chapter 4

1   See, for example, Liverpool University Department of Social Science, *The Dock Worker* (Liverpool University Press, 1956).
2   S. C. Newton and S. R. Parker, 'Who are the Temporary Workers?', *DE Gazette,* June 1975, p. 510.
3   K. Marx, *Capital*, vol. II (London: Dent, 1957) p. 708. For a more recent discussion, see H. Braverman, *Labor and Monopoly Capital* (New York: Monthly Review Press, 1974) pp. 386–401.
4   Newton and Parker, 'Who are the Temporary Workers?', pp. 507–8.
5   S. Parker and A. Sirker, *Temporary Workers* (London: Social Survey Division, OPCS, 1976) p. 3.
6   Parker and Sirker, *Temporary Workers*, pp. 13–14.
7   NBPI Report no. 89, 'Office Staff Employment Agencies Charges and Salaries' (London: HMSO, 1968) p. 2; T. K. Cobb, 'Quality in Temporary Services', *The Office*, vol. 73, no. 1 (January 1971).
8   NALGO Economic Committee discussion document, 13.7.74, p. 13.
9   In a speech delivered to the Confédération Internationale des Entreprises de Travail Temporaire (CIETT) annual conference, Copenhagen, 4 June 1971.
10   NBPI Report no. 89, p. 2.
11   Newton and Parker 'Who are the Temporary Workers?', p. 511.
12   Parker and Sirker, *Temporary Workers*, p. 32.
13   SOFRES (Government Survey Body), *Temporary Work in France* (Montrouge, 1973) pp. 12–13.
14   J. Campling, 'Jobs and Agencies', *New Society*, 23 May 1974, p. 445.
15   Gerry Bourne, European Manager for Manpower, quoted in M. Moore, 'The Temporary Help Service Industry: Historical Development, Operation and Scope', *Industrial and Labor Relations Review*, XVIII (July 1965) p. 556.
16   Moore, ibid., p. 556.
17   T. Doran, 'A Study of Employment Agencies, Registers, Selection Consultants, and Headhunters' (unpublished MSc dissertation, Durham University Business School, 1971).
18   Based on information supplied by the federation of Personnel Services, 7 April 1978, and by the *DE Gazette*, September 1977, p. 981.
19   Doran, 'Study of Employment Agencies'. Doran notes that turnover among agencies in the USA also stands at about 50 per cent.
20   C. Fulop, *Markets for Employment* (London: Institute of Economic Affairs, 1971) p. 39.
21   R. M. Jones, 'A Market for Labour and the Office Staff Sector', *British Journal of Industrial Relations*, vol. x, no. 2 (July 1972) p. 197.

22   NBPI Report no. 89, p. 3.

23   Jones, 'A Market for Labour', p. 201.

24   *New Society*, 11 August 1977, p. 293.

25   *DE Gazette*, September 1977, p. 981.

26   In a speech delivered to the CIETT annual conference, 4 June 1971.

27   Jones, 'A Market for Labour', p. 198.

28   V. L. Olesen and F. Katsuranis, 'Urban Nomads: Women in Temporary Clerical Services' in *Women Working*, ed. A. Stromberg and S. Harkess (Palo Alto, California: Mayfield, 1978) p. 323.

29   Administrative Management Society Survey, *Personnel*, January 1971, vol. 11, no.7, p. 6. Although many employers considered temps to be less efficient than regulars, 84 per cent considered that they nevertheless got good value in relation to other wages and costs.

30   SOFRES, *Temporary Work in France*, pp. 24–5.

31   NBPI Report no. 89, p. 4.

32   R. Silverstone, 'The Office Secretary' (unpublished PhD thesis, City University, London, 1974) pp. 454–6.

33   R. Pearson, *The Use of Temporary Staff* (Brighton: Institute of Manpower Studies, 1975) pp. 30–1.

34   Doran, 'A Study of Employment Agencies'.

35   Reported in the *Financial Times*, 19 August 1974, p. 6.

36   'The Great Agency Scandal', *Index to Office Equipment and Supplies*, 1 September 1973, p. 16.

37   Clive Jenkins, General Secretary of ASTMS, suggested that 'interviewers, in fact, do not generally last long in their jobs', in *Top Secretary*, October 1972.

38   *Financial Times*, 19 August 1974, p. 6.

39   J. Skeels, 'Perspectives on Private Employment Agencies', *Industrial Relations*, February 1969, p. 160.

40   Fulop, *Markets for Employment*, pp. 111–12.

41   *Evening News*, 26 May 1978.

42   The fact that the service is free to the applicant does not, in the opinion of some groups, particularly the unions, exonerate the agencies. To the extent that agencies profit from the sale of the temporary's labour power, there are inevitably many organisations, including the ILO, which maintain a resolute opposition to their existence.

43   Silverstone, 'Office Secretary', p. 461.

44   P. Riddell, 'Temps Provide a Cushion', *Financial Times*, 24 October 1975, p. 11.

45   According to Eric Hurst, speaking at the tenth CIETT annual conference in May 1977, 'the number of temporaries fell at the very worst by forty per cent'.

46   *The Times*, 27 August 1977, p. 17.

47   *Evening Standard*, 18 September 1978.

48   *Evening Standard*, 13 April 1978.

49   *Evening Standard*, 9 March 1978.

50   *Evening Standard*, 13 June 1977.

51   NALGO discussion document, p. 13.

52   B. Jerman, 'Temporary Mums', *Guardian*, 14 December 1974.

Chapter 5

1   For an extended discussion of the impact of both patriarchy and capitalism upon female wage labour, see Women's Studies Group, Centre for Contemporary Cultural Studies, *Women Take Issue* (London: Hutchinson, 1978) pp. 54–71.

2   *Observer*, 8 January 1978.
3   A. Hunt, *A Survey of Women's Employment*, vol. 1 (London: HMSO, 1968) p. 30.
4   Alfred Marks Bureau; *The Ideal Job* (London, April 1976) p. 20.
5   *Evening Standard*, 25 July 1977.
6   *Evening Standard*, 13 June 1977.
7   Federation of Personnel Services of Great Britain Ltd, *The Temporary*, (London, 1975) table XII.
8   Figures derived from Department of Employment, *Women and Work: A Statistical Survey* (London: HMSO, 1974) p. 55; Federation of Personnel Services, *The Temporary*, p. 6.
9   A. Hunt, *A Survey of Women's Employment*, vol. 11 (London: HMSO, 1968) p. 163.
10   The occupational classification used in Table 5.2 is based upon a scheme adopted by Goldthorpe *et al.* in their study *The Affluent Worker in the Class Structure* (Cambridge University Press, 1969) pp. 196–7. The only modification is a simplification of the classification used for manual workers. I should point out that when I designed my questionnaire in 1971, I adopted the conventional practice of asking for father's occupation only. This convention has now been widely challenged. In Table 5.2, and in subsequent tables, percentages have been rounded up.
11   M. Gannon and U. Brainin, 'Employee Tenure in the Temporary Help Industry', *Industrial Relations*, vol. 10 (May 1971) pp. 172–3. See also M. Gannon, 'An Analysis of Job Motivation among Clerical Temporary Help Employees' (unpublished paper. The author is Associate Professor in the College of Business and Management, University of Maryland).
12   Hunt, *Survey of Women's Employment*, p. 16.
13   According to a chi-square test of significance where p is less than or equal to 5 per cent (0.05).
14   Hunt, *Survey of Women's Employment*, p. 218.
15   Alfred Marks Bureau, *Machine Age Girls* (London, October 1974) p. 19.
16   According to Olesen and Katsuranis, in their study of American temporary clerical workers, there are indeed certain categories of persons who may turn to temporary employment because of an inability to procure or to cope with permanent work. These are people who are handicapped not by any lack of skill, but by physical disabilities or emotional problems. Such people, according to the authors, 'found temporary work tolerable in a work force that does not easily accept disabilities'. ('Urban Nomads: Women in Temporary Clerical Services' in *Women Working*, ed. A. Stromberg and S. Harkess (Palo Alto, California: Mayfield, 1978) pp. 332–3.)
17   Federation of Personnel Services, *The Temporary*, p. 6; Alfred Marks Bureau, *Temporarily at Work* (London, July 1973).
18   Hunt, *Survey of Women's Employment*, vol. 1, p. 50.
19   Alfred Marks Bureau, *A Profile of the Office Temp* (London, January 1971) p. 20.
20   Gannon and Brainin, 'Employee Tenure in the Temporary Help Industry', p. 175.
21   V. Olesen and F. Katsuranis, 'Urban Nomads', p. 322; Gannon, 'Analysis of Job Motivation', p. 5.
22   Alfred Marks Bureau, *A Profile of the Office Temp*, p. 20.
23   From K. Cole and D. Bain, *Girlpower* (Greenwich, Conn.: Fawcett, 1971) p. 26.
24   See, for example, the FPS survey of office temps, *The Temporary*, pp. 6–22.

25   Olesen and Katsuranis, 'Urban Nomads', p. 334.

26   DE Manpower Paper no.9, *Women and Work — A Statistical Survey* (London: HMSO, 1974) p. 10.

27   Olesen and Katsuranis, 'Urban Nomads', p. 326.

28   Ibid., p. 333.

29   M. Gannon and U. Brainin, 'Job Rotation and Employee Tenure Among Temporary Workers', *Academy of Management Journal*, vol. 14, no. 1 (March 1971) p. 144.

30   Taken from a brochure for business executives distributed by a leading temp help organisation.

31   Olesen and Katsuranis, 'Urban Nomads', p. 326.

32   Alfred Marks Bureau, *A Profile of the Office Temp*, p. 27.

33   S. Parker and A. Sirker, *Temporary Workers* (London: Social Survey Division, OPCS, 1976) pp. 37–8.

Conclusions

1   See, for example, D. Lockwood, *The Blackcoated Worker* (London: Allen and Unwin, 1958) p. 125, and E. Mumford and O. Banks, *The Computer and the Clerk* (London: Routledge and Kegan Paul, 1967) p. 21.

2   D. Silverman, *The Theory of Organisations* (London: Heinemann, 1970).

3   Women's Studies Group, Centre for Contemporary Cultural Studies, *Women Take Issue* (London: Hutchinson, 1978) pp. 65–6.

4   D. Morgan, *Social Theory and the Family* (London: Routledge and Kegan Paul, 1975) p. 168.

5   S. Rowbotham, *New Society*, vol. 44, no. 813 (4 May 1978) p. 267.

Bibliography

BAIN, G. S., *The Growth of White-collar Unionism* (Oxford University Press, 1970).

BAIN, G. S. and PRICE, R., 'Union Growth and Employment Trends in the UK 1964–70', *British Journal of Industrial Relations,* November 1972.

BARKER, D., and ALLEN, S. (eds), *Dependence and Exploitation in Work and Marriage,* (London: Longman, 1976).

BARRON, R. D., and NORRIS, G. M., 'Sexual Divisions and the Dual Labour Market', paper to the BSA annual conference, Aberdeen, 1974.

BEECHEY, V., 'Some Notes on Female Wage Labour in Capitalist Production', *Capital and Class,* no. 3, Autumn 1977.

BENET, M. K., *Secretary* (London: Sidgwick and Jackson, 1972).

BLACKBURN, R., *Union Character and Social Class* (London: Batsford, 1967).

BLAUNER, R., *Alienation and Freedom* (University of Chicago Press, 1964).

BLAXALL, M., and REAGAN, B. (eds), *Women and the Workplace* (University of Chicago Press, 1976).

BRAVERMAN, H., *Labor and Monopoly Capital* (New York: Monthly Review Press, 1974).

BROMAGE, N., and GRAVES, D., 'What Secretaries and Typists like about their Jobs', *Industrial and Commercial Training,* vol. 8, no. 9, September 1976.

BROWN, R., 'Women as Employees', in Barker, D. and Allen, S. (eds), *Dependence and Exploitation in Work and Marriage* (London: Longman, 1976).

CAMPLING, J., 'Jobs and Agencies', *New Society,* 23 May 1974.

Census of Population 1966: Great Britain (London: HMSO, 1968).

Census of Population 1971: Great Britain, Summary Tables – 1% sample (London: HMSO, 1973).

CHILD, J. (ed.), *Man and Organisation* (London: Allen and Unwin, 1973).

COLE, K., and BAIN, D., *Girlpower* (Greenwich, Connecticut: Fawcett, 1971).

Confédération Internationale des Entreprises de Travail Temporaire, Reports of Annual Conferences, 1971, 1977.

Cosmopolitan, December 1974.

COTGROVE, S., *The Science of Society* (London: Allen and Unwin, 1967).

CROMPTON, R., 'Approaches to the Study of White-collar Unionism', *Sociology,* vol. 10, no. 3 (September 1976).

CROZIER, M., *The Bureaucratic Phenomenon* (University of Chicago Press, 1964).

CROZIER, M., *The World of the Office Worker* (University of Chicago Press, 1971).

DALE, J. R. *The Clerk in Industry* (Liverpool University Press, 1962).

DAVIES, M., 'Woman's Place is at the Typewriter', *Radical America*, vol. 8, no. 4, July–August 1974.

DEPARTMENT OF EDUCATION AND SCIENCE, *Commercial Studies in Schools* (London: HMSO, 1970).

DEPARTMENT OF EMPLOYMENT, *Annual Abstract of Statistics 1974* (London: HMSO, 1974).

DEPARTMENT OF EMPLOYMENT, *New Earnings Survey, 1970* (London: HMSO, 1970).

DEPARTMENT OF EMPLOYMENT, *New Earnings Survey, 1976* (London: HMSO, 1977).

DEPARTMENT OF EMPLOYMENT, *Women and Work: A Review* (London: HMSO, 1975).

DEPARTMENT OF EMPLOYMENT, *Women and Work: A Statistical Survey* (London: HMSO, 1974).

Department of Employment Gazette, 'Young Persons Entering Employment 1973', May 1974.

Department of Employment Gazette, September 1977.

Department of Employment Gazette, October 1977.

DORAN, T., 'A Study of Employment Agencies, Registers, Selection Consultants, and Headhunters' (unpublished MSc dissertation, Durham University Business School, 1971).

ELLIOTT, R. F., 'The Growth of White-collar Employment in Great Britain 1951–1971', *British Journal of Industrial Relations*, vol. xv, no. 1.

ELMER, M.C., *A Study of Women in Clerical and Secretarial Work in Minneapolis, Minnesota;* (University of Minnesota, 1925).

FEDERATION OF PERSONNEL SERVICES OF GREAT BRITAIN, *The Temporary* (London: FPS, 1975).

Financial Times 19 August 1974.

FOGARTY, M., ALLEN, A. J., ALLEN, I., and WALTERS, P., *Women in Top Jobs* (London: Allen and Unwin, 1971).

FOX, A., *A Sociology of Work in Industry* (London: Collier-Macmillan, 1971).

FUGE, M. (ed.), *Careers and Vocational Training* (London: Arlington, 1967).

FULOP, C., *Markets for Employment* (London: Institute of Economic Affairs, 1971).

GANNON, M., 'An Analysis of Job Motivation among Clerical Temporary Help Employees', unpublished paper.

GANNON, M., 'A Profile of the Temporary Help Industry and its Workers', *Monthly Labor Review,* May 1974.

GANNON, M., and BRAININ, U., 'Employee Tenure in the Temporary Help Industry', *Industrial Relations*, May 1971.

GANNON, M., and BRAININ, U., 'Job Rotation and Employee Tenure among Temporary Workers', *Academy of Management Journal*, vol. 14, no. 1, March 1971.

GOLDTHORPE, J., LOCKWOOD, D., BECHHOFER, F., and PLATT, J., *The Affluent Worker in the Class Structure* (Cambridge University Press, 1969).

GREER, G., *The Female Eunuch* (London: MacGibbon and Kee, 1970 and London: Paladin, 1971).

Guardian, 28 March 1974.

Guardian, 29 August 1974.

HARRIS, A., and CLAUSEN, R., *Labour Mobility in Great Britain 1953-63* (London: Government Social Survey, HMSO, 1966).

L. HARRIS INTERNATIONAL, *Secretaries and Typists in London* (London: L. Harris International, 1973).

HUNT, A., *A Survey of Women's Employment*, vols I and II (London: HMSO, 1968).

HUTCHINGS, D., and CLOWSLEY, J., 'Why do Girls Settle for Less?', *Further Education* vol. 11, no. 1, Autumn 1970.

INCOMES DATA SERVICES, *Women's Pay and Employment* (London: IDS, 1975).

Index to Office Equipment and Supplies, 'The Great Agency Scandal', 1 September 1973.

JERMAN, B., 'Temporary Mums', *Guardian*, 14 December 1974.

JONES, R. M., 'A Market for Labour and the Office Staff Sector', *British Journal of Industrial Relations*, vol. X, no. 2, July 1972.

KLEIN, V., *Britain's Married Women Workers* (London: Routledge and Kegan Paul, 1965).

KORDA, M., *Male Chauvinism: How it Works* (London: Barrie and Jenkins, 1974).

LEWIS-SMITH, S., *But Will She Be a Good Secretary?* (London: Harrap, 1974).

Listener, 19 and 26 December 1974.

LIVERPOOL UNIVERSITY, *The Dockworker* (Liverpool University Press, 1956).

LOCKWOOD, D., *The Blackcoated Worker* (London: Allen and Unwin, 1958).

LONG LAWS, J., 'Work Aspiration of Women: False Leads and New Starts' in Blaxall, M. and Reagan, B. (eds), *Women and the Workplace* (Chicago, London: University of Chicago Press, 1976).

LOVE, M., *The Health Hazards of Office Work*, Pamphlet produced for a conference of women office workers, New York City, October 1973.

LUMLEY, R., *White-collar Unionism in Britain* (London: Methuen, 1973).

MACKIE, L., and PATTULLO, P., *Women at Work* (London: Tavistock, 1977).

ALFRED MARKS BUREAU, *The Battery Birds* (London, April 1971).

ALFRED MARKS BUREAU, *The Boss Speaks Out*, (London, July 1972).

ALFRED MARKS BUREAU, *The Ideal Job*, (London, April 1976).

ALFRED MARKS BUREAU, *Machine Age Girls*, (London, October 1974).

ALFRED MARKS BUREAU, *Married Women in the Office*, (London, January 1972).

ALFRED MARKS BUREAU, *Motives for Movement*, (London, April 1974).

ALFRED MARKS BUREAU, *A Profile of the Office Temp*, (London, January 1971).

ALFRED MARKS BUREAU, *Right Hand Women*, (London, January 1974).

ALFRED MARKS BUREAU, *Temporarily at Work*, (London, July 1973).

MARX, K., *Capital*, vol. II (London: Dent, 1957).

MERCER, D. E., and WEIR, D., 'Attitudes to Work and Trade Unionism among White-collar Workers', *Industrial Relations Journal*, vol. 3, no. 2, *Summer 1972*.

MINISTRY OF LABOUR, *Computers in Offices* (London: HMSO, 1965).

MOORE, M., 'The Temporary Help Service Industry: Historical Development, Operation and Scope', *Industrial and Labor Relations Review*, XVIII, July 1965.

MORGAN, D., *Social Theory and the Family* (London: Routledge and Kegan Paul, 1975).

MORSE, N., *Satisfactions in the White-Collar Job* (University of Michigan, Institute for Social Research, 1953).

MUMFORD, E., and BANKS, O., *The Computer and the Clerk* (London: Routledge and Kegan Paul, 1967).

NATIONAL BOARD FOR PRICES AND INCOMES, *Report No. 89, Office Staff Employment Agencies Charges and Salaries* (London: HMSO, 1968).

New Society, 11 August 1977.

NEWTON, S. C., and PARKER, S. R., 'Who are the Temporary Workers?, *DE Gazette*, June 1975.

OAKLEY, A., *The Sociology of Housework*, (Bath: Martin Robertson, 1974).

Observer, 8 May, 1977.

Observer, 8 January 1978.

OLESEN, V. L., and KATSURANIS, F., 'Urban Nomads: Women in Temporary Clerical Services', in Stromberg, A. H., and Harkess, S. (eds), *Women Working* (Palo Alto, California: Mayfield, 1978).

PARKER, S., and SIRKER, A., *Temporary Workers* (London: Social Survey Division, OPCS, 1976).

PEARSON, R., *The Use of Temporary Staff* (Brighton: Institute of Manpower Studies, 1975).

Personnel, vol. 11, no. 7, January 1971.

PETTMAN, B. O., 'Some Factors Influencing Labour Turnover: A Review of Research Literature', *Industrial Relations Journal*, vol 4, no. 3, 1973.

PIEPMEIER, K., and ADKINS, T., 'The Status of Women and Fertility', *Journal of Biosocial Science*, vol. 5, October 1973.

PRICE, R., and BAIN, G. S., 'Union Growth Revisited: 1948–1974 in Perspective' *British Journal of Industrial Relations*, vol. XIV, no. 3.

RHEE, H. A., *Office Automation in Social Perspective* (Oxford: Blackwell, 1968).

RIDDELL, P., 'Temps Provide a Cushion', *Financial Times*, 24 October 1975.

ROWBOTHAM, S., (review article), *New Society*, vol. 44, no. 813, 4 May 1978, p. 267.

ROWBOTHAM, S., *Woman's Consciousness, Man's World* (Harmondsworth: Penguin, 1973).

ROWE, B., *The Private Secretary* (London: Museum Press, 1958, 1967).

SCHOOLS COUNCIL SIXTH FORM ENQUIRY, *Sixth Form Pupils and Teachers*, 1970.

SCOTT, K., and DEERE, M., *Office Staff: Holidays, Turnover and Other Procedures* (London: Institute of Administrative Management, 1975).

SEEAR, N., ROBERTS, V., and BROCK, J., *A Career for Women in Industry?* (London: Oliver and Boyd, 1964).

SHARPE, S., *Just Like a Girl* (Harmondsworth: Penguin, 1976).

SHAW, M., ELSY, V., and BOWEN, P., *Office Girls: Education and Job Choice*, unpublished paper, 1975.

SILVERMAN, D., 'Clerical Ideologies: A Research Note', *British Journal of Sociology*, vol. 19, 1968.

SILVERMAN, D., *The Theory of Organisations* (London: Heinemann, 1970).

SILVERSTONE, R., 'Just a Sec?', *Personnel Management*, vol. 7, no. 6, June 1975.

SILVERSTONE, R., 'The Office Secretary', unpublished PhD thesis, City University, London, 1974.

SKEELS, J., 'Perspective on Private Employment Agencies', *Industrial Relations*, February 1969.

SMITH, R., 'Sex and Occupational Role on Fleet Street', in Barker, D., and Allen, S., (eds), *Dependence and Exploitation in Work and Marriage* (London: Longman, 1976).

Social Trends 1976 (London: HMSO, 1976).

SOFRES (Government Survey Body), *Temporary Work in France* (Montrouge, 1973).

Spare Rib, no. 24, June 1974.

Spare Rib, no. 27, September 1974.

Spare Rib, no. 68, March 1978.

STANDINGFORD, O., *Office* (London: BBC Publications, 1972).

STANSFIELD, R. G., 'Typing Pools: a Study in Satisfaction in Work', unpublished manuscript, 1948. Cited in Silverstone, R., 'The Office Secretary', unpublished PhD thesis, City University, London, 1974.

STASSINOPOULOS, A., *The Female Woman* (London: Davis–Poynter, 1973).

STROMBERG, A., and HARKESS, S. (eds), *Women Working* (Palo Alto, California: Mayfield, 1978).

SULLEROT, E., *Woman, Society and Change* (London: Weidenfeld and Nicolson, 1971).

Sunday Times, 7 April 1974.

Sunday Times, 22 January 1978.

THACKRAY, J., 'The Secret of Secretaries', in *Management Today*, April 1972.

The Times, 29 January 1974.

The Times, 29 April 1974

The Times, 'A Special Report on Office Efficiency', 13–17 September 1976.

The Times, 27 August 1977.

The Times, 'A Guide to Productivity in the Office', 12–16 September 1977.

Top Secretary, October 1972.

WESTERGAARD, J., and RESLER, H., *Class in a Capitalist Society* (London: Heinemann, 1975 and Harmondsworth: Penguin, 1976).

WHITCOMB, H. and J., *Strictly for Secretaries* (London: Hurst and Blackett, 1959).

WILD, R., and HILL, A. B., *Women in the Factory* (London: Institute of Personnel Management, 1970).

WILLIAMS, R., and ROOT, M., 'Has Your Company got Secretary Appeal?, *Personnel Management*, November 1971.

WINTER, E., *Your Future as a Temporary Office Worker* (New York: Richards Rosen Press, 1968).

WOMEN'S STUDIES GROUP, Centre for Contemporary Cultural Studies, *Women Take Issue* (London: Hutchinson, 1978).

WRIGHT MILLS, C., *White Collar* (New York: Oxford University Press, 1951).

YOUNG, M., (ed.), *Knowledge and Control* (London: Collier-Macmillan, 1971).

YOUNG, M., and WILLMOTT, P., *Family and Kinship in East London* (Harmondsworth: Penguin 1962).

ZWEIG, F., *Women's Life and Labour* (London: Gollancz, 1952).

Index